MASTERPIEC
URDU NAZM

This book is intended to introduce the reader to the best specimens of the Urdu *Nazm*, as distinguished from the *ghazal*. It contains English translations of 42 *nazms*, chosen from the works of 19 famous poets, such as Mir Taqi Mir, Nazir Akbarabadi, Shauq Lucknavi, Iqbal, Josh, Hafeez, Akhtar Sheerani, Majaaz, Faiz, and Sahir. The poets are presented in chronological order, and each is introduced with an authentic portrait, and a brief biographical-cum-critical note. The "Introduction" attempts in lucid prose a definition of the *nazm*, and describes its characteristic features as an art form.

The layout of the book is methodical. Each poem is first given in Urdu calligraphics, followed on the opposite page by its translation in lucid, rhythmical language which, in turn, is succeeded by the romanized version of the Urdu text. The transliteration should enable even the non-Urdu-knowing reader to have a feel of the Urdu language. All the poems selected for translation are among the classics of Urdu poetry. They deal with all sorts of themes, and represent a variety of styles and stanzaic forms. It is thus a fairly representative collection which, taken together with the author's three earlier volumes on the *ghazal* and the *rubai*, should offer to the reader the best of Urdu poetry in English translation.

K.C. Kanda *has taught English literature for over 30 years at Delhi University. He holds a doctorate in English from the University of Delhi, and Master's degrees from Punjab and Nottingham Universities. He is also a first class M.A. in Urdu from Delhi University. While English poetry has been his speciality professionally, Urdu poetry has been his great love since his schooldays. His publications include:* An Anthology of English Poetry *(Arnold Heinemann, 1976);* The Two Worlds of Tennyson *(Doaba House, 1985);* Masterpieces of Urdu Ghazal *(1991);* Masterpieces of Urdu Rubaiyat *(1994);* Urdu Ghazals: An Anthology *(1994) — all three published, like the present volume, by Sterling Publishers, New Delhi. Dr. Kanda is currently working on a translation of Mir Taqi Mir, one of the grest classics of Urdu poetry. Two of his critical studies:* Dramatic Monologues of Robert Browning, *and* Tennyson's In Memoriam *have recently been released by Sterling.*

Excerpts from the reviews

Masterpieces of Urdu Ghazal

"It is a miracle that despite the strait-jacket in which it was enclothed, the ghazal not only survived but flourished through the centuries.... I recommend this anthology to lovers of Urdu poetry."

—*Khushwant Singh, Sunday*

"All in all, it is a book for the shelves of both who know and love Urdu and would like to be conversant with its best form of poetry."

—*The Pioneer*

"Mr. Kanda, in his well-researched volume, has painstakingly brought out the best of Urdu Ghazal, and this concise volume could well be considered a boon for research scholars in Urdu Poetry."

—*The Hindu*

Urdu Ghazals: An Anthology

"Mr. K.C. Kanda has painstakingly included in the anthology an excellent selection of Urdu ghazals, not only in Urdu (Persian) script, the English translation of a high quality, but, more importantly, the transcription in Roman as well. The volume would rank high among other works of a similar nature."

—*The Hindu*

Masterpieces of Urdu Rubaiyat

This book contains English translations of 269 *rubaies,* chosen from the works of 25 famous poets, chronologically arranged. It covers a wide spectrum of Urdu poetry, from Mir and Sauda in the 18th century to Josh and Firaq in the 20th century.

—*Globe*

MASTERPIECES OF
URDU NAZM

K.C. KANDA

STERLING

STERLING PAPERBACKS
An imprint of
Sterling Publishers (P) Ltd.
Regd. Office: A1/256 Safdarjung Enclave,
New Delhi-110029. CIN: U22110DL1964PTC211907
Tel: 26387070, 26386209; Fax: 91-11-26383788
E-mail: mail@sterlingpublishers.in
www.sterlingpublishers.in

Masterpieces of Urdu Nazm
© 1997, K.C. Kanda
ISBN 978 81 207 1952 1
Reprint 1998, 2000, 2003, 2010, 2018

All rights are reserved.
No part of this publication may be reproduced, stored in a retrieval system or transmitted, in any form or by any means, mechanical, photocopying, recording or otherwise, without prior written permission of the original publisher.

Printed and Published in India by

Sterling Publishers Pvt. Ltd.,
Plot No. 13, Ecotech-III, Greater Noida - 201306, U. P. India

To
My Children

ARUN & KIRAN
RANJANA & YOGESH

اے اہلِ نظر آؤ یہ جاگیر سنبھالو
میں مملکتِ لوح و قلم بانٹ رہا ہوں

فراق

Come, ye discerning minds, take over your heritage,
Lo, I bequeath to you the wealth of pen and page.

PREFACE

This book may be treated as a complement to my earlier books: *Masterpieces of Urdu Ghazal* (1990), *Masterpieces of Urdu Rubaiyat* (1994) and *Urdu Ghazals: An Anthology* (1994), all of which are intended to introduce the readers, more particularly, of the non-Urdu-knowing class, to the best specimens of Urdu poetry in various genres. The present anthology contains English translations of 42 "nazms", chosen from the works of 19 famous poets, including such master-poets as Mir Taqi Mir, Nazir Akbarabadi, Shauq Lucknavi, Iqbal, Josh, Hafeez, Akhtar Sheerani, Majaz, Faiz and Sahir. The poets are presented in a chronological order, and each poet is introduced with an authentic portrait, and a biographical-cum-critical note. In the opening chapter of the book, I have attempted a definition of the "nazm", as distinguished from "ghazal", and briefly described the origin, development, and special features of this poetic form.

All the poems presented in this selection are now counted among the classics of Urdu poetry. They deal with all sorts of themes, and represent a variety of styles and stanzaic forms, including also a few specimens of the Urdu "nazm" in blank verse and free-verse. This volume may thus be called a fairly representative collection of Urdu "nazm" in English translation. The present-day living poets of the "nazm" are, however, outside the scope of this book. The constraint of space has obliged me to curtail the length of some longer poems, such as the "masnavis" of Mir and Shauq, Iqbal's "Shikwa" and "Jawab-e-Shikwa", and some of the poems of Josh Malihabadi. I have taken care not to leave out, in the process of abridgement, any lines or passages which have a direct bearing on the essentials of the narrative, or are poetically outstanding.

While translating these poems my aim has been to preserve the sense and spirit of the original, though it may involve an occasional departure from the literal accuracy of the text. Knowing that an important source of the pleasure of Urdu poetry lies in the music of its lines and rhymes, I have attempted rhymed verse in my translations, though I do not hesitate to substitute assonance for rhyme when a suitable rhyme-word is not easily traceable.

The layout of the book is similar to the pattern of my earlier volumes. Each poem is first given in Urdu calligraphics, followed, on the opposite page, by its English translation which, in turn, is succeeded by the Romanised version of the text (in italics). The Romanised transliteration should give a feel of the Urdu language even to those readers who are not conversant with Urdu in the Persian script. It may even prove to be of practical help to the learners of Urdu.

I am beholden to all my friends and counsellors who have helped me in the preparation of this book. On the top of this list is my never-failing friend, Dr. J. S. Neki, a man of sound judgement and wide erudition, who has always been generous in sparing his time and attention for my needs. I am bounden to him for his valuable aid and encouragement. I owe hearty thanks to Professor Gopi Chand Narang, the noted Urdu scholar and National Professor of Urdu, who has helped me in this project in more ways than one :by lending me books from his personal library, by guiding me in the selection of poets and poems, and by providing me with some of the rare photographs of the poets. For my source material I have drawn largely on the library of *Jamia Millia Islamia*, New Delhi, and I express my gratitude to its librarian and the library staff who allowed me free access to their bookshelves. I must also thank my son, Dr. Arun Kanda who, as always, diligently scrutinised the manuscript and corrected the proofs of this book. I would be failing in my duty if I do not express my special thanks to Mr S. K. Ghai, Managing Director, Sterling Publishers, who has shown special care and zeal in the publication of this book, thereby demonstrating his genuine interest in the promotion and popularisation of Urdu literature.

K. C. Kanda

CONTENTS

Preface	vii
Introduction: Urdu Nazm	1
MOHAMMED QULI QUTAB SHAH (1565-1611)	11
Gori	15
Piari	17
Basant	19
Barsaat	21
MIR TAQI MIR (1723-1810)	23
Khwab-O-Khayaal (Abridged)	27
NAZIR AKBARABADI (1732-1830)	51
Banjara Nama	55
Aadmi Nama	63
Burhapa	71
Rotian	89
NAWAB MIRZA SHAUQ LUCKNAVI (1783-1871)	97
Zahr-e-Ishq (Abridged)	101
SALAMAT ALI DABIR (1803-1875)	133
Hazrat Hussain Asks For Water For Ali Asghar (Excerpt)	137
BABAR ALI ANEES (1804-1874)	141
The Burning Plain of Karbala (Excerpt)	145
KHWAJA ALTAF HUSSAIN HALI (1837-1914)	151
Chup ki Daad (Abridged)	155
AKBAR HUSSAIN AKBAR ALLAHABADI (1846-1921)	167
Miss Seemein Badan	171
Majnun's Reply to Laila's Mother	175
SIR MOHAMMED IQBAL (1873-1938)	177
Shikwa (Abridged)	181
Jawab-e-Shikwa (Abridged)	193

Saqi Nama (Excerpts)	205
Tarana-e-Hind	215
Naya Shivala	217
Ram	219
BRIJ NARAIN CHAKBAST (1882-1926)	**221**
A Scene from Ramayana	225
TILOK CHAND MEHROOM (1885-1966)	**235**
Nur Jahan ka Mazaar	239
SHABIR HASSAN JOSH MALIHABADI (1898-1982)	**247**
Baghawat (Abridged)	251
Kissan (Abridged)	263
Husn aur Mazdoori	271
ABU-AL-ASAR HAFEEZ JULLUNDHARY (1900-1982)	**277**
Raqasa	281
Abhi tau Main Jawan Hun (Abridged)	291
AKHTAR SHEERANI (1905-1948)	**297**
Aurat	301
Ai Ishq Hamen Barbad na Kar	305
Reehana	313
NAZAR MOHAMMED RASHID (1910-1975)	**319**
Sharabi	323
Be Karan Raat ke Sannate Mein	325
SANA ALLAHA SANI DAAR MEERAJI (1912-1949)	**329**
Mujhe Ghar Yaad Aata Hai	333
Samundar Ka Bulawa	337
ASRAR-UL-HAQ MAJAZ (1911-1955)	**341**
Aawara	345
Khwab-e-Sehar	353
FAIZ AHMED FAIZ (1911-1984)	**357**
Mujh se Pehli si Mahabbat Miri Mehboob na Maang	361
Mire Humdum, Mire Dost	363
Lahu Ka Suragh	367
ABDUL HAIE SAHIR LUDHIANVI (1922-1980)	**369**
Taj Mahal	373
Chakley	377
Index of First Lines	382

INTRODUCTION : URDU *NAZM*

Poetry may be roughly divided into two broad categories: the subjective and the objective. In the subjective kind of poetry the poet looks within himself and finds his inspiration in his own thoughts, emotions and experiences. In the objective kind, on the contrary, the poet goes out of himself, observes the world of men and manners, and records its actions and events, its sights and sounds, without reference to his own personality or predilections. These two categories, however, are not water-tight, for no poet can be purely subjective, or simply objective. In every lyric (which is another name for subjective poetry) there is an occasional intrusion of the objective spirit in the form of description, reflection, or philosophic comment; and in every objective poem, be it narrative or descriptive, there is an element of subjectivity, for the poet's very choice of a particular subject, be it 'Taj Mahal", or 'The Tomb of Nurjahan", is dictated by his inner impulse or interests. But if a poem is to be judged by the totality of its mood or mode, it can generally be classified as objective or subjective.

The *ghazal* in Urdu represents the most popular form of subjective poetry, while the *nazm* exemplifies the objective kind, often reserved for narrative, descriptive, didactic or satirical purposes. Under the broad head of the *nazm* we may also include the classical forms of poems known by specific names such as *masnavi* (a long narrative poem in rhyming couplets on any theme: romantic, religious, or didactic), *marsia* (an elegy traditionally meant to commemorate the martyrdom of Hazrat Imam Hussain and his comrades of the Karbala fame), or *qasida* (a panegyric written in praise of a king or a nobleman), for all these poems have a single presiding subject, logically developed and concluded.

However, these poetic species have an old world aura about their subject and style, and are different from the modern *nazm*, supposed to have come into vogue in the later part of the nineteenth century.

In order to understand the distinguishing features of the *nazm* it will be helpful to place it by the side of the *ghazal* and mark the points of contrast and resemblance between the two. The *ghazal*, as is well-known, is a short poem, generally of seven, nine, or at most, of a dozen couplets in the same metre. It always opens with a rhyming couplet called "matla", and ends with the "maqta", which often includes the pen-name of the poet. It follows a set rhyming pattern: aa, ba, ca, da, and so on. The *nazm* is not bound by any such considerations of length or rhyme scheme. There could be a long *nazm* like Iqbal's "Shikwa", which contains as many as 186 lines, or a short one like Iqbal's "Ram", with only twelve lines. Further, the poet of the *nazm* is free to adopt any metrical arrangement that suits his subject or mood. A large number of *nazms*, such as Mir's "Khwab-O-Khayal", or Josh Malihabadi's "Kissan", are written in separately rhyming couplets which, however, observe the discipline of a uniform metre throughout the poem. Some *nazms* like Chakbast's "Ramayan ka ek scene", or Mehroom's "Noor Jahan ka Mazaar", use another popular poetic measure called "musaddas", a unit of six lines, consisting of a rhyming quatrain and a couplet on a different rhyme. Iqbal's poem, "Ram", follows the rhyming pattern of the *ghazal* in all the couplets but the last, which, to give the effect of finality, makes use of a new and different rhyme. And all the poems of Quli Qutab Shah included in this volume adhere to the pattern of the *ghazal*, complete with "matla" and "maqta". The poet of the *nazm* thus enjoys a greater measure of freedom in the choice of rhyme scheme and length of the poem, as against the practitioner of the *ghazal*, and this enables him to match his style with the subject, and adjust the tone and pace of his verse to reflect the undulations of mood and situation.

A group of progressive writers of the early decades of the 20th century have successfully exploited the freedom and flexibility of the *nazm*. Taking a cue from English poets like T. S. Eliot and Ezra Pound, they reject the rigidity of the regular rhyme, dispense with "radif" and "qafia", and opt for the medium of blank verse or free verse. A poem written in blank verse is called "nazm-e-muarra" in Urdu. Such a poem breaks with the tradition of "radif" and "qafia", but observes the sanctity of metre, and sticks to lines of equal length. The free-verse poem called "Azad Nazm" goes a step further, for it not only discards the rhyme, but also feels free to use lines of unequal length in the same poem, or even in the same stanza. With the skilful manipulation of the internal pause, and by avoiding the frequent use of end-stopped lines, the practitioner of this form can give a greater degree of flexibility and naturalness to his lines, so as to bring them as close as possible to the intonation and rhythms of natural speech. However, even the poet of the "Azad Nazm" is careful to preserve the inner rhythm and cadence of his verse and obeys the laws of metre, without which his poem may forfeit its claim to be classed as poetry. It may not be out of place to mention that despite the outstanding achievement of "free verse" poems in the hands of poets like N. M. Rahid and Meeraji, the traditional kind of *nazm* continues to delight the readers with the incantation of its musical measures.

The *nazm* differs from the *ghazal* in another important way. The *ghazal* prides itself, among other things, on the detachability and completeness of its individual verses, which retain their sense and effectiveness even when divorced from their context in the poem. The verses are not bound by the law of unity and consistency. The poet of the *ghazal* is at liberty to talk about love in the first verse, death in the second, envy in the third, mysticism in the fourth, and so on. Such is not the case with the *nazm* which owes its strength and identity to the logical evolution of thought and theme. A *nazm* must have a controlling thought or idea, discussed, developed and concluded, with due regard to the laws of poetic composition. That's why a *nazm*, as against the *ghazal*, always carries a title summing up its central theme The various units of the *nazm*, besides subserving the need of the central thought, must be mutually interlinked, so as to contribute to the forward movement of narration which should culminate in an aesthetically satisfying close. And this reminds us of the etymological meaning of *nazm*, an Arabic term implying a stringing together of pearls, or an artistic ordering of words and lines.

Although the *nazm*, in the aforesaid sense of a specific theme logically developed and metrically presented, has existed in Urdu poetry since the very early times, as can be evidenced by the *nazms* of Quli Qutab Shah (1565-1611) or of Nazir Akbarabadi (1732-1830), the *nazm* in its modern form may be said to have begun in the later part of the 19th century. One cause for the revival and popularisation of the *nazm* was the growing realisation among the poets and readers that the traditional *ghazal* was too narrow and restrictive to serve the larger interests of life and society. No doubt, the *ghazal*, in the hands of the master-poets like Mir, Sauda, Zauq or Ghalib, has demonstrated its capacity to deal with the whole range of human experience, its one staple subject has been love: love, earthy or ethereal, which it treats, because of the exigencies of its form, in a characteristically condensed and suggestive manner, with the aid of images and allusions, without stating its case directly or in detail. Ghalib was apparently alluding to the restrictive form of the *ghazal* when he wrote:

بقدرِ شوق نہیں ظرفِ تنگنائے غزل
کچھ اور چاہیئے وسعت مرے بیاں کے لئے

Narrow is the mould of *ghazal*, too compressed and cramped,
I need a larger space to spell out my thoughts.

The narrowness of the *ghazal* becomes widely conspicuous by a comparison of this form with the English poetry of the 19th century written by the Romantics like Wordsworth, Coleridge or Shelley, or by the Victorian poets such as Tennyson, Browning or Arnold. There is obviously no scope in the *ghazal* for poems like the "Immortality Ode", the "West Wind", or "The Ancient Mariner", the poems which, apart from drawing our attention to the beauty and witchery of nature, express the eternal verities of life in a thoughtful and thought-provoking manner. As more and more of Indian readers got exposed to Western thought and literature, the traditional Urdu *ghazal* with its perpetual involvement with the locks and cheeks of the beloved, and enclosed in the same metrical straitjacket, began to appear stale and decadent, unrelated to the ever expanding needs of life. Consequently, under the leadership of men like Sir Sayyed Ahmed Khan, some younger enthusiasts such as Altaf Hussain Hali and Mohammed Hussain Azad decided to give a new direction to Urdu poetry, by broadening its base and harnessing its energies for the larger purposes of life.

The foundation of the modern *nazm* was formally laid on 30 June, 1874, when, under the aegis of the "Anjuman-e-Urdu", a new kind of "mushaira", called "Munazama" (literally, a symposium of *nazms*), was organised at Lahore (Pakistan). This was a unique symposium for the reason that it gave to the participating poets not a "tarah misra" (a line of poetry which was to serve them as a model for their poetical exertions, in terms of mood, metre, and rhyme), but a specific topic to build their poems upon. In fact, the "munazama" extended the freedom of the poets not only in the choice of the size and shape of the poems, but also in the matter of subject and theme. The poet of the *nazm* could now write on any subject under the sun, provided it stirred his imagination, and contained the potential for striking a responsive chord in the hearts of the readers. The first topic prescribed for this poetical gathering was "Zamistan" (Winter Season), which shows a turning towards the poetry of nature from an age-long obsession with amatory themes. Mohammed Hussain Azad read his poem, "Shab-e-Qadar", on this occasion, which was highly acclaimed. Ismael Meeruti, another pioneering poet of the movement criticised in one of his poems the crippling conservatism of the traditional *ghazal*, and made a plea for change:

سخن وران زماں کی بھی ہے یہی حالت
کہ اس قدیم ڈگر کو نہ چھوڑتے زنہار
سوائے عشق نہیں سوجھتا کوئی مضموں
سو وہ بھی محض خیالی گھڑت کا طومار

Men of letters in this age are all convention-bound,
Nothing can persuade them to quit the old groove,
Love is their sole concern, love is their refrain,
Which too is fancy-fed, far removed from truth.

But it was Altaf Hussain Hali, who in his poems like "Hub-e-Watan", "Barkha Rut", "Chup ki Daad", and "Bewa ki Munajaat", as also in his masterpiece, "Musaddis-a-Hali", blazed a new trail, and used the long Urdu *nazm* as an instrument of social and moral reform. Hali also used the *nazm* for interpreting the beauties of nature—a theme which was more or less neglected, or treated marginally by the poets of the classical *ghazal*. It was he again who in his prose treatise, "Muqaddama-e-Shair-o-Shairi", underscored the limitations of the classical *ghazal* and pointed out the hollowness of its hackneyed themes, thus putting the *nazm* on a surer path of progress.

Hali's poems draw into focus an important feature of the *nazm*. While the *ghazal* has been primarily used as an instrument of aesthetic and intellectual pleasure, and a source of courtly entertainment, the *nazm* combines pleasure with purpose, and expends its resources in the service of society. It is a more useful, more pragmatic, more earth-bound form of poetry, loaded generally with a moral and a message. It believes in the dictum of art for life sake, as against the aesthetic creed of art for art sake. This is as true of the poems of Hali, as of Akbar Allahabadi, Chakbast, Mohammed Iqbal, Josh Malihabadi, or, for that matter, of the poems of Nazir Akbarabadi, which, though written long before the revival of the *nazm* in the modern form, are all addressed to the needs of the common man, and deal with issues of universal import, in a language that may truly be called the language of every-day speech. Nevertheless, as can be ascertained by a perusal of the poems presented in this anthology, each poet has his special area of interest and his favourite mode of expression. What Hali says in plain and direct terms, is stated ironically, with the aid of humour and satire, by Akbar Allahabadi. Also, Iqbal's emphasis on selfhood and self-respect, couched in philosophical words, is basically a call for national and individual awakening, harking back to Hali and anticipating several other later-day poets such as Josh Malihabadi, Faiz, Firaq, Hafeez or Sahir, all of whom have the good of the nation at their heart, though each one has his own concept of what is good for the people.

There is another relevant point to be noted. The *nazm* which began as a reaction against the domination of the *ghazal* gives precedence to reason over imagination, and not vice versa, as was done heretofore. Instead of taking the reader into the intricate depths of the human mind, or on flights of fancy beyond this world, the *nazm* prefers to keep its feet planted on this earth, which is the earth of all of us, and is content to portray real life in a relatively realistic way. Mirza Ghalib's assertion:

آگہی دام شنیدن ہے جس قدر چاہے بچھا ئے
مدّعا عنقا ہے اپنے عالمِ تقریر کا

Let reason do its very best to comprehend my sense,
Subtle like the fabled phoenix is the purport of my speech—

might be true for the *ghazal*, but not generally for the *nazm* which ought to be intelligible and easily accessible to an average reader. A peculiar beauty of the *ghazal* lies in its brevity and suggestiveness, in its ability to express in just two lines what will need a much longer space if stated directly and in detail. As the *nazm* is not bound by the restriction of length, or by the discipline of the rhyming order, it can afford a more discursive, and a more detailed exploration of its essential subject than the *ghazal*. The availability of a larger canvas enables the poet of the *nazm* to survey and record the vast panorama of life including the sights and scenes of nature, oddities and jealousies of man, vagaries of time and fate, atrocities of the strong and the sufferings of the poor, besides, of course, the all-important affairs of the heart. It is significant that Faiz Ahmed Faiz, when he turns to take stock of "problems other than those of love" (*Dukh aur bhi hain zamaane mein mahabbat ke siwa*), chooses the mould of the *nazm* in preference to that of the *ghazal*, though he is equally at home in both these genres. The capaciousness of the *nazm* makes it specially relevant to the modern world, riddled as it is with ever-new problems of social, cultural, or political sort. Sahir Ludhianvi's exhortation:

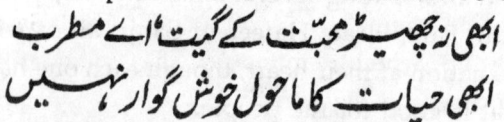

ابھی نہ چھیڑ محبّت کے گیت اے مطرب
ابھی حیات کا ماحول خوش گوار نہیں

Sing not, O lutanist, songs of love as yet,
Time is not congenial for such romantic themes—

is meant to remind the reader that the old lyrical mode, with its emphasis on love and romance, is out of tune with the realities of this trouble-tossed world. Coming out of the wonderland of the *ghazal*, we should turn towards more realistic strains, channelled through the more responsive form of the *nazm*.

That the form of the *nazm* is capable of responding to the changing needs of the times, is borne out by the works of several poets contained in this volume. When the movement for Home Rule was at its height, it found its voice in the poems of Chakbast, when Hindu Muslim unity was the need of the hour, poets like Hali and Iqbal came out with patriotic songs such as "Hub-e-Watan" and "Tarana-e-Hind"; when, under the leadership of Mahatma Gandhi, the flag of rebellion was unfurled against the British regime, Josh Malihabadi came to the fore with his stirring poems like "Baghawat", and "Zawal-e-Jahanbani", and when socialistic ideas gained currency among the Indian intelligentsia, a group of progressive poets such as Faiz, Sahir and N. M. Rashid emerged on the scene to defend the proletariat against the bourgeoisie, and to glorify the Red Revolution. The *nazm* as such has always measured up to the needs of the people, something which the *ghazal* alone could not have so successfully done.

Lest we overstate the useful and hortatory role of the *nazm*, we should read the poems of Akhtar Sheerani and Majaz Lucknavi, both of whom return with a vengeance to the world of love and lyricism, though this lyricism, in the case of Majaz at least, is mingled with a strong note of protest against the inequities of the social order. The romantic note insistently heard in their poems is meant to remind us that, despite our preoccupation with social and political issues, love will continue to play a pivotal role in the arena of art and life. And then there are poems like "Be Karan Raat ke Sannaate mein" (N. M. Rashid), and "Samunder ka Bulawa" (Meeraji), which demonstrate that the poet of the *nazm* has not surrendered his right to be introvert or introspective. He can, if his subject demands, take the reader into the interior realm of his mind and thought, and back again to the world of physical and social realities. All this speaks volumes for the sweep and scope of the *nazm*.

I would conclude this note with a word of caution. Despite the multiple merits of the *nazm*, and despite its relevance to the drama of real life, it holds no threat to the power and popularity of the *ghazal*, which in the hands of such consummate artists as Jigar, Asghar, Faiz, Fani or Firaq, has amply proved its worth as an imperishable art form, fully equipped to fathom the mysteries of the human mind, or tap the complexities of love and life. As a matter of fact, the *ghazal* and the *nazm* are complementary rather than mutually exclusive poetic forms, and their areas of artistic functioning have a tendency to overlap. The two together enable us to make the two essential voyages: the voyage within, to strange countries not visible to the actual senses, and the voyage without, in the external world of social, religious, natural, or political phenomenon.

Mohammed Quli Qutab Shah.
(1565-1611)

MOHAMMED QULI QUTAB SHAH
(1565-1611)

Sultan Mohammed Quli Qutab Shah, son of Ibrahim Qutab Shah, was the ruler of the state of Golconda, and founder of the city of Hyderabad. He was a contemporary of emperor Jalal-ul-din Akbar, and was, like Akbar, a liberal, kind-hearted ruler, a lover of peace and amity, and a patron and promoter of the fine arts of poetry, music and architecture. More than that, he was a great poet, the author of a rich collection of nearly 50,000 couplets, comprising *ghazals, nazms, masnavis, qasidas, rubaies* and *qitas*. It is now generally agreed that Quli Qutab Shah, rather than Wali Deccany, was the founding father of Urdu poetry. He may also be called the architect of Urdu language which he built by blending together Persian and Hindi, with a sprinkling of words and phrases drawn from Punjabi, Arabic, and local Deccany dialects. He, however, saw to it that the new product remained close to the language of common speech. He may truly be called the poet of the people who has written poems to celebrate the popular Indian festivals such as Holi, Diwali, Eid, Basant, Barsaat, the New Year Day, and the like. But he was basically, a lover and a poet of love. A man of romantic temperament, his privileged position as a ruler allowed him easy access to the society of women, and it was this amorous involvement with the fair sex that inspired the poet in him. In a series of poems he has chosen to dwell upon the graces and charms of his twelve mistresses who are remembered by such endearing names as "Piari", "Gori", "Nanhi", "Sanwli", "Chhabeeli", etc. Two of these *nazms*, "Piari", and "Gori", are also included in this anthology. Both these poems are written to praise the beauty of the poet's mistresses, and to persuade them to surrender their wealth of beauty at their lover's feet. It is interesting to recall that the city of Hyderabad founded by him was first named "Bhag Nagar" after the name of his beloved, Bhag Mati.

The third poem of this selection, *Basant,* relates to the Indian festival of spring, when the young and old give themselves up to the spirit of jollity, and sprinkle colours on each other with gay abandon. The fourth poem, *Barsaat,* describes the poet's amorous gambols against the background of the cloud-filled skies. All these poems are frankly sensuous and romantic, and all of them end with the praise of the Prophet, which, incidentally, points to the twin aspects of the poet's personality: the romantic and the religious.

It may also be noted that all these poems are written in the metrical pattern of the *ghazal,* which may be represented as aa, ba, ca, da, and so on.

Excessive drinking and a sensual way of life told heavily on Qutab Shah's health, and he died at the comparatively young age of 47. But he'll be remembered for his pioneering role in the development of Urdu poetry, and for founding the historic city of Hyderabad.

محمد قلی قطب شاہ

گوری

سہاتا ہے مکھ حُسن گوری کا شاب
او مکھ چند پہ چند کیاں ہیں لاجوں نقاب
او قد سروں یں ہے کندن کا نہال
جھمکتا ہے تو اُس سٹھے سورج کا تاب
توں رنگ رس کی باغ کی ہے کلی
تو چوتا ہے جیون کا تج مکھ سٹھے آب

رسالے ادھر ہیں ترے مد بھرے
سو کرتے ہیں عشاق دل کوں کباب
کہوں زلف یا تازہ سُنبل سہی
او مکھ پھول پر جوں کہ چند پر سحاب
تری چال بد مست سٹھے لاجیں گج
نہیں اُن میں اے بھید ہور اے شتاب
بنی صدقے قطبا سوں گوری ملی
تو گل با نہ دے اُس سوں پیوے شراب

Mohammed Quli Qutab Shah
Gori

It looks so charming, my Gori's beaming face,
The moon gets eclipsed, confronted with her grace.

She's not a cypress, but a plant of gold,
Like the radiant sun, emitting dazzling rays.

A bud you are of vernal grove, with hue and sap imbued,
Copious drops of nectar flow down your face.

Intoxicating are your lips, with purple wine aglow,
Which with their passionate heat set my heart ablaze.

Are these the locks of hair, or tasselled hyacinth?
Which like the lunar clouds hang about your face.

You put the elephants to shame with your drunken gait,
For they cannot emulate your winsome pace and grace.

To the Prophet's holy grace, I owe the gift of Gori's love,
Drink, O Qutaba, draughts of wine holding her in your embrace!

Suhaata hai mukh husn Gori ka shaab,
O mukh chand pe chand kiyaan hain la jon niqaab.

O sarv qad nahin hai kundan ka nihal,
Jhamakta hai tu us the sooraj ka taab.

Tun rang ras ki baagh ki hai kali,
Tochota hai jeevan ka tuj mukh the aab.

Rasaale adhar hain tire madh bhare,
So karte hain ushaaq dil kon kabab.

Kahun zulaf ya taaza sumbal suhi,
O mukh phool par jun ke chand par sahaab.

Tiri chaal mad mast the laajen gaj,
Nahin un mein aeh bhed hor aeh shataab.

Nabi sadqe Qutaba son Gori mili,
Tu gal baande us son peeve sharaab.

قلی قطب شاہ
پیاری

پیاری نکر توں سبھن سوں منم
جو جاگی جوانی تو پھر ہوگی خم
یقیں جان جگ میں اے بات ہے
کہ گوہر پُھٹے پر ہوتا مول کم
جوانی و جوبن ہے سب پاؤنا
کہ تجھ بتھے ہو وے عیش سائیں کوں جم
میا آپ سائیں کا رکھ اپنے دل
کہ رتج بتھے ہو وے عیش سائیں کوں جم
چھنداں سیتی سنگار کر آئی دھن
سُہے مکھ اُپر خوی کہ جوں پھل پہ نم
پنواتے ہیں سکیاں میں اپ حسن کوں
او چاہے ہیں خوباں میں اپنا علم
بنی صدقے قطب آ ہے رتج نیہہ تھے مست
سہے سب بتاں میں توں اُس کا صنم

Quli Qutab Shah
Piari

Be not proud, O love, of your beauteous brow,
This fleeting youth will leave you broken like a bow.

Everyone in the world this truth doth know,
That a pearl, when broken, forfeits its glow.

No use are youth and beauty, you, my love, should know,
Unless you let your lover drink away the bowls.

Let your heart be fully charged with my love, O sweet,
Let your lord bathe and bask in your radiant glow.

There you arrive on the scene decked and dressed with grace,
Lo, they sparkle like the dew, the drops of sweat on your brow.

Surfeiting your playmates, with your beauty's wine,
You raise your standard over the beauty's show.

Qutaba revels in your love by the Prophet's grace,
In the beauties' circle, his love steals the show.

Piari nakar tun sajan son manam.
Jo jaagi jawaani tau phir hogi kham.

Yaqin jaan jag mein aeh baat hai,
Ke gohar phute par hota mol kam.

Jawaani-o-joban hai sab paaona,
Ke tujh the howe aish saaien ko jam.

Meea aap saaien ka rakh apne dil,
Ke tuj the howe aish saaien ko jam.

Chhandan saity singaar kar aai dhan,
Suhe mukh upar khui ke jun phul pe nam.

Panwaate hain sakian mein ap husn kon,
Ochaae hain khubaan mein apna alam.

Nabi sadqe Qutba hai tuj neh the mast,
Suhe sab butaan mein tun uska sanam.

قلی قطب شاہ
بسنت

بسنت کھیلیں عشق کی آپ پیارا
تمہیں ہیں چاند میں ہوں جوں ستارا
نخیل کندن کے تاراں انگ مجھ نا
بندی ہوں چھند بندسوں کر سنگارا
بسنت کھیلیں ہمن ہور سا جنایوں
کہ اسماں رنگ شفق پایا ہے سارا
پیا پگ پر ملا کر لیا ئی پیاری
بسنت کھیلی ہوا رنگ رنگ سنگارا
جوبن کے حوضخانے رنگ مدن بھر
سور و ماروم چرکیاں لائے دھارا
بھیگی چولی میں بھٹین نس نشانی
عجب سورج میں ہے کیوں نس کوں ٹھارا
بسنت ونت جھد سو کندن گال اوپر
پھولایا آگ کیسر کی بہارا
نبیؐ صدقے بسنت کھیلیا قطب شہ
رنگیلا ہور رہیا ترلوک سارا

Quli Qutab Shah
Basant

Let us celebrate Basant, the fest of love and life,
You, my love, are the moon, I, a star on high.

My body is all aglow, like the purest, shining gold,
Here I come decked and draped, armed and fortified.

I and my darling sweet should give in to the vernal mood,
Drench ourselves in colours rich, like the tinted twilight sky.

After bowing to her lord, Piari joins the floral show,
Plays the sport with such a zest, all her robes get richly dyed.

Charging both her beauteous bowls with the wine of love,
Striking like the lightning flash, my inner being she electrifies.

Her nipples beneath her dripping bra, like the sable night
    appear,
How can the night withstand the sun, I'm utterly mystified.

So it seems from golden cheeks and bodies yellow-splashed,
That the blazing saffron bloom is now at its golden height.

Qutab has enjoyed Basant, glory be to the Prophet's name,
The universe, from end to end, with colours gay is beautified.

Basant khelen ishq ki aa payara,
Tumhin hain chaand, main hun joon sitara.

Nachhil kundan ke taaraan ank jhona,
Bandi hun chhand band son kar singaara.

Basant khelen haman hor saajana yun,
Ke aasmaan rang shafaq paaya hai saara.

Peeaa pag par mila kar liyai Piari,
Basant kheli, hua rang rang singara.

Joban ke hauzkhane rang madan bhar,
So roma rom chirkiyan laae dhara.

Bhiki choli mein bhuten nis nishani,
Ajab sooraj mein hai kyon nis kon thara.

Basant want jhad so kundan gaal upar,
Phoolaya aag kesar ki bahara.

Nabi sadqe basant khelia Qutab Shah,
Rangila ho rahya trilok saara.

قلی قطب شاہ
برسات

رُوت آیا کلیاں کا ہوا راج
ہری ڈال سر پھولاں کے تاج
مینہوں بُند کا لیو ہِت پیالا
رُوت ناریاں ساجیں ایکس تھے یک راج
تن تھنڈ ت لرزت، جوبن گرجت
پیا مکھ دیکھت کنپکی کس کبسے آج
ناری مکھ جھمکے جیسے بجلی
انجل باوک میں سہے اُس لاج
کیس پھول دیسے ستارے اسماں
اس زمانے کی پری پدمنی آئے آج
چوند ہر گرجت ہور مینہوں برست
عشق کے چمنے چمن موراں کا ہے راج
حضرت مصطفیٰ کے صدقے آیا برش کالا
قطب شہ عشق کر و دن دن راج

Quli Qutab Shah
Barsaat

With the birth of rainy season begins the reign of buds,
Green branches now will don crowns of roses on their heads.

Hold the cups in your hands, fill them with the drops of rain,
There they come, fervour-charged, beauties richly decked and dressed.

Their bodies quiver in chilly air, their bosoms bounce and throb,
As they see their love approach, their stays, it seems, would snap and burst.

The damsel's face emits a glow like the lightning flash,
And she draws over her face the mantle slipping from her head.

The flowers that adorn her hair shine like the stars on high,
She is Padmini of to-day, dressed in her charming best.

Thunder and lightning fill the sky, heavily doth it pour,
The peacocks with their lilting songs set the grove aburst.

Glory be to Prophet the great, who sent the rains from heaven,
May your reign flourish, O Qutaba, your amorous court be blessed!

Rut aaya kaliaan ka hua raaj,
Hari daal sir phoolan ke taaj.

Meinhun bund ka laio hat payala,
Rut naariaan saajen ekas the yak saaj.

Tan thandat larzat, joban garjat,
Peeaa mukh dekhat kanchiky kas bakse aaj.

Naari mukh jhamke jaise bijly,
Anjal baauk mein suhe us laaj.

Kes phool dese sitaare asmaan,
Is zamane ki pari Padmini aae aaj.

Chaundhir garjat hor meinhon barsat,
Ishq ke chamne chaman moran ka hai raaj.

Hazrat Mustifa ke sadqe, aaya barsh kala,
Qutab Shah ishq karo din din raaj.

Mir Taqi Mir
(1723-1810)

MIR TAQI MIR
(1723-1810)

Mir Taqi Mir is one of the immortals among Urdu poets. A specialist of the *ghazal*, he has left behind six poetical collections called *Dewans*, containing a total of 13,585 couplets. He has also written *masnavis*, *marsias*, and *qasidas*, besides a *Dewan* in Persian poetry, and at least three important works in Persian prose—*Nikaat-ul-Shora*, containing lives of Urdu poets, *Zikar-e-Mir*, an autobiography, and *Faiz-e-Mir*, a book specially written for the edification of the poet's son.

Mir is basically a poet of love, more specially, of love unfulfilled, which has lent to his poetry a peculiar tinge of sadness, not depressing or morbid, but soothing and humanising. Transience of life, hollowness of earthly achievements, inevitability of death, immanence of God, helplessness of man, and value of humanity, humility, and compassion, are some of the recurrent themes of his poetry. His chief strength lies in expressing deep thoughts in a simple, conversational style, which seemingly artless, yet represents the acme of poetic skill and perfection. Mir is also one of the early architects of the Urdu language. He lived at a time when Urdu poetry was at a formative stage—its language was getting reformed, and its texture was being enriched with borrowings from Persian imagery and idiom. Aided by his aesthetic instincts, Mir struck a fine balance between the old and the new, the indigenous and the imported elements. Knowing that Urdu is essentially an Indian language, he retained the best in native Hindi speech, and leavened it with a sprinkling of Persian diction and phraseology, so as to create a poetic language at once simple, natural and elegant, acceptable alike to the elite and the common folk.

It is a commonplace criticism that Mir is a poet of pathos and melancholia. His pathos, it should be remembered, is compounded of personal and public causes. His life was a long struggle against unfavourable circumstances. He lost his father, Mohd. Ali Mataqqi, at the age of 10, and his godfather, Sayed Aman Allah, at about the same age. Thus orphaned, he moved from Agra to Delhi, and went from pillar to post in search of financial and emotional support.

At the age of 17 Mir suffered a stroke of madness, a consequence of cumulative mental tension, precipitated, one may surmise, by frustration in love. In this state of manic depression the boy-poet would be haunted by a fairy-faced apparition, that would descend to him every night from the moon, and disappear at dawn, leaving him restless during the day. This hallucinatory experience is the basis of Mir's *masnavi*, "Khwab-o-Khayal", which is included in this book in an abridged form. Apart from being a fine piece of narrative art, this poem contains a moving account of the plight of a psychic patient, and the callous way this sickness was treated in the past. It is remarkable that even when the poet is passing through the worst phase of mental and physical agony, he doesn't lose his hold on love and beauty which glimmer every now and then through the generally dark imagery of this poem, as in the following couplet:

Carking cares of life my mental peace did foil,
My luck, like my darling's locks, was always caught in coils.

Mir's sorrows were further strengthened by the circumstances of his age. He lived at a time when Delhi was subjected to the devastating raids of Nadir Shah and Ahmed Shah. Mir was a helpless witness to these traumatic events which have left a deep imprint on his mind and art. When life became unbearable in Delhi, Mir, like many other peace-loving folk, migrated to Lucknow, but so sensitive was he to his personal honour, and so attached to the streets of Delhi, that he felt ill-at-ease in the new dispensation. He died in Lucknow in 1810 at the age of 87.

میر تقی میر
خواب و خیال

خوشا حال اُس کا جو معدوم ہے
کہ احوالِ اپنا تو معلوم ہے
رہیں جانِ غم ناک کو کاہشیں
گئیں دل سے نومید سو خواہشیں
زمانے نے رکھا مجھے متّصل
پراگندہ روزی پراگندہ دل
نہ گئی کب پریشانیِ روزگار
رہا میں تو ہم طالعِ زلفِ یار
وطن میں نہ اِک صبح میں شام کی
نہ پہنچی خبر مجھ کو آرام کی
اُٹھاتے ہی سر پر پڑا اتّفاق
کہ دشمن ہوئے سارے اہلِ وفاق
زمانے نے آوارہ چاہا مجھے
مری بے کسی نے نباہا مجھے
رفیقوں سے دیکھی بہت کوتہی
غریبی نے اِک عمر کی ہم سری

Mir Taqi Mir
Khwab-O-Khayal (Dream and Fancy)

He alone is happy whom we do not know,
My plight, of course, everyone doth know.

My sad and weary life was always trouble-tossed,
Unrealized remained my dreams and my noble thoughts.

The world and its crooked ways drove me to the wall,
Always I was hard-pressed, always broken-heart.

Carking cares of life my mental peace did foil,
My luck, like my darling's locks, was always caught in coils.

I didn't ever spend at home a single peaceful day,
No welcome news, no relief ever came my way.

Hardly had I raised my head, when I got a blow,
The entire world, en bloc, suddenly turned my foe.

I was forced out of home to turn a vagrant waif,
My only friend, my helplessness, watched me night and day.

I was treated by my friends in a callous way,
Adversity gave me company all along the way.

Khusha haal uska jo maadum hai,
Ke ahwaal apna tau maalum hai.

Rahin jaan-e-ghamnaak ko kaahshen,
Gaien dil se naumeed sau khwahishen.

Zamane ne rakhha mujhe mutsil,
Praganda rozi, praganda dil.

Gai kab pareshani-e-rozgaar,
Raha main tau hum-taala-e-zulaf-e-yaar.

Watan mein na ik subah main sham ki,
Na pahunchi khabar mujhko aaraam ki.

Uthate hi sar par para ittefaaq,
Ke dushman hue saare ahl-e-wafaaq.

Zamane ne awara chaha mujhe,
Miri be kasi ne nibaha mujhe.

Rafiqon ne dekhi bahut kotahi,
Gharibi ne ik umar ki humsari.

میر تقی میر

مجھے یہ زمانہ جدھر لے گیا
غریبانہ چندے بسر لے گیا
بندھا اِس طرح آہ بارِ سفر
کرے زادہ راہ کچھ نہ بارِ سفر
چلا اکبر آباد سے جس گھڑی
در و بام پر چشمِ حسرت پڑی
دلِ مضطرب اشکِ حسرت ہوا
جگر رخصتانے میں رخصت ہوا
پس از قطع رہ لائے دِلّی میں بخت
بہت کھینچے یاں میں نے آزارِ سخت
جگر جورِ گردوں سے خوں ہو گیا
مجھے رُکتے رُکتے جنوں ہو گیا
ہوا خبط سے مجھ کو ربطِ تمام
لگی رہنے دہشت مجھے صبح و شام
کبھو کف بہ لب مست رہنے لگا
کبھو سنگ در دست رہنے لگا

Mir Taqi Mir

Wherever I was driven by the tide of time,
Penury stared me in the face, alien was the clime.

Thus, alas, I set out on my wild exile,
Unequipped and unprovided for the game of life.

I left Akbarabad with a heavy heart,
Casting a lingering look on the roofs and walls.

In a flood of wistful tears my heart did burst,
Pain of parting nibbled away all my strength and guts.

I was brought to Delhi by my evil stars,
Where I suffered miseries, untold, unthought.

The tyranny of the heavens made my vitals bleed,
I grew insane, suppressing down my grief.

Rapt in frenzy wild, morn and eve I lay,
To wild hallucinations I fell a prey.

Sometimes with my hand on lips I would sit withdrawn,
Or, with a stone in hand cause a deep alarm.

Mujhe yeh zamana jidhar le gaya,
Gharibana chande basar le gaya.

Bandha istarah, aah, baar-e-safar,
Kare zaad-e-rah kuchh na baar-e-safar.

Chala Akbarabad se jis ghari,
Dar-o-baam par chashm-e-hasrat pari.

Dil-e-muzterib ashk-e-hasrat hua,
Jigar rukhsatane mein rukhsat hua.

Pas az qata rah laae dilli mein bakht,
Bahut kheinche yaan main ne azaar sakht.

Jigar jaur-e-gardoon se khoon ho gaya,
Mujhe rukte rukte janoon ho gaya.

Hua khabt se mujh ko rabt-e-tamam,
Lagi rahne wahshat mujhe subah-o-sham.

Kabho kaf balab mast rahne laga,
Kabho sang dar dast rahne laga.

میر تقی میر

کبھو غرقِ بحرِ تحیّر رہوں
کبھو سر بہ جیبِ تفکر رہوں
یہ وہم غلط کاریاں تک کھنچا
کہ کارِ جنوں آسماں تک کھنچا
مہ چاردہ کار آتش کرے
ڈروں یاں تلک میں کہ جی غش کرے
توہّم کا بیٹھا جو نقشی دُرست
لگی ہونے وسواس سے جان سُست
نظر آئی اِک شکل مہتاب میں
کمی آئی جس سے خور و خواب میں
اگر چند پرتوسے مہ کے ڈروں
ولیکن نظر اس طرف ہی کروں
ڈروں دیکھ مائل اسے اس طرف
بہ حدے کہ آجائیں ہونٹوں پہ کف
رہی فکرِ جاں میرے احباب کو
اڑا دیویں سب گھر کے اسباب کو

Mir Taqi Mir

Sometimes I would sit utterly lost and dazed,
At other times with downcast head and abstracted gaze.

The spell of wild delusions stretched itself so far,
That my manic state spanned the sky and stars.

The sight of the rounded moon scalded me like fire,
So that I would faint with fear, well-nigh expire.

When with delusions vague my mind was deep-impressed,
Taking false for true, I lost my living zest.

But when I saw a shape in the moon ensconced,
I lost my appetite, I lost my calm.

Though I was afraid of the image in the beam,
I couldn't help but gaze and gaze at that silver gleam.

That lunar shape, on me intent, awakened deep dread,
So much so, my mouth and lips began to foam and fret.

My friends felt concerned about my very life,
Everything in the room was hastily shoved aside.

Kabho gharq-e-bahr-e-tahayyur rahun,
Kabho sar ba jeb-e-tafakkur rahun.

Yeh waham-e-ghalt kaar yaan tak khincha,
Ke kaar-e-janoon aasmaan tak khincha.

Mah-e-chaar-dah kaar-e-aatish kare,
Darun yaan talak main ke ji ghash kare.

Tawahum ka baitha jo naqsh-e-darust,
Lagi hone wiswas se jaan sust.

Nazar aai ik shakal mahtaab mein,
Kami aai jis se khur-o-khwab mein.

Agarchand partaw se mah ke darun,
Wa lekin nazar us taraf hi karun.

Darun dekh maail use is taraf,
Ba hadde ke aa jaaen honton pe kaf.

Rahi fikr-e-jaan mere ahbab ko,
Ura dewen sab ghar ke asbab ko.

میر تقی میر

ہوئے پاس کوئی تفاوت سے ہو
سراسیمہ کوئی محبت سے ہو
کوئی فرطِ اندوہ سے گریہ ناک
گریباں کسو کا مرے غم سے چاک
جو دیکھوں تو آنکھوں سے لوہو بہے
نہ دیکھوں تو جی پر قیامت رہے
کہے چشم بنائی کو ہر بار غیر
ولے منزلِ دل میں اس مہ کی سیر
اگر ہوش میں ہوں ولے بے خبر
وہ صورت رہے میرے پیشِ نظر
اُسے دیکھوں جیدھر کروں میں نگہ
وہی ایک صورت ہزاروں جگہ
نگہ گردشِ چشم سے فتنہ ساز
مژہ آفتِ روزگارِ دراز
جو آنکھ اس کی بینی سے جا کر لڑے
دمِ تیغ پر راہ چلنی پڑے

Mir Taqi Mir

Someone would approach me tremulous with fear,
Others with love extreme enfolded me and cheered.

Someone overwhelmed with grief shed copious tears,
Another would rend his cloak, or his collar tear.

If I gazed at that shape my eyes streamed blood,
If I took my eyes away, ill-at-ease I felt.

The eye didn't believe in what it really saw,
The lunar shape, all the time, my inner self did gnaw.

Be it the state of consciousness, or a fainting fit,
That shape refused my inner mind to quit.

I saw that elfin face wherever I gazed,
That shape confronted me in every nook and place.

Calamitous was the glance of her rolling eyes,
Her eye-lashes could easily the gazer mesmerize.

If on her plaited locks you cast your eye,
You feel as if a dagger across your path doth lie.

Hue paas koi tafaawat se ho,
Saraseema koi mahabbat se ho.

Koi fart-e-andoh se giriya naak,
Garebaan kaso ka mere ghum mein chaak.

Jo dekhun tau aankhon se lohu bahe,
Na dekhun tau ji par qayamat rahe.

Kahe chashm binaai ko har baar ghair,
Wale manzil-e-dil mein us mah ki sair.

Agar hosh mein hun, wale be khabar,
Woh soorat rahe mere pesh-e-nazar.

Use dekhun jeedhar karun mein nigah,
Wohi ek soorat hazaaron jagah.

Nigah gardish-e-chashm se fitna saaz,
Mizha aafat-e-rozgaar-e-daraaz.

Jo aankh us ki beeni se ja kar lare,
Dam-e-tegh par raah chalni pare.

میر تقی میر

مکان کنجِ لب خواہشِ جان کا
تبسّم سبب کاہشِ جان کا
دہن دیکھ کر کچھ نہ کہیے کہ آہ
سخن کی نکلتی ستی مشکل سے راہ
گلِ تازہ شرمندہ اس روسے ہو
نخل مشک ناب اس کے گیسوٗ سے ہو
سراپا میں جس جا نظر کیجیے
وہیں عمر اپنی بسر کیجیے
کہیں مہ کا آئینہ در دست ہے
کہیں بادۂ حُسن سے مَست ہے
کہیں نقشِ دیوار دیکھا اسے
کہیں گرم رفتار دیکھا اسے
کہیں دل بری اُس کو درپیش ہے
کہیں مائلِ خوبیِ خویش ہے
کہیں جملہ تن مہر صرفِ سلوک
کہیں مجھ سے سرگرم حرفِ سلوک

34

Mir Taqi Mir

The corner of her lips housed deep desire,
Enough was her smile to ruin you entire.

The beauty of her mouth lay beyond description,
Hardly was there scope to open conversation.

Her lovely face would put to shame freshly blossomed rose,
Eglantine would hang her head seeing her locks afloat.

Captivating was her beauty right from top to toe,
Wherever your eye doth rest, there you want to live and grow.

Now you find her gazing in the mirror of moon,
Drunk with the wine of beauty she would strut eftsoons.

Sometime she would seem a painting on the wall,
Sometime on feet agile walk about the hall.

Sometimes she would be seen to play the lover's part,
Sometimes in self-praise she was seen absorbed.

Every word of her speech was with sweetness charged,
Often she would talk to me with fond regard.

Makaan kunj-e-lab khwahish-e-jaan ka,
Tabassum sabab kaahsh-e-jaan ka.

Dahan dekh kar kuchh na kahieye ke aah,
Sakhun ki nikalti thi mushkil se raah.

Gul-e-taaza sharminda us roo se ho,
Khajil mushk-e-naab us ke gaisu se ho.

Saraapa mein jis naa nazar kijieye,
Wahin umar apni basar kijeye.

Kahin mah ka aaeena dar dast hai,
Kahin baada-e-husn se mast hai.

Kahin naqsh-e-deewar dekha use,
Kahin garm raftaar dekha use.

Kahin dil bari us ko darpesh hai,
Kahin maail-e-khoobi-e-khesh hai.

Kahin jumla tan mehar sarf-e-salook,
Kahin mujh se sar garm harf-e-salook.

میر تقی میر

کبھوُ صورتِ دل کش اپنی دکھائے
کبھوُ اپنے بالوں میں مُنھ کو چھپائے
کبھوُ گرم کینہ کبھوُ مہرباں
کبھوُ دوست نکلے کبھوُ خصمِ جاں
گلے میں مرے ہاتھ ڈالے کبھوُ
طرح دشمنی کے نکالے کبھوُ
کبھوُ چیں بہ ابرو کبھوُ ہنس کے بات
کبھوُ بے وفائی، کبھوُ التفات
جو میں ہاتھ ڈالوں وہاں کچھ نہیں
بہ جُز شکل وہی عیاں کچھ نہیں
ہر اِک رات چندے یہ صورت رہی
اسی شکل وہی سے صحبت رہی
دمِ صبح ہو گرم رہ سوئے ماہ
کہ در پیش آوے یہ روزِ سیاہ
کہ جھوما کروں بیدِ مجنوؤں کی طرز
رہے یاد اس سرو موزوؤں کی طرز

Mir Taqi Mir

Now she'uld reveal to me her attractive face,
Now behind her falling locks veil her sweet visage.

Now extremely critical, now supremely kind,
Now warm and friendly, now a foe divine.

Now she'd enfold me deep within her arms,
Then, out of spite, try to hurt and harm.

Now in a ruffled mood, now scattering smiles,
Now full of kindness, now full of guile.

But when I tried to catch her, nothing could I find,
A mere hallucination, a fiction of the mind.

I suffered the same fate, night after night,
That fairy shape, every day, took me for a ride.

At dawn that child of fancy would set out for the moon,
Casting on the rising day a thick pall of gloom.

Passion-crazed I would sit, shaking like a bamboo frail,
Remembering that cypress shape, and her elfin ways.

Kabho soorat-e-dilkash apni dikhaae,
Kabho apne baalon mein munh ko chhipaae.

Kabho garm keena, kabho meharbaan,
Kabho dost nikle, kabho khasm-e-jaan.

Gale mein mire haath dale kabho,
Tarah dushmani ke nikale kabho.

Kabho cheen-ba-abroo, kabho hans ke baat,
Kabho be-wafai, kabho iltefaat.

Jo main haath daaloon, wahan kuchh nahin,
Ba juz shakl-e-wahmi ayaan kuchh nahin.

Har ik raat chande yeh soorat rahi,
Isi shakl-e-wahmi se suhbat rahi.

Dam-e-subah ho garm rah soo-e-mah,
Ke darpesh aawe yeh roz-e-seaah.

Ke jhooma karun bed-e-majnun ki tarz,
Rahe yaad us sarw-e-mauzoon ki tarz.

میر تقی میر

رہوں زرد میں گاہ بیمار سا
پریشاں سخن گہہ پری وار سا
پری خوان کو کوئی افسوں پڑھائے
کسیؤ سے کوئی جا کے تعویذ لائے
طبیبوں کو آخر دکھایا مجھے
نہ پینا جو کچھ تھا پلایا مجھے
دوا جو لکھی سو خلافِ مزاج
کھنچا اس خرابی سے کارِ علاج

دروں خود بخود بے حواسی رہی
پریشاں دلی اور اداسی رہی
سروں بے کلی جاؤں تاہر کہیں
نہ گھر میں لگے جی نہ باہر کہیں
قیامت جنوں کا رہے سر میں شور
کھنچا جائے دل کوہ و صحرا کی اور
رہے شوق سر در گریبانِ دل
ہوا کھینچے صحرا کو دامانِ دل

Mir Taqi Mir

I became sick and pale, my speech turned to drawl,
As if an evil spirit held my soul in thrall.

Some approached the sorcerer to get my spell annulled,
Some brought an amulet my inner heat to quell.

I was shown around to the physicians wise,
Who made me drink the potions which I deep disliked.

My system wouldn't accept the potions they prescribed,
Prolonged was my treatment, but I had no respite.

I felt deep disturbed, by saner sense betrayed,
Drowned in depression, distracted, dismayed.

I wandered from place to place, restlessness besieged,
Nor at home, nor out of home, could I feel at ease.

I could hear within my mind a wild frenzic roar,
Something egged me on towards the barren wolds.

Passion-crazed was my head, deep-depressed my heart,
The desert wind beckoned me to its wild resorts.

Rahun zard main gah beemar sa,
Pareshan sakhun, gah pari dar sa.

Pari khwan ko koi afsun parhaae,
Kaso se koi jaa ke taaweez laae.

Tabibon ko aakhir dikhaya mujhe,
Na peena jo kuchh tha pilaya mujhe.

Dawa jo likhi so khilaf-e mizaaj,
Khincha is kharabi se kaar-e-ilaaj.

Daroon khud bakhud be hawasi rahi,
Pareshan dili aur udaasi rahi.

Karun be kali jaaoon ta har kahin,
Na ghar mein lage ji, na bahar kahin.

Qayamat janoon ka rahe sar mein shor,
Khincha jaae dil koh-o-sahra ki oar.

Rahe shauq sar dar gareban-e-dil,
Hawa kheinche sahra ko damaan-e-dil.

میر تقی میر

جنوں آہ در پہ ہوا جاں ان کے
مجوز ہوئے یار زنداں کے
کیا بند اِک کوٹھڑی میں مجھے
کہ آتشِ جنوں کی مگر واں بجھے
لبِ نان اِک بار دینے لگے
دمِ آب دشوار دینے لگے
کہاں علم کا کسبِ فرصت نہ آہ
ہوا کا کبھی واں گشت روزن کی راہ
نہ آوے کوئی ڈر سے میرے کنے
کہ کیا جانیے کیسی صحبت بنے
وہ آشفتہ سرہوش مندی سے دور
نہیں رابط مقتضائے شعور
وہ حجرہ جو تھا گور سے تنگ تر
در اُس کا نہ کھلتا تھا دو دو پہر
سرِ شام بیٹھا تھا میں ایک روز
افاقت نہ آئی تھی مجھ کو ہنوز

40

Mir Taqi Mir

When my madness threatened to drain away my life,
That I be kept confined, so my friends advised.

In a narrow dungeon I was then encaged,
So that my raging fire might get assuaged.

I was given food to eat only once a day,
Even for the drinking water I had to beg and pray.

Where was there time or scope to sit, think, or read,
Rarely through the ventilator came a whiff of breeze.

None would approach me, they were so afraid,
How would I treat them, none could anticipate.

There I sat demented, of all my wits relieved,
Devoid of sense and logic were my words and deeds.

Narrower than the grave was that dungeon dark,
Whose door for hours long remained securely barred.

As I sat inside my cell one day at eve,
When my manic sickness hadn't lost its heat,

Janoon, aah, darpai hua jaan ke,
Mujawwiz hue yaar zindaan ke.

Kiya band ik kothri mein mujhe,
Ke aatish janoon ki magar waan bujhe.

Lab-e naan ik baar dene lage,
Dam aab dushwar dene lage.

Kahan ilam ka kasb-e-fursat na aah,
Hawa ka bhi waan gasht rozan ki raah.

Na aawe koi dar se mere kane,
Ke kya jaaneye kaisi suhbat bane.

Woh aashufta sar hoshmandi se door,
Nahin raabta muqtzaae shaoor.

Woh hujra jo tha gor se tang tar,
Dar uska na khulta tha do do pahr.

Sar-e-sham baitha tha main ek roz,
Afaqat na aai thi mujh ko hanooz.

میر تقی میر

کہ یاروں نے برجستہ تدبیر کی
مرے خون میں کچھ نہ تقصیر کی
اگر چند کہنے کو خوں کم کیا
لیا لوہو اتنا کہ بے دم کیا
بڑی دیر تک خون جاری رہا
میں بے ہوش وہ رات ساری رہا
جگایا سحر مجھ کو اک شور سے
کھلی آنکھ میری بڑے زور سے

وہی دستِ فصاد میں نشتر
وہی رنگ صحبت کا پیشِ نظر
وہی لوہو لینے کا ہنگامہ پھر
وہی ترلہو میں مرا جامہ پھر
لگے نشتر ایسے کہ لگتے نہیں
چبھے جیسے مژگاں کسو کے تئیں
ہوا خون سے دامن و جیب تر
رگِ جاں تلک زخم پہنچا مگر

Mir Taqi Mir

Some friends got together and then prescribed,
The letting out of my blood that was running wild.

Though they said they simply had extracted excess blood,
Yet this act of blood-letting left me nearly dead.

Bleeding continued for long after I was incised,
Unconscious I lay in bed all through the night.

One day I was roused by a sudden alarm,
I flung open my eyes in the twilight dawn.

The same cruel hand I saw with a lancet sharp,
The same gory prospect made me wince and start.

The uproar of blood-letting filled the air again,
My cloak, through and through, was drenched in blood again.

Cruel piercing lancets were thrust into my veins,
Like a sharp eye-lash causing immense pain.

Both my skirt and collar got blood-stained,
The wound spreading out reached the jugular vein.

Ke yaaron ne barjasta tadbir ki,
Mire khoon mein kuchh na taqsir ki.

Agar chand kahne ko khoon kam kiya,
Liya lohu itna ke be dam kiya.

Bari der tak khoon jaari raha,
Main be-hosh woh raat saari raha.

Jagaya sahar mujh ko ik shor se,
Khuli aankh meri bare zor se.

Wohi dast-e-fassad mein neshtar,
Wohi rang suhbat ka pesh-e-nazar.

Wohi lohu lene ka hangama phir,
Wohi tar lahu mein mera jama phir.

Lage nishtar aise ke lagte nahin,
Chubhe jaise mizhgan kaso ke taein.

Hua khoon se daaman-o-jeb tar,
Rag-e-jaan talak zakhm pahuncha magar.

میر تقی میر

سخن ضعف سے سخت دشوار تھا
پلک کا اٹھانا بھی اِک بار تھا
کھڑا ہوں اگر پاؤں لغزاں رہے
بدن بید کی طرح لرزاں رہے
چلا جائے سر پاؤں بقدر بقدر کرے
نسیم سحد کار صر صر کرے
پس از چند آنکھیں ٹھہرنے لگیں
نگاہیں بھی کچھ کام کرنے لگیں
بندھا ناتوانی کا رختِ سفر
کیا طاقتِ رفتہ نے مُنھ ادھر
کسے تھا مری زندگانی کا دھیان
ولیکن نہایت تھا میں سخت جان
لگی جان سے آنے اعضا کے بیچ
کوئی روز رہنا تھا دنیا کے بیچ
پھر ناتواں میں بہت دور سے
کہ نزدیک تھا عالمِ گور سے

Mir Taqi Mir

I couldn't stir or speak, I'd grown so weak,
Even to lift my eye-lids was a trying feat.

If I tried to stand, my feet beneath would shake,
My body would tremble, my limbs would quake.

My legs would totter, my head would reel,
Blast-like appeared to me even the gentle breeze.

Slowly my faculties began to stabilize,
Day by day I regained my clearer sense of sight.

Debility from my body did at last depart,
With the vigour returning, life resumed its part.

Who was there, after all, concerned about my life,
But for my tenacious will I would sure have died.

My body's failing strength at last revived,
I wasn't fated, so it seemed, so soon to die.

I had staged a comeback from the farthest end,
From the very edge of grave I had been returned.

Sakhun zuef se sakht dushwar tha,
Palak ka uthana bhi ik baar tha.

Khara hun agar paaon laghzan rahe,
Badan baid ki tarah larzan rahe.

Chala jaae sar paaon thar thar kare,
Naseem-e-sahar kaar-e-sar sar kare.

Pas az chand aankhen thahrne lagin,
Nigahen bhi kuchh kaam karne lagin.

Bandha natawaani ka rakht-e-safar,
Kiya taaqat-e-rafta ne munh idhar.

Kise tha miri zindagani ka dhayan,
Walekin nihayat tha main sakht jaan.

Lagi jaan si aane aaza ke beech,
Koi roz rahna tha duniya ke beech.

Phira natawan main bahut door se,
Ke nazdik tha aalam-e-gor se.

میر تقی میر

وہ صورت کا وہم اور دیوانگی
لگی کرنے در پردہ بے گانگی
نہ دیکھے مری اور اس پیارے سے
غریبانہ سر مارے دیوار سے
کہیں ٹک تسلّی کہیں بے قرار
کہیں شوق سے میرے بے اختیار
کہیں واسطے میرے روتی ہے خوں
کہیں دستِ زیرِ زنخ ہے ستوں
کہیں دل کو اپنے دکھاوے مجھے
مری بے وفائی جتاوے مجھے
کہیں دست بر دل وہ رشکِ قمر
کہیں حسرت آلودہ مجھ پر نظر
کہیں مجھ سے کہتی ہے رخصت مجھے
کہ مطلق نہیں غم کی طاقت مجھے
کبھو بے ادائی و دشنام ہے
کبھو باد کے ہاتھ پیغام ہے

Mir Taqi Mir

Rarely that illusory shape sprang before my sight,
I would catch a glimpse of her, albeit, once a while.

She wouldn't look at me with love, as heretofore,
Despairingly she beat her head against the walls and doors.

Sometimes she felt becalmed, sometimes ill-at-ease,
Sometimes, maddened in my love, restless would she reel.

Tears of blood for my sake sometime she would spill,
Or with her chin in hand stare statue-still.

Now she would point out her broken heart to me,
Or charge me to my face with infidelity.

Now with her hand on heart stood that moon-like shape,
Now she'd cast on me a longing, wistful gaze.

Now she was found bidding me adieu,
Saying that this woeful life she couldn't endure.

Now she was callous and full of foul abuse,
Now sent messages through the wind that blew.

Woh soorat ka wahm aur deewanagi,
Lagi karne dar parda be-ganagi.

Na dekhe miri oar us payaar se,
Gharibana sar maare deewar se.

Kahin tuk tasalli, kahin be qarar,
Kahin shauq se mere be ikhtiar.

Kahin waaste mere roti hai khoon,
Kahin dast-e-zer-e-zanakh hai satoon.

Kahin dil ko apne dikhawe mujhe,
Miri be wafai jitawe mujhe.

Kahin dast bar dil woh rashk-e-qamar,
Kahin hasrat aaluda mujh par nazar.

Kahin mujh se kahti hai rukhsat mujhe,
Ke mutliq nahin ghum ki taqat mujhe.

Kabho be adaai-o-dushnaam hai,
Kabho baad ke haath paigham hai.

میر تقی میر

غرض نا امیدانہ کر اِک نگاہ
وہ نقشِ توہّم گیا سوئے ماہ
نہ آیا کبھو پھر نظر اس طرح
نہ دیکھا اُسے جلوہ گر اس طرح
مگر گاہ سایہ سا مہتاب میں
کبھو وہم سا عالمِ خواب میں
دلِ خو پذیر وصالِ دوام
رہے خواب میں روز و شب صبح و شام
خیال اس کا آوے کہ سُن ہو رہوں
تلے سر کے پتھر رکھوں سو رہوں
مجھے آپ کو یوں ہی کھوتے گئی
جوانی تمام اپنی سوتے گئی
دکھایا نہ اُس نے مرے رُو خواب میں
نہ دیکھا پھر اس کو کبھو خواب میں
نہ دیکھا کبھو میرؔ پھر وہ جمال
وہ صحبت تھی گویا کہ خواب و خیال

48

Mir Taqi Mir

In short, with a despairing gaze,
Moonwards went that illusory face.

Never again I saw that sight,
That fairy face would not oblige.

A shadowy something in the moon sometimes I descried,
Or, a gleam in my dreams flitted across my eyes.

But my heart which at bottom eternal union sought,
Ever remained submerged in her dreams and thoughts.

The moment I think of her my sense and soul freeze,
Throwing myself on my bed, I strive hard to sleep.

Thus my whole past life was a total waste,
My youth has slipped away in a sleepy state.

Never did she show her face even in my dreams,
Never again could I see that changeling gleam.

Never again, O Mir, that beauteous vision I saw,
As if that encounter was a dream, a wishful thought.

Gharz na umeedana kar ik nigah,
Woh naqsh-e-tawahham gaya soo-e-mah.

Na aaya kabho phir nazar ustarah,
Na dekha use jalwa gar is tarah.

Magar gah saya sa mahtaab mein,
Kabho wahm sa aalam-e-khwab mein.

Dil-e-khoo pazir wisal-e-madaam,
Rahe khwab mein roz-o-shab, subah-o-sham.

Khayal us ka aawe ke sunn ho rahun,
Tale sar ke pathhar rakhun, so rahun.

Mujhe aap ko yunhi khote gai,
Jawani tamam apni sote gai.

Dikhaya na us mah ne roo khwab mein,
Na dekha phir usko kabho khwab mein.

Na dekha kabho, Mir, phir woh jamaal,
Woh suhbat thi goya ke khwab-o-khayal.

Abridged

Nazir Akbarabadi
(1732-1830)

NAZIR AKBARABADI
(1732-1830)

Nazir's date of birth is shrouded in uncertainty. Some chroniclers of Urdu literature place his birth in 1732, while others suggest that he was born in 1739 or 1740, around the time of Nadir Shah's raid on Delhi. When, a few years later, Ahmed Shah Abdali let loose a reign of terror in Delhi, Nazir, like many other contemporaries, migrated to Agra (Akbarabad), where he lived for the rest of his life. As a young man, he led a carefree life, enjoying the fun and frolic of the town, and participating in the then fashionable sports of chess,"chausar", and kite-flying. But later in life he sobered down and led a simple, saintly life believing in and preaching the virtues of love, compassion and piety. He was a broad-minded humanist, free from the rancour of fanaticism. That's why he could celebrate, with equal eclat, the festivals of both the communities, and eulogise the life and thought not only of Muslim saints and seers, but also of Hindu religious figures like Ram and Krishna. His poetry holds a mirror to the community of life and culture that existed in those days.

Nazir lived a long life of 98 years, because of which he cannot be fitted into any one school of poetic thought or style. He can be said to have shared the poetic milieu of Mir and Sauda, of Insha and Jurrat, as well as of Ghalib and Momin. Yet his poetry is uniquely independent of the influence of any of these poets. In the first place, Nazir is essentially a poet of the *nazm*, whereas all the above-mentioned poets are specialists of the *ghazal*. Secondly, his verse is entirely free from the superficial elegance and verbal acrobatics of the Lucknow school, as also from the Persianised grandeur of Ghalib or Momin. Both in its thought and style, Nazir's poetry is rooted deep in the Indian soil. He talks about the common concerns of man in a language which in the real sense is the language of the common people. Moreover, unlike the other Urdu poets, he never sought the patronage of kings and courts, but found his inspiration in the company of his like-minded friends. He can truly be called the poet of the common people.

Another distinguishing mark of Nazir lies in the didactic and moralistic flavour of his poetry. In nearly all his major poems, be it "Banjara Nama" or "Admi Nama" we can hear the voice of a saintly man urging the readers to shed their greed and lust, and seek their salvation in the grace of God. At the same time there is a touch of healthy humour in his poetry which endears him to his readers. We may read his "Burhapa" to get a taste of his humour which emboldens him to laugh not only at others, but also at himself. Nazir has also made a significant contribution to the development of Urdu lauguge. He has invested everyday diction with literary dignity by using it in his poetry. For him no word is unpoetical, and no subject, if it concerns human life, is too low to be treated in verse. Because of his talent for natural description, and his interest in national events, Nazir harks back to Quli Qutab Shah, anticipating on the other hand, later-day poets like Hali and Azad. He is a master of popular poetic measures, and smooth, singing rhythms.

نظیر اکبرآبادی

بنجارا نامہ

ٹٹک حرص و ہوا کو چھوڑ میاں، مت دیس بدیس پھرے مارا
قزّاق اجل کا لوٹے ہے دن رات، بجا کر نقارا
کیا بدھیا، بھینسا، بیل، شتر، کیا گوئیں، پلاّ سربھارا
کیا گیہوں، چاول، موٹھ، مٹر، کیا آگ، دھواں کیا انگارا
سب ٹھاٹھ پڑا رہ جاوے گا، جب لاد چلے گا بنجارا

گر تو ہے لکھتی بنجارا، اور کھیپ بھی تیری بھاری ہے
اے غافل! تجھ سے بھی چڑھتنا، اک اور بڑا بیوپاری ہے
کیا شکر، مصری، قند، گری، کیا سانبھر، میٹھا، کھاری ہے
کیا داکھ، منقّٰی، سونٹھ، مرچ، کیا کیسر، لونگ، سپاری ہے
سب ٹھاٹھ پڑا رہ جاوے گا، جب لاد چلے گا بنجارا

تو بدھیا لادے، بیل بھرے، جو پورب پچھم جاوے گا
یا سود بڑھا کر لاوے گا، یا ٹوٹا، گھاٹا، پاوے گا
قزّاق اجل کا رستے میں، جب بھالا مار گراوے گا
دھن، دولت، نانی، پوتا کیا، اک کنبہ کام نہ آوے گا
سب ٹھاٹھ پڑا رہ جاوے گا، جب لاد چلے گا بنجارا

Nazir Akbarabadi
Banjara Naama (Annals of the Pedlar)

Leave your lust and greed, O man, wander not in distant lands,
The fiend of death will rob your wealth, there he stands with drum and band;
Bulls, buffaloes, cows and camels, bags, bushels, and cans,
Wheat, rice, peas and pulses, smoke, spark, or brand,
This pomp and show will help no more, when the pedlar packs and goes.

If you are a millionaire with richly loaded stores,
Know, ye ignorant, your rival has much more,
Sugar, candy, jaggery, nuts; salt, sour dough,
Raisins, grapes, pepper, ginger, saffron, betel, cloves,
This pomp and show will help no more when the pedlar packs and goes.

With your loaded bulls and oxen you will travel East and West,
To return with richer coffers, or with depleted wealth,
When enroute, the shade of death, with bayonet sharp will pierce your chest,
Pelf or power, friends or family—nothing will revive your breath;
This pomp and show will help no more when the pedlar packs and goes.

Tuk hirs-o-hawa ko chhor mian, mat des bades phire mara,
Qazzaq ajal ka loote hai din raat, baja kar naqqara;
Kya bidhiya, bhainsa, bel, shutar, kya goien, palla, sarbhara,
Kya gehun, chawal, moth, matar, kya aag, dhuan, kya angara,
Sab thath para rah jawega jab laad chalega banjara.

Gar tu hai lakhhi banjara, aur khep bhi teri bhari hai,
Ai ghafil; tujh se bhi charhta ik aur bara beopari hai,
Kya shakkar, misri, qand, giri, kya sambhar, meetha, khari hai,
Kya daakh, munaqqa, saunth, mirch, kya kesar, laung, supari hai
Sab thath para rah jawega jab laad chalega banjara.

Tu bidhiya laade, bel bhare, jo purab pachhim jawega,
Ya sood barha kar lawega, ya tota, ghata, pawega,
Qazzaq ajal ka raste mein jab bhala mar girawega,
Dhan, daulat, naati, pota kya, ik kunba kaam na aawega,
Sab thath para rah jawega jab laad chalega banjara.

نظیر اکبرآبادی

ہر منزل میں اب ساتھ ترے یہ جتنا ڈیرا ڈنڈا ہے
زر، دام، درم کا بھانڈا ہے، بندوق، سپر اور کھانڈا ہے
جب نایک تن کا نکل گیا، جو ملکوں ملکوں ہانڈا ہے
پھر ہانڈا ہے، نہ بھانڈا ہے، نہ حلوا ہے، نہ مانڈا ہے
سب ٹھاٹھ پڑا رہ جاوے گا، جب لاد چلے گا بنجارا
جب چلتے چلتے رستے میں، یہ گون تری ڈھل جاوے گی
اک بدھیا تیری مٹی پر، پھر گھاس نہ چرنے آوے گی
یہ کھیپ جو تو نے لادی ہے، سب حصوں میں بٹ جاوے گی
دھی، پوت، جنوائی، بیٹیا، کیا، بنجارن پاس نہ آوے گی
سب ٹھاٹھ پڑا رہ جاوے گا، جب لاد چلے گا بنجارا
یہ کھیپ بھرے جو جاتا ہے، یہ کھیپ میاں مت گن اپنی
اب کوئی گھڑی، پل، ساعت میں، یہ کھیپ بدن کی ہے کھپنی
کیا تھال کٹورے چاندی کے، کیا پیتل کی ڈبیا، ڈھپنی
کیا برتن سونے روپے کے، کیا مٹی کی ہنڈیا، چپنی
سب ٹھاٹھ پڑا رہ جاوے گا، جب لاد چلے گا بنجارا

Nazir Akbarabadi

These paraphernalia which follow you at every step,
The pots full of guineas and gold, gun, shield, and axe,
When your pilot leaves the body that has wandered East and West,
Loaves and puddings, pans and pots,—every thing will lose its zest,
This pomp and show will help no more when the pedlar packs and goes.

When with daily het and wet, this money bag will lighter grow,
Your withering fields will not attract a single browsing cow,
The loads of wealth by you amassed will be owned by other folks,
Son, daughter, son-in-law, nay, your wife will colder grow;
This pomp and show will belp no more, when the pedlar packs and goes.

The bag that you stuff and fill, is it yours? think not so,
Any hour, minute or moment, this wind bag is bound to blow,
These silver cups and plates, the brazen boxes all aglow,
These china pots, this earthenware, these vessels of glittering gold,
This pomp and show will help no more, when the pedlat packs and goes.

Har manzil mein ab saath tire yeh jitna dera daanda hai,
Zar, Daam, daram ka bhanda hai, bandooq, sapar our khanda hai,
Jab naik tan ka nikal gaya, jo mulkon mulkon handa hai,
Phir handa hai, na bhanda hai, na halwa hai, na manda hai.
Sab thath para rah jawega jab laad chalega banjara.

Jab chalte chalte raste mein, yeh goon tiri dhal jawegi,
Ik bidhiya teri mitti par phir ghaas na charne aawegi,
Yeh khep jo tu ne laadi hai, sab hisson mein bat jawegi,
Dhi, put, janwai, beta kya, banjaran paas na aawegi;
Sab thath para rah jawegi, jab laad chalega banjara.

Yeh khep bhare jo jata hai, yeh khep mian mat gin apni,
Ab koi ghari, pal saait mein, yeh khep badan ki hai khapni,
Kya thal, katore chandi ke, kya peetal ki dabia, dhapni,
Kya bartan sone, rupe ke, kya mitti ki handia, chapni,
Sab thath para rah jawega jab laad chalega banjara.

نظیر اکبرآبادی

یہ دھوم دھڑکا ساتھ لیے، کیوں پھرتا ہے جنگل جنگل
اک تنکا ساتھ نہ جاوے گا، موقوف ہوا جب اُن اور جل
گھر بار، اٹاری، چوبارے، کیا خاصا، تن سُکھ اور مخمل
سیا چھلوں، پردے، فرشش نئے، کیا لال پلنگ اور رنگ محل
سب ٹھاٹھ پڑا رہ جاوے گا، جب لاد چلے گا بنجارا

کیوں جی پر بوجھ اٹھاتا ہے اِن گونوں بھاری بھاری کے
جب موت لتیڑا آن پڑا، چھپر دونے ہیں بیوپاری کے
کیا ساز جڑاؤ، زر، زیور، کیا گوٹے، ثقان کناری کے
کیا گھوڑے زین سنہری کے، کیا ہاتھی لال عماری کے
سب ٹھاٹھ پڑا رہ جاوے گا، جب لاد چلے گا بنجارا

مغرور نہ ہو تلواروں پر، مت پھول بھروسے ڈھالوں کے
سب پتا توڑ کے بھاگیں گے منہ دیکھ اجل کے بھالوں کے
کیا دبے موتی ہیرول کے، کیا ڈھیر خزانے مالوں کے
کیا بقچے ہاتاش، مشجّر کے، کیا تختے شال دوشالوں کے
سب ٹھاٹھ پڑا رہ جاوے گا جب لاد چلے گا بنجارا

Nazir Akbarabadi

Carrying along this boom and bang, why roam thou in the wilds?
Not a straw will go with you when the fateful time arrives,
Velvet, chintz, or brocades, bungalows, buildings high,
Pleasure domes or purple beds, curtains, blinds, or tiles,
This pomp and show will help no more when the pedlar packs and goes.

Why do you load your heart with bulging bags and sacks,
Your rivals will grab your goods when robber-death attacks,
Stone-studded jewellery, robes lace-attached,
Richly caparisoned elephants, golden-saddled pads,
This pomp and show will help no more when the pedlar packs and goes.

Boast ye not of your sword, do not flaunt your shield,
Seeing the sharp fangs of death, everyone will take to heels,
Boxes full of diamonds, treasures safely sealed,
Gold cloth and floral velvet, shawls of delicate weave,
This pomp and show will help no more when the pedlar packs and goes.

Yeh dhoom dharakka saath lieye, kyon phirta hai jungle, jungle,
Ik tinka saath na jawega, mauqoof hua jab un aur jal,
Ghar baar atari, chaubare, kya khasa, tan sukh, aur makhmal,
Kya chilwin, parde, farash naye, kya lal palang aur rang mahal,
Sab thath para rah jaega jab laad chalega banjara.

Kyon ji par bojh uthata hai in goonon bhari bhari ke,
jab maut lutera aan para, phir doone hain beopari ke,
Kya saaz jaraoo, zar, zewar, kya gote than kinari ke,
Kya ghore zeen sunehri ke, kya haathi lal amari ke,
Sab thath para rah jawega jab laad chalega banjara.

Maghroor na ho talwaron par, mat phool bharose dhalon ke,
Sab patta tor ke bhagenge, munh dekh ajal ke bhalon ke,
Kya dibbe moti hiron ke, kya dher khazane maalon ke,
Kya bughche taash, mushbahr ke, kya takhte shaal do shaalon ke,
Sab thath para rah jawega jab laad chalega banjara.

نظیر اکبرآبادی

ہر آن نفع اور ٹوٹے میں، کیوں مِتا پھرتا ہے بَن بَن
ٹھیک غافل دل میں سوچ ذرا، ہے ساتھ لگا تیرے دشمن
کیا لونڈی، باندی، دائی، دوا، کیا بندہ چیلا نیک چلن
کیا مندر، مسجد، تال، کنواں، کیا گھاٹ، سرا، کیا باغ چمن
سب ٹھاٹھ پڑا رہ جاوے گا، جب لاد چلے گا بنجارا

جب مرگ پھر آ کر چابک کو، یہ بیل بدن کا ہانکے گا
کوئی ناج سمیٹے گا تیرا، کوئی گون سیے اور ٹانکے گا
ہودہ ڈھیرا کیلا جنگل میں، تو خاک لحد کی پھانکے گا
اُس جنگل میں پھر آہ نظیر، اک بھنگا آن نہ جھانکے گا
سب ٹھاٹھ پڑا رہ جاوے گا، جب لاد چلے گا بنجارا

Nazir Akbarabadi

Why with gain and loss obsessed, wander thou o'er hill and
    dale?
Can't you notice, O thou fool, the enemy moving on your trail?
Nurse, maid or medicine, servant, loyal slave,
Mosque, shrine, well-spring, inn, shore, or lake,
This pomp and show will help no more when the pedlar packs
    and goes.

When death, brandishing its lash, goads you forward on its
    track,
This one will collect your stores, that one sew the bag,
You'll eat the dust of grave, turned to humble ash,
Even a worm will not peep, where, Nazir, you lie enwrapped.
This pomp and show will help no more when the pedlar packs
    and goes.

Har aan nafa aur tote mein, kyon marta phirta hai ban ban,
Tuk ghafil dil mein soch zara, hai saath laga tere dushman,
Kya laundi, baandi, daai, dawa, kya banda, chela nek chalan,
Kya mandir, masjid, taal, kuan, kya ghaat, sara, kya bagh chaman
Sab thath para rah jawega jab laad chalega banjara.

Jab marg phira kar chabuk ko, yeh bel badan ka haanke ga,
Koi naaj sametega tera, koi goon sieye aur tankega,
Ho dher akela jungle mein, tu khak lahad ki phaankega,
Us jungle mein phir aah, Nazir, ik bhunga aan na jhankega.
Sab thath para rah jawega jab laad chalega banajara.

نظیر اکبرآبادی

آدمی نامہ

دنیا میں بادشاہ ہے، سو ہے وہ بھی آدمی
اور مفلس و گدا ہے، سو ہے وہ بھی آدمی
زردار، بے نوا ہے، سو ہے وہ بھی آدمی
نعمت جو کھا رہا ہے، سو ہے وہ بھی آدمی
ٹکڑے جو مانگتا ہے، سو ہے وہ بھی آدمی

ابدال و قطب وغوث و ولی، آدمی ہوئے
مُنکر بھی آدمی ہوئے، اور کفر کے بھرے
کیا کیا کرشمے کشف و کرامات کے کیے
حتیٰ کہ اپنے زہد و ریاضت کے زور سے
خالق سے جا ملا ہے، سو ہے وہ بھی آدمی

فرعون نے کیا تھا جو دعویٰ خدائی کا
شدّاد بھی بہشت بنا کر ہوا خدا
نمرود بھی خدا ہی کہاتا تھا برملا
یہ بات ہے سمجھنے کی، آگے کہوں میں کیا
یاں تک جو ہو چکا ہے، سو ہے وہ بھی آدمی

62

Nazir Akbarabadi
Aadmi Naama (Annals of Man)

He who is a king crowned, is but a man,
A beggar and a medicant both represent a man.
The affluent and the indigent both, in fact, are man,
He who rolls in luxury, what is he? a man.
And he who lives on charity passeth for a man.

Sufi, savant, priest, prophet—all belong to Adam's breed,
Atheist and the infidel, spring from human seed;
Those with supernal powers, doing miraculous deeds,
Who by their spiritual might great heights achieved,
And attained to Godhead,—represent the race of man.

Faroun who in olden times declared himself a God,
Shaddad who built his Paradise and imitated the Lord,
Nimrod who by one and all a very god was thought,
A hint to the wise, why dwell at large?
All who were drunk with pride were the type of man.

Duniya mein baadshah hai, so hai woh bhi aadmi,
Aur muflis-o-gada hai, so hai woh bhi aadmi;
Zardaar, be-nawa hai, so hai woh bhi aadmi,
Naimat jo kha raha hai, so hai woh bhi aadmi,
Tukre jo maangta hai, so hai woh bhi aadmi.

Abdaal-o-qutab-o-ghaus-o-wali, aadmi hue,
Munkir bhi aadmi hue, aur kufr ke bhare,
Kya kya karishme kishf-o-karamaat ke kieye,
Hatta ke apne zuhd-o-rayazat ke zor se
Khaliq se ja mila hai, so woh bhi hai aadmi.

Faroun ne kiya tha jo dawa khudaai ka,
Shaddad bhi bahisht bana kar hua khuda,
Namrod bhi khuda hi kahata tha barmala,
Yeh baat hai samajhne ki, aage kahun main kya?
Yaan tak jo ho chuka hai, so hai woh bhi aadmi.

نظیر اکبرآبادی

یاں آدمی ہی نار ہے، اور آدمی ہی نور
یاں آدمی ہی پاس ہے، اور آدمی ہی دور
کُل آدمی کا حُسن و قبیح میں ہے یاں ظہور
شیطاں بھی آدمی ہے، جو کرتا ہے مکر و زور
اور ہادی، رہنما ہے، سو ہے وہ بھی آدمی
مسجد بھی آدمی نے بنائی ہے یاں میاں
بنتے ہیں آدمی ہی امام اور خطبہ خواں
پڑھتے ہیں آدمی ہی قرآں اور نمازیاں
اور آدمی ہی اُن کی چُراتے ہیں جوتیاں
جو اُن کو تاڑتا ہے، سو ہے وہ بھی آدمی
یاں آدمی پہ جان کو وارے ہے آدمی
اور آدمی ہی تیغ سے مارے ہے آدمی
پگڑی بھی آدمی کی اُتارے ہے آدمی
چلّا کے آدمی کو پکارے ہے آدمی
اور سُن کے دوڑتا ہے، سو ہے وہ بھی آدمی

Nazir Akbarabadi

Man is the scorching fire, man the light sublime,
Everywhere, far and near, man alone doth shine;
Good as well as evil reside in human mind,
The cunning and the wily, and the Satanic kind,
The priest and the pontif—are all shades of man.

He who builds the mosque is none else but man,
Man delivers sermons, heads the priestly clan;
Man intones prayers, reads the Koran,
Man steals shoes when others go in trance;
And he who detects the thief is also called a man.

Man gives his life for others,
Man kills and slays his brothers,
Man insults us, makes us shudder,
Man calls on man when in deep trouble,
Man provides succour to the suffering man.

Yaan aadmi hi naar hai, aur aadmi hi noor,
Yaan aadmi hi paas hai, aur aadmi hi door,
Kul aadmi ka husn-o-qubah mein hai yaan zahoor,
Shaitan bhi aadmi hai jo karta hai makr-o-zoor;
Aur haadi, rahnuma hai, so hai woh bhi aadmi.

Masjid bhi aadmi ne banai hai yaan miaan,
Ban-te hain aadmi hi imam aur qutba khwan,
Parhte hain aadmi hi Koraan aur namaz yaan,
Aur aadmi hi unki churate hain jootian;
Jo un ko tarta hai, so hai woh bhi aadmi.

Yaan aadmi pe jaan ko ware hai aadmi,
Aur aadmi hi tegh se maare hai aadmi,
Pagri bhi aadmi ki utare hai aadmi,
Chilla ke aadmi ko pukare hai aadmi;
Aur sun ke daurta hai, so hai woh bhi aadmi.

نظیر اکبر آبادی

چلتا ہے آدمی ہی مسافر ہو، لے کے مال
اور آدمی ہی مارے ہے، پھانسی گلے میں ڈال
یاں آدمی ہی صید ہے، اور آدمی ہی جال
سچا بھی آدمی ہی نکلتا ہے میرے لال
اور جھوٹ کا بھرا ہے، سو ہے وہ بھی آدمی

یاں آدمی ہی لعل، جواہر ہے بے بہا
اور آدمی ہی خاک سے بدتر ہے ہوگیا
کالا بھی آدمی ہے کہ الٹا ہے جوں توا
گورا بھی آدمی ہے کہ ٹکڑا سا چاند کا
بدشکل و بدنما ہے، سو ہے وہ بھی آدمی

اک آدمی ہیں جن کے یہ کچھ زرق برق ہیں
روپے کے ان کے پانو ہیں، سونے کے فرق ہیں
جھمکے تمام غرب سے لے تا بہ شرق ہیں
کمخواب، تاش، شال دوشالوں میں غرق ہیں
اور چیتھڑوں لگا ہے، سو ہے وہ بھی آدمی

66

Nazir Akbarabadi

Man goes on travels carrying merchandise,
Man robs him on the way, relieves him of his life,
Man is the victor, man the victimised,
Man is the apostle of truth, we must realise,
That he who preaches falsehood is also a man.

Man is the precious pearl on earth,
Man is worse than way-side dust,
Man, the rival of moon on earth,
Man, the baking plate, reversed;
Ugliness and beauty lie compressed in man.

Here he flaunts his glittering robes,
Rolls in riches, swims in gold,
From East to West his reign doth hold,
Furs, brocades, finery—make him dashing bold,
And he who lies in tatters calls himself a man.

Chalta hai aadmi hi musafir ho le ke maal,
Aur aadmi hi maare hai phaansi gale mein dal,
Yaan aadmi hi said hai, aur aadmi hi jaal,
Sachcha bhi aadmi hi nikalta hai mere laal,
Aur jhoot ka bhara hai, so hai woh bhi aadmi.

Yaan aadmi hi lal jawahar hai be baha,
Aur aadmi hi khak se bad tar hai ho gaya,
Kala bhi aadmi hai ke ulta hai joon tawa,
Gora bhi aadmi hai ke tukra sa chand ka,
Bad shakal-o-bad numa hai, so hai woh bhi aadmi.

Ik aadmi hain jin ke yeh kuchh zarq barq hain,
Rupe ke un ke paaon, sone ke farq hain,
Jhamke tamam gharb se le ta ba sharq hain,
Kamkhwab, taash, shaal do shaalon mein gharq hain,
Aur cheethron laga hai, so hai woh bhi aadmi.

نظیر اکبرآبادی

مرنے میں آدمی ہی کفن کرتے ہیں تیّار
نہلا دُھلا اُٹھاتے ہیں کاندھے پہ کر سوار
کلمہ بھی پڑھتے جاتے ہیں ڈروتے ہیں زار زار
سب آدمی ہی کرتے ہیں مُردے کا کاروبار
اور وہ جو مر گیا ہے، سو ہے وہ بھی آدمی

اشراف اور کمینے سے لے، شاہ تا وزیر
ہیں آدمی ہی صاحبِ عزّت بھی اور حقیر
یاں آدمی مرید ہیں، اور آدمی ہی پیر
اچھا بھی آدمی ہی کہاتا ہے اے نظیر
اور سب میں جو بُرا ہے، سو ہے وہ بھی آدمی

Nazir Akbarabadi

Man prepares the coffin when dreadful death arrives,
Bathes the corpse and carries it on his shoulders high;
Man reads the verse, man sobs and sighs,
Performs for the departed all the funeral rites;
And who sleeps the sleep of death was also once a man.

From the king to the clown, from the noble to the mean,
Man is many-faceted,—ignominous, esteemed;
Man is the proud preceptor, man the disciple meek,
Man is loved and praised for his virtuous deeds,
And the worst of living beings bears the name of man.

Marne mein aadmi hi kafan karte hain tayyaar,
Nahla dhula uthate hain kaandhe pe kar sawaar,
Kalma bhi parhte jaate hain, rote hain zaar zaar,
Sab aadmi hi karte hain murde ka karobaar;
Aur woh jo mar gaya hai, so hai woh bhi aadmi.

Ashraaf aur kameene se le, shah ta wazir,
Hain aadmi hi sahib-e-izzat bhi aur haqir,
Yaan aadmi mureed hain, aur aadmi hi pir,
Achha bhi aadmi hi kahata hai, ai Nazir,
Aur sab mein jo bura hai, so hai woh bhi aadmi.

نظیر اکبرآبادی

بڑھاپا

کیا قہر ہے یارو، جسے آجائے بڑھاپا
اور عیشِ جوانی کے تئیں کھائے بڑھاپا
عشرت کو ملا خاک میں، غم لائے بڑھاپا
ہر کام کو، ہر بات کو ترسائے بڑھاپا
سب چیز کو ہوتا ہے بُرا ہائے بڑھاپا
عاشق کو تو اللہ نہ دکھلائے بڑھاپا

جو لوگ خوشامد سے بٹھاتے تھے گھڑی بہر
چھاتی سے لپٹتے تھے، محبت کی جتا لہر
اب آکے بُڑھاپے نے کیا ہائے یہ کچھ قہر
اب جن کے کنے جاتے ہیں، لگتے ہیں انھیں زہر
سب چیز کو ہوتا ہے بُرا ہائے بڑھاپا
عاشق کو تو اللہ نہ دکھلائے بڑھاپا

آگے تھے جہاں گُل بدن و یوسفِ ثانی
دیتے تھے ہمیں پیار سے چھلّوں کی نشانی
مر جائیں، تو اب منہ میں نہ ڈالے کوئی پانی
کِس دکھ میں ہمیں چھوڑ گئی، ہائے جوانی

70

Nazir Akbarabadi
Burhapa (Old Age)

Friends, 'tis a terrible thing to fall a prey to age,
Which destroys without remorse, joys of youthful days.
Which brings griefs galore, destroys all delights,
Makes us always yearn for things, now beyond our might.
Old age is the deadly foe of every charm and grace,
Never should a lover, O Lord, old age embrace!

Those who used to welcome us with a smiling face,
And hugged us tight out of love in their warm embrace,
O, the curse of old age! those who loved us deep,
Keep us at an arm's length, like a fell disease.
Old age is the deadly foe of every charm and grace,
Never should a lover, O Lord, old age embrace!

They called us "rose", and "Yousaf's peer",
They gave us rings as souvenir,
None will give us water now even if we die,
Ah youth, you have left us in a state of death-in-life.

Kya qahr hai yaaro jise aa jaae burhapa,
Aur aish-e-jawani ke taein khaae burhapa,
Ishrat ko mila khak mein ghum laae burhapa,
Har kaam ko, har baat ko tarsaae burhapa.

Sab cheez ko hota hai bura haae burhapa,
Aashiq ko tau allah na dikhlaae burhapa.

Jo log khushamid se bithate the ghari, pahr,
Chhati se lipat-te the mahabbat ki jita lahr,
Ab aa ke burhape ne kiya haae yeh kuchh qahr,
Ab jin ke kane jaate hain, lagte hain unhen zahr.

Sab cheez ko hota hai bura haae burhapa,
Aashiq ko tau Allah na dikhlaae burhapa.

Aage the jahan gulbadan-o-Yousaf-e-saani,
Dete the hamen payaar se chhallon ki nishani,
Mar jaaen, tau ab munh mein na daale koi paani,
Kis dukh mein hamen chhor gai, haae jawani!

نظیر اکبرآبادی

سب چیز کو ہوتا ہے بُرا ہائے بُڑھاپا
عاشق کو تو اللہ نہ دکھلائے بُڑھاپا
یاد آتے ہیں ہم کو جو جوانی کے وہ ہنگام
اور جام، دل آرام، مزے، عیش اور آرام
ان سب میں جو دیکھو تو نہیں ایک کا اب نام
کیا ہم پہ ستم کر گئی یہ گردشِ ایّام !
سب چیز کو ہوتا ہے بُرا ہائے بُڑھاپا
عاشق کو تو اللہ نہ دکھلائے بُڑھاپا
مجلس میں جوانوں کی تو ساغر ہیں چھلکتے
چھلکیں ہیں، بہاریں ہیں، پری رُو ہیں جھمکتے
ہم اُن کے تئیں دور سے ہیں رشک سے تکتے
وہ عیش و طرب کرتے ہیں ہم سر ہیں پٹکتے
سب چیز کو ہوتا ہے بُرا ہائے بُڑھاپا
عاشق کو تو اللہ نہ دکھلائے بُڑھاپا
جب عیش کے مہمان تھے، اب غم کے ہوئے ضَیف
اب خونِ جگر کھاتے ہیں، جب پیتے تھے سو کَیف

Nazir Akbarabadi

Old age is the deadly foe of every charm and grace,
Never should a lover, O Lord, old age embrace!
Ah, the gala days of youth now beyond recall,
That time of song and dance, of rich delights and balls,
Not a trace is left behind, all's in the past,
What a cruel deal is dealt by Time, whirling fast!
Old age is the deadly foe of every charm and grace,
Never should a lover, O Lord, old age embrace!
Brimming cups clink and clash at the youthful meets,
Amorous dances, sparkling beauties, rare, delicious treats,
We watch it from afar, and with envy burn,
They revel in drink and dance, we squeal and squirm.
Old age is the deadly foe of every charm and grace,
Never should a lover, O Lord, old age embrace!
Then we were by luxury lapped, now a prey to grief,
Now we drink our life-blood, then we drained the goblets sweet;

Sab cheez ko hota hai bura haae burhapa,
Aashiq ko tau Allah na dikhlaae burhapa.
Yaad aate hain hum ko jo jawani ke woh hangam,
Aur jaam, dil aaraam, maze, aish aur aaraam,
In sab mein jo dekho tau nahin ek ka ab naam,
Kya hum pe sitam kar gai yeh gardish-e-ayyam!
Sab cheez ko hota hai bura haae burhapa,
Aashiq ko tau Allah na dikhlaae burhapa!
Majlis mein jawanon ki tau saaghir hain chhalakte,
Chuhlen hain, baharen hain, pari roo hain jhamakte,
Hum un ke taein door se hain rashk se takte,
Woh aish-e-o-tarab karte hain, hum sar hain patakte.
Sab cheez ko hota hai bura haae burhapa,
Aashiq ko tau Allah na dikhlaae burhapa!
Jab aish ke mehman the, ab ghum ke hue zaif,
Ab khoon-e-jigar khate hain, jab peete the sau kaif;

نظیر اکبرآبادی

جب اینٹھ کے چلتے تھے، اسپر باندھ اٹھا سیف
اب ٹیک کے لاکھٹی کے تئیں چلتے ہیں، صد حیف
سب چیز کو ہوتا ہے بُرا ہائے بڑھاپا
عاشق کو تو اللہ نہ دکھلائے بُڑھاپا

پوچھیں جسے، کہتا ہے وہ، کیا پوچھے ہے بُڈّھے
آویں، تو یہ غل ہو کہ، کہاں آوے ہے بُڈّھے
بیٹھیں، تو یہ ہو دھوم، کہاں بیٹھے ہے بُڈّھے
دیکھیں جسے، کہتا ہے وہ، کیا دیکھے ہے بُڈّھے
سب چیز کو ہوتا ہے بُرا ہائے بڑھاپا
عاشق کو تو اللہ نہ دکھلائے بڑھاپا

کیا یار و کہیں، گو کہ بُڑھاپا ہے ہمارا
پر، بوڑھے کہانے کا نہیں تو بھی سہارا
جب، بوڑھا، ہمیں، ہائے جہاں کہہ کے پکارا
کافر نے کلیجے میں گویا تیر سا مارا
سب چیز کو ہوتا ہے بُرا ہائے بڑھاپا
عاشق کو تو اللہ نہ دکھلائے بڑھاپا

Nazir Akbarabadi

Then we walked with upright head, armed with sword and shield,
Now we hold a stick as prop, how tragic indeed!
Old age is the deadly foe of every charm and grace,
Never should a lover, O Lord, old age embrace!

When we speak, we are snubbed: "What say you, aged rag?"
When we approach they jeer at us: "Whither, O broken back?"
When we sit they shout and roar: "No room for you to squat;"
When we watch, "What watchest thou, O decrepit dad?"

Old age is the deadly foe of every charm and grace,
Never should a lover, O Lord, old age embrace!

We have grown old, nodoubt, but what to say?
The appellation, "aged man", heavily on us weighs.
When the world calls us old, we squirm and start,
As if an arrow sharp has pierced through the heart.

Old age is the deadly foe of every charm and grace,
Never should a lover, O Lord, old age embrace!

Jab ainth ke chalte the, sapar baandh, utha saif,
Ab tek ke laathi ke taein chalte hain, sad haif!

Sab cheez ko hota hai bura, haae, burhapa,
Aasiq ko tau Allah na dikhlaae burhapa!

Puchhen jise kahta hai woh, kya poochhe hai budhe?
Aawen tau yeh ghul ho ke kahan aawe hai, budhe?
Baithen tau yeh ho dhoom, kahan baithe ho budhe?
Dekhen jise, kahta hai woh, kya dekhe hai budhe?

Sab cheez ko hota hai bura, haae burhapa,
Aashiq ko tau Allah na dikhlaae burhapa!

Kya yaaro kahen, go ke burhapa hai hamara
Par, burhe kahane ka nahin tau bhi sahara,
Jab boorha hamen, haae, jahan kah ke pukara,
Kafir ne kaleje mein goya tir sa maara.

Sab cheez ko hota hai bura, haae, burhapa,
Aashiq ko tau Allah na dikhlaae burhapa!

نظیر اکبر آبادی

بوڑھوں میں اگر جاویں تو لگتا نہیں واں دل
واں کیوں کے لگے، دل تو ہے محبوبوں کا مائل
محبوبوں میں جاویں، تو وہ سب جھپٹے ہیں مل مل
کیا سخت مصیبت کی پڑی ان کے مشکل
سب چیز کو ہوتا ہے بُرا ہائے بُڑھاپا
عاشق کو تو اللہ نہ دکھلائے بُڑھاپا

پنگھٹ کو ہماری اگر اسواری گئی ہے
تو واں بھی لگی سانتھ یہ ہنسی خواری گئی ہے
سنتے ہیں کہ کہتی ہوئی پنہاری گئی ہے
"لو دیکھو، بُڑھاپے میں یہ مت ماری گئی ہے"
سب چیز کو ہوتا ہے بُرا ہائے بُڑھاپا
عاشق کو تو اللہ نہ دکھلائے بُڑھاپا

پگڑی ہو اگر لال، گلابی تو یہ آفت
کہتا ہے ہر اک دیکھ کے "دیکھ کیا خوب ہے رنگت"
ٹھٹھے سے کوئی کہتا ہے، کر شکل پہ رحمت
لاحول ولا، دیکھیے بُڑھے کی حماقت"

76

Nazir Akbarabadi

If we go to the old men's haunts, we feel dismayed,
How could it be otherwise, our hearts are beauty's slaves,
If we woo the beauties, they mock us in the face,
We are in a predicament, deadly intricate.
Old age is the deadly foe of every charm and grace,
Never should a lover, O Lord, old age embrace!
If we visit the well-side, riding astride a mare,
There too a similar fate in our face doth stare;
"A water-woman thus did speak," we are told by folks,
"The old man has lost his wits, how he raves and dotes!"
Old age is the deadly foe of every charm and grace,
Never should a lover, O Lord, old age embrace!
If we don a turban red, they mock us and malign,
Old age and ruddy robes! What a sight sublime!
Someone says in a jesting way: "To your age be kind,
By God this hoary head has sure lost his mind."

Boorhon mein agar jawen tau lagta nahin waan dil,
Waan kyonke lage, dil tau hai mehboobon ka maail,
Mehboobon mein jawen tau woh sab chheren hain mil mil,
Kya sakht museebat ki pari aan ke mushkil.

Sab cheez ko hota hai bura, haae burhapa,
Aashiq ko tau Allah na dikhlaae burhapa!

Panghat ko hamari agar aswari gai hai,
Tau waan bhi lagi saath yehi khwaari gai hai,
Sunte hain ke kahti hui pinhaari gai hai,
"Lo, dekho, burhape mein yeh mat maari gai hai."

Sab cheez ko hota hai bura, haae burhapa,
Aashiq ko tau Allah na dikhlaae burhapa!

Pagri ho agar lal, gulabi, tau yeh aafat,
Kahta hai har ik dekh ke, "kya khub hai rangat!"
Thathe se koi kahta hai, "kar shakal pe rahmat,
"Lahaul wila, dekhieye burhe ki hamaqat."

نظیر اکبرآبادی

سب چیز کو ہوتا ہے بُرا ہائے بڑھاپا
عاشق کو تو اللہ نہ دکھلائے بڑھاپا
گر بیاہ میں جاویں، تو یہ ذلّت ہے اُٹھانا
چھٹتے ہی بنے باپ نکاحی کا نشانا
رنڈوں میں اگر جاویں، تو مشکل ہے پھر آنا
افسوس، کسی جا نہیں بوڑھے کا ٹھکانا
سب چیز کو ہوتا ہے بُرا ہائے بڑھاپا
عاشق کو تو اللہ نہ دکھلائے بڑھاپا
دریا کے تماشے کو اگر جاویں، تو یارو
کہتا ہے ہر اک دیکھ کے، "جاتے ہو کہاں کو؟"
اور ہنس کے شرارت سے کوئی پوچھے ہے بدخو
"کیوں خیر ہے، کیا خضر سے ملنے کو چلے ہو؟"
سب چیز کو ہوتا ہے بُرا ہائے بڑھاپا
عاشق کو تو اللہ نہ دکھلائے بڑھاپا
نقلیں کوئی اِن پوپلے ہونٹوں کی بناوے
چل کر کوئی کُبڑے کی طرح، قد کو جھکاوے

Nazir Akbarabadi

Old age is the deadly foe of every charm and grace,
Never should a lover, O Lord, old age embrace.

If we join a wedding feast we are but disgraced,
The bride and the bridesmaids target our age;
If we visit some tavern, we cannot return,
We the old men, alas, are everywhere spurned.

Old age is the deadly foe of every charm and grace,
Never should a lover, O Lord, old age embrace.

If we visit the river bank, we are mocked again,
"Whither do you wend your way?" queries every swain,
Someone with a naughty grin, cunningly doth jibe,
Are you going out to meet, Khizar of the endless life?"

Old age is the deadly foe of every charm and grace,
Never should a lover, O Lord, old age embrace.

Someone apes out of fun our hollow, lisping lips,
Someone plays the hunchback, bending on his hips.

Sab cheez ko hota hai, bura, haae burhapa,
Aashiq ko tau Allah na dikhlaae burhapa.

Gar biaah mein jawen, tau yeh zillat hai uthana,
Chhut-te hi bane baap nikahi ka nishana,
Rindon mein agar jawen, tau mushkil hai phir aana,
Aphsos kisi ja nahin boorhe ka thikana.

Sab cheez ko hota hai bura, haae, burhapa,
Aashiq ko tau Allah na dikhlaae burhapa!

Darya ke tamashe ko agar jawen tau yaaro,
Kahta hai har ik dekh ke, "jaate ho kahan ko?"
Aur hans ke sharart se koi puchhe hai bad khoo,
Kyon khair hai, kya khizar se milne ko chale ho?"

Sab cheez ko hota hai bura, haae, burhapa,
Aashiq ko tau Allah na dikhlaae burhapa.

Naqlen koi in pople honton ki banawe,
Chal kar koi kubre ki tarah qad ko jhukawe,

نظیر اکبرآبادی

داڑھی کے کنے انگلی کو لالا کے نچاوے
یہ خواری تو اللہ کسی کو نہ دکھاوے
سب چیز کو ہوتا ہے بُرا ہائے بڑھاپا
عاشق کو تو اللہ نہ دکھلائے بُڑھاپا

تھے جیسے جوانی میں کیے دھوم دھڑکّے
ویسے ہی بُڑھاپے میں چھٹّے آن کے چھکّے
سب اُڑ گئے کافر وہ نظارے وہ جھمکّے
اب عیش جوانوں کو ہیں، اور بوڑھوں کو دھکّے
سب چیز کو ہوتا ہے بُرا ہائے بُڑھاپا
عاشق کو تو اللہ نہ دکھلائے بُڑھاپا

گر حرص سے داڑھی کو خضاب اپنی لگاویں
جھُرّی جو پڑی مُنھ پہ، اسے کیونکے مٹاویں
گو مکر سے، ہنسنے کے تیں، دانت بندھاویں
گردن تو پڑی ہلتی ہے، کیا خاک چھپاویں
سب چیز کو ہوتا ہے بُرا ہائے بُڑھاپا
عاشق کو تو اللہ نہ دکھلائے بُڑھاپا

Nazir Akbarabadi

Another tickles our beard with his fingers lithe,
Save us all, O gracious Lord, from such ignonimous plight.
Old age is the deadly foe of every charm and grace,
Never should a lover, O Lord, old age embrace!
How we jumped and roared in youth, O, we flew so high!
Decrepit age has brought us low, debunked our pride,
All those maddening sights and sounds are now dispersed
    and gone,
The young enjoy all delights, age is held in scorn.
Old age is the deadly foe of every charm and grace,
Never should a lover, O Lord, old age embrace!
We may sometime dye our beard just for vanity sake,
But we cannot wish away the wrinkles on our face,
We may flaunt a denture new, wear a false smile,
But this flaccid, flimsy neck is so hard to hide.
Old age is the deadly foe of every charm and grace,
Never should a lover, O Lord, old age embrace!

Daarhi ke kane ungali ko la la ke nachaawe,
Yeh khwaari tau Allah kisi ko na dikhawe.
Sab cheez ko hota hai bura, haae, burhapa,
Aashiq ko tau Allah na dikhlaae burhapa!
The jaise jawani mein kieye dhoom dharakke,
Waise hi burhape mein chhute aan ke chhakke,
Sab ur gaye kafir woh nazzare, woh jhamakke,
Ab aish jawanon ko hain, aur boorhon ko dhakke.
Sab cheez ko hota hai bura, haae, burhapa,
Aashiq ko tau Allah na dikhlaae burhapa!
Gar hirs se daarhi ko khizab apni lagawen,
Jhurri jo pari munh pe, use kyonke mitawen,
Go makr se hansne ke taein, daant bandhawen,
Gardan tau pari hilti hai, kya khak chhupawen.
Sab cheez ko hota hai bura, haae burhapa,
Aashiq ko tau Allah na dikhlaae burhapa!

نظیر اکبرآبادی

یہ ہونٹھ جواب پو پلے یار وہیں ہمارے
اِن ہونٹوں نے بوسوں کے بہت رنگ میں مارے
ہوتے تھے جوانی میں تو پریوں کے گزارے
اور اب تو چڑیل آن کے، اِک لات نہ مارے
سب چیز کو ہوتا ہے بُرا ہائے بُڑھاپا
عاشق کو تو اللہ نہ دکھلائے بُڑھاپا

تھے جیسے جوانی میں پئے جام سبو کے
ویسے ہی بُڑھاپے میں پئے گھونٹ لہو کے
جب آ کے گلے لگتے تھے محبوب بھبو کے
اب کہیے، تو بُڑھیا بھی کوئی مُنھ پہ نہ تھو کے
سب چیز کو ہوتا ہے بُرا ہائے بُڑھاپا
عاشق کو تو اللہ نہ دکھلائے بُڑھاپا

محفل میں وہ مستی سے بگڑنا نہیں بھولے
ساقی سے پیالوں پہ جھگڑنا نہیں بھولے
ہنس ہنس کے پری زادوں سے لڑنا نہیں بھولے
وہ، گالیاں، وہ بوسوں پہ اڑنا نہیں بھولے

Nazir Akbarabadi

These lips which, O friend, now loosely hang,
Do you know how many kisses in yonder days they drank?
In days of youth we were beseiged by numerous fairy dames,
Today even a vile witch dreads to hear our name.

Old age is the deadly foe of every charm and grace,
Never should a lover, O Lord, old age embrace!

As then we drank from brimming cups, with foaming purple beads,
So now we sup at our heart, which day and night bleeds;
In our youth glowing beauties held us in embrace,
Even a hag doesn't now spit at our face.

Old age is the deadly foe of every charm and grace,
Never should a lover, O Lord, old age embrace!

We recall that getting cross without offence or cause,
That wrangling with the saqi for yet another glass.
We remember those amorous fights with bewitching dames,
We would clamour for kisses, they would cry: "shame."

Yeh hont jo ab pople yaaro hain hamare,
In honton ne boson ke bahut rang hain maare;
Hote the jawani mein tau parion ke guzaare,
Aur ab tau churel aan ke, ik laat na maare.

Sab cheez ko hota hai bura, haae burhapa,
Aashiq ko tau Allah na dikhlaae burhapa.

The jaise jawani mein pieye jaam saboo ke,
Waise hi burhape mein pieye ghoont lahu ke,
Jab aa ke gale lagte the mehboob bhabhooke,
Ab kaheye tau burhiya bhi koi munh pe na thooke.

Sab cheez ko hota hai bura, haae, burhapa,
Aashiq ko tau Allah na dikhlaae burhapa!

Mehfil mein woh masti se bigarna nahin bhoole,
Saqi se piaalon pe jhagarna nahin bhoole,
Hans hans ke pari zaadon se larna nahin bhoole,
Woh gaalian, woh boson pe arna nahin bhoole.

نظیر اکبرآبادی

سب چیز کو ہوتا ہے بُرا ہائے بُڑھاپا
عاشق کو تو اللہ نہ دکھلائے بُڑھاپا
کیا دَور تھا، سر دُکھنے کا ہوتا تھا حد افسوس
ہر غنچہ دہن دیکھ کے کرتا تھا حد افسوس
اب مر بھی اگر جائیں، تو ہوتا ہے کہ افسوس
افسوس، صد افسوس، صد افسوس صد افسوس!
سب چیز کو ہوتا ہے بُرا ہائے بُڑھاپا
عاشق کو تو اللہ نہ دکھلائے بُڑھاپا
وہ کوشش نہیں، جس کے کوئی خوف سے دہلے
وہ زعم نہیں، جس سے کوئی بات کو سہہ لے
جب پھوس ہوئے ہاتھ، تھکے پاؤ بھی پہلے
پھر جس کے جو کچھ شوق میں آوے سو ہی کہہ لے
سب چیز کو ہوتا ہے بُرا ہائے بُڑھاپا
عاشق کو تو اللہ نہ دکھلائے بُڑھاپا
کرتے تھے جوانی میں تو سب آپ سے آ، چاہ
اور حُسن دکھاتے تھے وہ سب آن کے دل خواہ

Nazir Akbarabadi

Old age is the deadly foe of every charm and grace,
Never should a lover, O Lord, old age embrace!
When we complained of headache, ah! woe betide!
A host of blooming beauties rushed to sympathise,
If to-day we pass away, none would feel the loss,
What a fate, O my friends, alas! alas! alas!

Old age is the deadly foe of every charm and grace,
Never should a lover, O Lord, old age embrace!
Spent is all that fire which made the others quail,
Gone is the might of pride which on others prevailed,
When our hands have lost their vigour, feet sink and fail,
They can say whatever they like, we can only wail.

Old age is the deadly foe of every charm and grace,
Never should a lover, O Lord, old age embrace!
When we were young, they sought us out, our sweethearts,
    unasked,
They unlocked their beauteous wealth of their own accord.

Sab cheez ko hota hai, bura, haae, burhapa,
Aashiq ko tau Allah na dikhlaae burhapa!

Kya daur tha sar dukhne ka hota tha jad afsos,
Har ghuncha dahan dekh ke karta tha had afsos,
Ab mar bhi jaaen agar tau hota hai kad afsos,
Afsos, sad afsos, sad afsos, sad afsos!

Sab cheez ko hota hai bura, haae burhapa,
Aashiq ko tau Allah na dikhlaae burhapa!

Woh josh nahin, jis ke koi khauf se dahle,
Woh zuhm nahin, jis se koi baat ko sahle;
Jab phoos hue haath, thake paaon bhi pahle,
Phir jis ke jo kuchh shauq mein aawe, so hi kah le.

Sab cheez ko haota hai bura, haae, burhapa,
Aashiq ko tau Allah na dikhlaae burhapa.

Karte the jawani mein sab aap se aa, chaah,
Aur husn dikhate the woh sab aan ke dil khwah;

نظیر اکبرآبادی

یہ قہر بُڑھاپے نے کیا، آہ نظیر آہ!
اب کوئی نہیں پوچھتا، اللہ ہی اللہ
سب چیز کو ہوتا ہے تبرا ہائے بُڑھاپا
عاشق کو تو اللہ نہ دکھلائے بُڑھاپا

Nazir Akbarabadi

What a terrible blow is dealt by hoary age, alas!
None is there to help or heed, save, Nazir, our God.

Old age is the deadly foe of every charm and grace,
Never should a lover, O Lord, old age embrace!

Yeh qahr burhape ne kiya, ah Nazir, ah!
Ab koi nahin puchhta, Allah hi Allah!

Sab cheez ko hota hai bura, haae burhapa,
Aashiq ko tau Allah na dikhlaae burhapa!

نظیر اکبرآبادی

روٹیاں

جب آدمی کے پیٹ میں آتی ہیں روٹیاں
پھولی نہیں بدن میں سماتی ہیں روٹیاں
آنکھیں پری رُخوں سے لڑاتی ہیں روٹیاں
سینے پر بھی ہاتھ چلاتی ہیں روٹیاں
جتنے مزے ہیں سب یہ دکھاتی ہیں روٹیاں

روٹی سے جس کا ناک تلک پیٹ ہے بھرا
کرتا پھرے ہے کیا وہ اُچھل کود جا بجا
دیوار پھاند کر کوئی کوٹھا اُچھل گیا
ٹھٹھا، ہنسی، شراب، صنم، ساقی، اِس سوا
سو سو طرح کی دھوم مچاتی ہیں روٹیاں

جس جا پہ ہانڈی، چولھا، توا اور تنور ہے
خالق کی قدرتوں کا اُسی جا ظہور ہے
چولھے کے آگے آنچ جو جلتی حضور ہے
جتنے ہیں نور، سب میں یہی خاص نور ہے
اِس نور کے سبب، نظر آتی ہیں روٹیاں

Nazir Akbarabadi
Rotian (Chapaties)

When chapaties fill a man's stomach right to the brim,
He feels puffed up with joy, makes a merry din;

Chapaties rouse romantic longings, chapaties make us bold
To touch and tickle the bosoms, to play with cheeks and chins.

Chapaties are the mainspring of all the joys of life!
He who is feted with chapaties to his fill,
Will leap and bound in joy everywhere at will.

There he jumps across the wall, scales the roofs and hills,
Wine, beauty and saqi, pranks, jokes and thrills,

Chapaties bring to man sundry other delights!
Where you find all together, hearth, oven, pot and plate,
There lies manifest God's bounteous grace.

The fire burning in the hearth, beneath the cooking plate,
Spreads its warm radiance all around the place.

In this radiant light chapaties spring to sight.

Jab aadmi ke pet mein aati hai rotian,
Phooli nahin badan mein samati hain rotian.

Aankhen pari rukhon se larati hain rotian,
Seene upar bhi haath chalati hain rotian.

Jitne maze hain sab yeh dikhati hain rotian.

Roti se jiska naak talak pet hai bhara,
Karta phire hai kya woh uchhal kood, ja baja;

Deewar phand kar koi kotha uchhal gaya,
Thatha, hansi, sharab, sanam, saqi, is siwa,

Sau sau tarah ki dhoom machati hain rotian.

Jis ja pe haandi, choolha, tawa aur tanoor hai,
Khaliq ki qudraton ka usi ja zahoor hai.

Choolhe ke aage aanch jo jalti hazoor hai,
Jitne hain noor, sab mein yehi khas noor hai.

Is noor ke sabab, nazar aati hain rotian.

نظیر اکبرآبادی

آوے توے، تنور کا جس جازباں یہ نام
یا چکی چولہے کا جہاں گل زار ہو تمام
واں سر جھکا کے کیجیے ڈنڈوت اور سلام
اِس واسطے کہ خاص یہ روٹی کے ہیں مقام
پہلے اِنہی مکانوں میں آتی ہیں روٹیاں

اِن روٹیوں کے نُور سے سب دل ہیں پُر نور
آٹا نہیں ہے، چھلنی سے چھن چھن گرے ہے نور
پیڑا ہے ایک اُس کا ہے برفی و موتی چور
ہرگز کسی طرح نہ بجھے پیٹ کا تنور
اِس آگ کو مگر یہ بجھاتی ہیں روٹیاں

پوچھا کسی نے یہ کسی کامل فقیر سے
"یہ مہر و ماہ حق نے بنائے ہیں کاہے کے؟"
وہ سُن کے بولا "وہ بابا! خدا تجھ کو خیر دے
ہم تو نہ چاند سمجھیں، نہ سورج ہیں جانتے
بابا! ہمیں تو یہ نظر آتی ہیں روٹیاں"

Nazir Akbarabadi

Where they talk with respect of hearth and hot plate,
There where the grinding mill sweetly reverberates,

There should we bow our heads, lie prostrate,
This is the home of chapaties, this their birthplace.

This is where the chapaties first of all arrive.

Chapaties brighten every heart, keep it mighty pleased,
'Tis not the flour but rays of light that filter through the sieve,

Every ball of dough is a rare, delicious treat,
The fire of hunger will not let us sit at ease,

Chapaties quench this fire, leave us satisfied.

Someone put this question to a wise sage,
"How did the gracious God sun and moon create?"

"Bless ye, sir," the sage replied, "Let me humbly state:
We know naught about the sun, or the moon in space,

We can only see in them chapaties round and bright."

*Aawe tawe tanoor ka jis ja zaban pe naam,
Ya chakki choolhe ka jahan gulzar ho tamaam,*

*Waan sar jhuka ke kijeye dandwat aur salaam,
Is waste ke khas yeh roti ke hain maqaam;*

Pehle inhi makanon mein aati hain rotian.

*In rotion ke noor se sab dil hain poor, poor,
Aata nahin hai, chhalni se chhan, chhan gire hai noor;*

*Pera har ek uska hai, barfi-o-moti choor,
Hargiz kisi tarah na bujhe pet ka tanoor,*

Is aag ko magar yeh bujhati hain rotian.

*Poochha kisi ne yeh kisi kaamil faqir se,
"Yeh mehar-o-maah haq ne banae hain kaahe ke?"*

*Woh sun ke bola, "Baba! Khuda tujh ko khair de,
Hum tau na chaand samjhen, na suraj hain jaante,*

Baba! hamen tau yeh nazar aati hain rotian."

نظیر اکبرآبادی

پھر پوچھا اس نے کہیے، یہ ہے دل کا نور کیا؟
اِس کے مشاہدے میں ہے کھلتا ظہور کیا؟
وہ بولا اس کے " تیرا گیا ہے شعور کیا!
کشفُ القلوب اور یہ کشفُ القبور کیا؟
جتنے ہیں کشف، سب یہ دکھاتی ہیں روٹیاں"

روٹی جب آئی پیٹ میں، سو قند کھل گئے
گل زار کھلے پھولے آنکھوں میں، اور عیش مل گئے
دو ترنوالے پیٹ میں جب آ کے ڈھل گئے
چودہ طبق ہے، جتنے تھے، سب بھید کھل گئے
یہ کشف، یہ کمال،، دکھاتی ہیں روٹیاں

روٹی نہ پیٹ میں ہو، تو پھر کچھ جستن نہ ہو
میلے کی سیر، خواہشِ باغ و چمن نہ ہو
بھوکے، غریب دل کی، خدا سے لگن نہ ہو
سچ ہے کہا کسی نے کہ، بھوکے کے بھجن نہ ہو
اللہ کی بھی یاد دلاتی ہیں روٹیاں

Nazir Akbarabadi

Then he asked, "Tell us, thou, what's this inner light?
What does it reveal, what signifies?"

"Have you lost your wits?" thus the sage replied,
Why talk of spiritual lore, mysteries of death and life,
All occult knowledge from chapaties alone derives.

As chapaties fill the stomach, a hundred sweets provide the feast,
Gardens blossom in the eyes, luxuries offer lavish treats,

When a couple of buttered morsels glide into the belly deep,
The secret of all the dishes suddenly stands revealed.

Chapaties work miracles, wonders and delights!

An empty stomach finds no joy in any festive meet,
Garden picnics cannot a hungry man please,

A famished man cannot meditate in peace,
Such a man, 'tis rightly said, cannot even tell the beads.

Chapaties makes us think of God, remind us of His might.

Phir poochha us ne, "kahieye, yeh hai dil ka noor kya?
Is ke mushahde mein hai khulta zahoor kya?"

Woh bola sun ke: "Tera gaya hai shaoor kya!
Kashaf-ul-qaloob aur yeh kashaf-ul-qaboor kya?

Jitne hain kashaf, sab yeh dikhati hain rotian.

Roti jab aai pet mein sau qand ghul gaye,
Gulzar phoole aankhon mein aur aish tul gaye,

Do tar niwale pet mein jab aa ke dhul gaye,
Chaudah tabaq ke, jitne the, sab bhed khul gaye.

Yeh kashaf, yeh kamal, dikhati hain rotian.

Roti na pet mein ho, tau phir kuchh jatan na ho,
Mele ki sair, khwahish-e-bagh-o-chaman na ho,

Bhooke, gharib dil ki, khuda se lagan na ho,
Sach hai kaha kisi ne ke bhooke bhajan na ho.

Allah ki bhi yaad dilaati hain rotian.

نظیر اکبرآبادی

کپڑے کسی کے لال ہیں، روٹی کے واسطے
لمبے کسی کے بال ہیں، روٹی کے واسطے
باندھے کوئی رومال ہیں، روٹی کے واسطے
سب کشف اور کمال ہیں روٹی کے واسطے
جتنے ہیں روپ، سب یہ دکھاتی ہیں روٹیاں

دُنیا میں اب بدی نہ کہیں اور نیکوئی ہے
نا دشمنی و دوستی، نا تنگ خوئی ہے
کوئی کسی کا، اور کسی کا نہ کوئی ہے
سب کوئی ہے اُسی کا کہ جس ہاتھ دوئی ہے
نوکر، نفر، غلام، بناتی ہیں روٹیاں

روٹی کا اب ازل سے ہمارا تو ہے خمیر
روکھی بھی روٹی، حق میں ہمارے ہے شہد و شیر
یا پتلی ہوویں، موٹی، خمیری ہو، یا فطیر
گیہوں کی، جوار، باجرے کی، جیسی ہو نظیر
ہم کو تو سب طرح کی خوش آتی ہیں روٹیاں

Nazir Akbarabadi

Someone wears ruddy robes, for chapaties' sake,
Someone wears his hair long, for chapaties' sake,
Another ties handkerchief, to win the chapaties' race,
All miracles and wonders, chapaties alone generate.

Chapaties manifest themselves in many a different guise.

There's nothing good or evil in the world today,
No amity, no enmity, nor flights of rage,

None belongs to anyone, none is our mate,
We befriend him alone who the ladle sways.

Chapaties make servants, slaves, cringing parasites!

Chapaties are the stuff with which the human frame is made,
For us even a dry crumb, Nazir, honey-like tastes.

Fat or slim, fresh or leavened, whatever be the shape,
Barley, wheat, or millet, whatever be the base,

Irrespective of their type, chapaties give us great delight.

Kapre kisi ke lal kain roti ke waste,
Lambe kisi ke bal hain, roti ke waste,

Baandhe koi rumaal hai, roti ke waste,
Sab kashaf aur kamal hain, roti ke waste.

Jitne hain roop, sab yeh dikhati hain rotian.

Duniya mein ab badi na kahin aur nakoi hai,
Na dushmani-o-dosti, na tund khooi hai,

Koi kisi ka, aur kisi ka na koi hai,
Sab koi hai uska ke jis haath doi hai,

Naukar, nafar, ghulam, banati hain rotian.

Roti ka ab azal se hamara tau hai khamir,
Rukhi bhi roti, haq mein hamare hai, shahd-o-shir,

Ya patli howe, moti, khamiri ho, ya fatir,
Gehun ki, jawar, bajre ki, jaisi ho Nazir,

Hum ko tau sab tarah ki khush aati hain rotian.

Nawab Mirza Shauq Lucknavi
(1783-1871)

NAWAB MIRZA SHAUQ LUCKNAVI
(1783-1871)

Hakim Tassadiq Hussain Khan, popularly known as Nawab Mirza Shauq, was born at Lucknow in 1783. He belonged to a family of *hakims* (practitioners of Unani medicine), and his father, Agha Ali Khan was a reputed *hakim* of Lucknow. Accordingly, Shauq's early education included, besides a grounding in language and literature, a training in the field of medicine, so that he came to be known as *Hakim* Nawab Mirza. Shauq was a tall, handsome, well-dressed man, imbued with aristocratic tastes. In addition, he was a man of romantic propensities, with a weakness for wine and women. It may not be wrong to conjecture that in the making of his romantic *masnavies* has entered his own experience of amorous attachments. Because of his romantic disposition he was at first denied admittance to the inner precincts of the royal palace; but Nawab Wajid Ali Shah, himself a deeply sensuous man, was specially fond of Shauq, and allowed him access to the royal household. Wajid Ali also granted him a monthly stipend of Rs. 500, which figure, according to some writers, seems rather exaggerated. But Nawab Mirza, we may recall, was both a poet and a royal physician. These twin qualifications must have enhanced his value in the eyes of his patron.

When Shauq grew up, the air of Lucknow was surcharged with poetry and music. Insha, Mushafi and Jurrat had outlived their productive periods, leaving the poetic field to Nasikh and Aatish. Shauq was specially impressed by the poetry of Aatish, and adopted him as his poetic mentor. Starting as a writer of the *ghazal*, Shauq soon changed over to *masnavi* (the long narrative poem), in which he has earned immortal fame. His poetic reputation rests mainly on three of his famous *masnavies*: *Fareb-e-*

Ishq, Bahar-e-Ishq, and *Zahar--e-Ishq,* all of which are inspired by the theme of romantic love, and are remarkable for a frank portrayal of youthful passion, now sincere, now deceitful, now happy and now tragic. His most successful *masnavi, Zahar-e-Ishq,* describes the story of a passionate romance which ends, because of social taboos and conventional restraints, in the tragic death of the heroine. Apart from their romantic content these poems are notable for their linguistic simplicity, rhythmic flow, and a skilful use of everyday idiom, especially of the women and courtesans of Lucknow. These poems, moreover, contain authentic pictures of the cultural and social life of Lucknow of the time of Wajid Ali Shah, the last ruler of Avadh.

نواب مرزا شوق لکھنوی
زہرِ عشق

ایک قصّہ عجیب لکھتا ہوں
داستانِ غریب لکھتا ہوں
تازہ اس طرح کی حکایت ہے
سننے والوں کو جس سے حیرت ہے
جس محلّے میں تھا ہمارا گھر
وہیں رہتا تھا ایک سوداگر
مردِ اشراف صاحبِ دولت
تاجروں میں کمال ذی عزّت
ایک دختر تھی اس کی ماہ جبیں
شادی اس کی نہیں ہوئی تھی کہیں
ثانی رکھتی نہ تھی وہ صورت میں
غیرتِ حور تھی حقیقت میں
اس سن و سال پر کمال خلیق
چال ڈھال انتہا کی نستعلیق
چشمِ بد دور وہ ئیں آنکھیں
رشکِ چشمِ غزال تھیں آنکھیں

Nawab Mirza Shauq Lucknavi
Zahar-e-Ishq (The Tragedy of Love)

A strange tale, lo, I inscribe,
A humble man's tale of life.

It is such a novel tale,
He who hears is left amazed.

In the street where I abode,
A merchant also lived and throve.

A rich, reputed gentleman,
Respected by the business clan.

He had a daughter moon-visaged,
As yet unmarried, still a maid.

Unrivalled was her tender grace,
Houri's envy was her face.

Though young she was a sober maid,
Her manners showed poise and grace.

Save, O God, from evil glance,
Her beauteous eyes that deer-like pranced!

Ek qissa ajib likhta hoon,
Daastaan-e-gharib likhta hoon;

Taaza is tarah ki hikayat hai,
Sun-ne walon ko jis se hairat hai.

Jis mahalle mein tha hamara ghar,
Wahin rahta tha ek saudagar.

Mard-e-ashraf sahib-e-daulat,
Tajron mein kamal zi izzat.

Ek dukhtar thi uski maah jabeen,
Shadi uski nahin hui thi kahin.

Sani rakhti na thi woh soorat mein,
Ghairat-e-hoor thi haqiqat mein.

Is san-o-saal par kamal khaliq,
Chal dhal inteha ki nustaleeq.

Chashm-e-badoor, woh haseen aankhen,
Rashk-e-chashm-e-ghazaal cheen aankhen.

شوق لکھنوی

تھا جو ماں باپ کو نظر کا ڈر
آنکھیں بھر کر نہ دیکھتے تھے ادھر
تھی زمانے میں بے عدیل و نظیر
خوش گلو، خوش جمال، خوش تقریر
ایک دن چرخ پر جو ابر آیا
کچھ اندھیرا سا ہر طرف چھایا
کھل گیا جب برس کے وہ بادل
قوس تب آسمان پہ آئی نکل
دل مرا بیٹھے بیٹھے گھبرایا
سیر کرنے کو بام پر آیا
خفقاں دل کا جو بہلنے لگا
اس طرف اُسے ٹہلنے لگا
دیکھا اک سمت جو اٹھا کے نظر
سامنے تھی وہ دُختِ سوداگر
ساتھ ہم جولیاں بھی تھیں دوچار
دیکھتی تھیں وہ آسماں کی بہار

102

Shauq Lucknavi

Lest it may cause some unknown bale,
Her parents would not at her gaze.

She was without a peer, unique,
Sweet in looks, in voice, in speech.

One day the sky was overcast,
The earth was also tinged with dark.

When the clouds had spent their might,
A rainbow spanned across the sky.

Tired of sitting all alone,
I climbed the stairs to gently roam.

As I felt relaxed, relieved,
I began to pace at ease.

When by chance my eyes were raised,
The merchant's daughter met my gaze.

A few of her friends stood beside,
They had come to watch the sight.

Tha jo maan baap ko nazar ka dar,
Aankhen bhar kar na dekhte the idhar.

Thi zamane mein be adil-o-nazir,
Khush gulu, khush jamal, khush taqrir.

Ek din charkh par jo abar aaya,
Kuchh andhera sa har taraf chhaya,

Khul gaya jab baras ke woh baadal,
Qaus tab aasmaan pe aai nikal.

Dil mira baithe baithe ghabraya,
Sair karne ko baam par aaya.

Khafqaan dil ko jo bahalne laga,
Is, us taraf tahalne laga.

Dekha ik samat jo utha ke nazar,
Saamne thi woh dukht-e-saudagar.

Saath humjolian bhi thin do chaar,
Dekhti thin woh aasman ki bahaar.

شوقؔ لکھنوی

بام سے کچھ اترتی جاتی تھیں
چھبیں آپس میں کرتی جاتی تھیں
رہ گئی جب اکیلی وہ گل رُو
نگراں سیر کو ہوئی ہر سُو
ہوئی میری جو اس کی چار نگاہ
منھ سے بے ساختہ نکل گئی آہ
حال دل کا نہیں کہا جاتا
خوب سنبھلا نہیں غشؔ آ جاتا
نہ ہوا گو کلام فی ما بین
روح قالب میں ہو گئی بے چین
سامنے وہ کھڑی تھی ماہ منیر
چُپ کھڑا تھا میں صورتِ تصویر
اسی صورت سے ہو گئی جب شام
لائی پاس ان کے اک کنیز پیام
بیٹھی ناحق بھی ہو ویس کھاتی ہیں
اماں جان آپ کو بلاتی ہیں

Shauq Lucknavi

In a while they were gone,
Laughing, jesting all along.

When the damsel was alone,
She began surveying around.

When by chance clashed our eyes,
I couldn't help but raise a sigh.

I can't express my inward state,
I was about to fall and faint.

Not a word betwixt us passed,
Yet my soul was deep distraught.

My radiant moon was just in front,
But I was like a statue, stunned.

As it was close to eventide,
Her maid with a word arrived;

"You mother feels concerned a lot,
Here she sends an urgent call."

Baam se kuchh utarti jati thin,
Chuhlen aapas mein karti jati thin.

Rah gai jab akeli woh gul roo,
Nigran sair ko hui har soo.

Hui meri jo uski char nigah,
Munh se be saakhta nikal gai aah.

Haal dil ka nahin kaha jaata,
Khub sambhla, nahin ghash aa jaata.

Na hua go kalaam fi ma bain,
Rooh qalib mein ho gai be chain.

Saamne khari thi woh mah-e-muneer,
Chup khara tha main soorat-e-taswir.

Isi soorat se ho gai jab sham,
Laai pass un ke ik kaneez payaam.

Baithi naahaq bhi haulen khati hain,
Amman jaan aap ko bulati hain.

شوقؔ لکھنوی

سُن کے لونڈی کے منھ سے یہ پیغام
گئی کوٹھے کے نیچے وہ گُل فام
اُس کا جلوہ نہ جب نظر آیا
میں بھی روتا ہوا اُتر آیا
شام سے پھر سحر کی مر مر کے
شب وہ کاٹی خدا خدا کر کے
پڑ گیا دل میں غم سے اِک ناسور
یہی اس دن سے پڑ گیا دستور
دن میں سو بار بام پر جانا
دیکھنا بھالنا چلے آنا
جب نہ دیکھا وہاں پہ وہ گُل رُو
فرطِ غم سے ٹپک پڑے آنسو
گزرے کچھ دن جو رنج کے مارے
زرد رُخسار ہو گئے سارے
ہو گئی پھر تو ایسی حالت زار
جیسے برسوں کا ہو کوئی بیمار

Shauq Lucknavi

Obeying her mother's anxious call,
She left the roof and down did dart.

When I failed to see her sight,
I too perforce withdrew inside.

Sighing and crying I spent the night,
Ah, how I yearned to see daylight!

Grief consumed my heart away,
This is how I spent my days:

On terrace I would often stay,
Survey around and come away.

Oh, my eyes would drip and flow,
When I failed to see my rose.

As a result of ceaseless grief,
Pale became my rosy cheeks.

I had grown so weak and lean,
For years I've been sick, it seemed.

Sun ke laundi ke munh se yeh paigham,
Gai kothe ke neeche woh gul faam.

Uska jalwa na jab nazar aaya,
Main bhi rota hua utar aaya.

Sham se phir sahr ki mar mar ke,
Shab woh kaati Khuda Khuda karke.

Par gaya dil mein ghum se ik naasoor,
Yehi is din se par gaya dastoor.

Din mein sau bar baam par jaana,
Dekhna bhalna, chale aana.

Jab na dekha wahan pe woh gulroo,
Fart-e-ghum se tapak pare aansu.

Guzre kuchh din jo ranj ke maare,
Zard rukhsaar ho gaye saare.

Ho gai phir tau aisi hualat-e-zaar,
Jaise barson ka ho koi beemaar.

شوقؔ لکھنوی

دیکھے ماں باپ نے جو یہ انداز
روح قالب سے اُڑ گئی پرواز
پوچھا مجھ سے یہ کیا ہے حال ترا
کس طرف ہے بندھا خیال ترا
سچ بتا دے کہ دھیان کس کا ہے
دل میں غم میری جان کس کا ہے
کون سے ماہ رُو پہ مرتے ہو
سچ کہو کس کو پیار کرتے ہو
کھاتے ہو، پیتے ہو، نہ سوتے ہو
روز اُٹھ اُٹھ کے شب کو روتے ہو
یوں تو برباد تو شباب نہ کر
مٹی ماں باپ کی خراب نہ کر
باتیں یہ والدین کی سُن کر
اور اک قلب پر لگا نشتر
شرم کے مارے منہ کو ڈھانپ لیا
کچھ نہ ماں باپ کو جواب دیا

Shauq Lucknavi

When my parents saw my plight,
They felt the biggest shock of life.

"What ails thee, O dear?" they asked,
"Where have you embroiled your heart?

Who has, in sooth, your fancy caught?
Whose grief is nibbling at your heart?

Which moon-like face is your desire?
Who has set your heart on fire?

You neither eat, nor drink, nor sleep,
But keep awake at night and weep.

Waste not, dear, your youth this way,
Rob us not of peace, we pray."

My parents' deep distressful talk,
Further lacerated my heart.

No reply to them I made,
Whelmed by grief I hid my face.

Dekhe maan baap ne jo yeh andaaz,
Rooh qalib se kar gai parwaaz.

Puchha mujh se yeh kya hai haal tira,
Kis taraf hai bandha khayal tira.

Sach bata de ke dhayan kis ka hai,
Dil mein ghum meri jaan kiska hai?

Kaun se maah roo pe marte ho,
Sach kaho kis ko payaar karte ho.

Khate ho, peete ho, no sote ho,
Roz uth uth ke shab ko rote ho.

Yun tau barbaad tu shabab na kar,
Mitti maan baap ki kharab na kar.

Baaten waalden ki sun kar,
Aur ik qalb par laga nishtar.

Sharm ke maare munh ko dhaamp liya,
Kuchh na maan baap ko jawab diya.

شوق لکھنوی

گزرا یاں تک تو یہ ہمارا حال
اب بیاں ان کا ہوتا ہے احوال
میں تو کھائے ہوئے تھا عشق کا تیر
پر ہوئی ان کے دل پہ بھی تاثیر
درد و غم آگیا جو دل کو پسند
سونا راتوں کو ہوگیا سوگند
ہوگئی جب کمال حالتِ زار
جی میں باقی رہا نہ صبر و قرار
لکھنے پڑھنے کا تھا جو اس کو ذوق
سوچ کر دل میں لکھا اک خطِ شوق
"ہو یہ معلوم تم کو بعدِ سلام
غمِ فرقت سے دل ہے بے آرام
اپنے کوٹھے پہ تو نہیں آتا
دل ہمارا بہت ہے گھبراتا
شکل دکھلا دے کبریا کے لئے
بام پر آ ذرا خدا کے لئے"

Shauq Lucknavi

Thus far I have told my tale,
Now hear, how the other behaved.

Love, no doubt, did wound my heart,
But she too felt the poignant dart.

Inured to the pangs of grief,
She forgot her rest or sleep.

But when she felt extremely sore,
She lost content and self-control.

As she loved to read and write,
She put her thoughts in black and white;

"I wish you well and then inform,
My heart with parting pain is stormed.

When on roof I see you not
My restless heart is torn apart.

For God's sake, show your face,
Come to the roof, bless ye, Grace!"

Guzra yaan tak tau yeh hamara haal,
Ab bayaan unka hota hai ahwaal.

Main tau khaae hua tha ishq ka teer,
Par hui un ke dil par bhi taseer.

Dard-o-ghum aa gaya jo dil ko pasand,
Sona raaton ko hao gaya saugand.

Ho gai jab kamal haalat-e-zaar,
Ji mein baqi raha na sabar-o-qaraar.

Likhne parhne se tha jo usko zauq,
Soch kar dil mein likha ik khat-e-shauq.

"Ho yeh maalum tum ko baad-e-salaam,
Ghum-e-furqat se dil hai be aaraam.

Apne kothe pe tu nahin aata,
Dil hamara bahut hai ghabrata.

Shakal dikhla de kibriya ke lieye,
Baam par aa zara Khuda ke lieye."

شوقؔ لکھنوی

پڑھ کے میں نے لکھا یہ اُن کو جواب
"کیا لکھوں تم کو اپنا حالِ خراب
بن گئی یاں تو جان پر میری
خوب لی آپ نے خبر میری
ہجر میں مرکے زندگانی کی
اب بھی پوچھا تو مہربانی کی
عشق کا ہے مرے اثر واللّٰہ!
ورنہ تم لکھتیں یہ، معاذ اللّٰہ!
تم تو وہ لوگ ہوتے ہو جلّاد
نہیں سنتے کوئی کرے فریاد
ہو بلا سے کسی کا حال بُرا!
کوئی مر جائے تم کو کیا پروا؟
اب میں لکھتا ہوں آپ کو یہ حضور!
وصل کی فکر چاہیئے ہے ضرور
اس میں غفلت جو تُو نے کی اے ماہ
حال ہوگا مرا کمال تباہ"

112

Shauq Lucknavi

Thus to her I gave reply:
Know thee not my wretched plight?

My very life is at stake,
For you haven't shown your face.

Without you I but pine and yearn,
Thank you for your kind concern.

Love indeed has miracle wrought,
A billet doux from you, my God!

Murderers are ye folks, indeed,
Deaf to the lovers' plaintive pleas.

You care two hoots for the others' plight,
It matters not if someone dies.

May I now request you please,
We should find a way to meet.

If you ignore my plea, my moon,
Surely it will cause my doom.

Parh ke main ne likha yeh unko jawab:
Kya likhun tumko apna haal-e-kharab.

Ban gai yaan tau jaan par meri,
Khoob li aap ne khabar meri.

Hijar mein mar ke zindagani ki,
Ab bhi puchha tau meharbani ki.

Ishq ka hai mere asar, wallah!
Warna tum likhtin yeh, maaz-Allah!

Tum tau woh log hote ho jallad,
Nahin sunte koi kare faryaad.

Ho bala se kisi ka haal bura,
Koi mar jaae tum ko kya parwah?

Ab main likhta hun aap ko yeh hazoor,
Wasal ki fikar chahieye hai zaroor.

Is mein ghaflat jo tu ne ki, ai, maah,
Haal hoga mera kamal tabaah.

شوقؔ لکھنوی

پھر کیا یہ جواب میں تحریر!
"کچھ قضا تو نہیں ہے دامنگیر!
ذکر اِن باتوں کا یہاں کیا تھا؟
چھیڑنے کو ترے یہ لکھا تھا
تم پہ میں مرتی! کیا قیامت تھی
کیا مرے دشمنوں کی شامت تھی؟
تجھ پہ مرتے بھی گر مرے بدخواہ
یوں نہ لکھتی کبھی معاذ اللہ!
جان پا پوش سے نکل جاتی
پر طبیعت نہ یوں بدل جاتی
طالبِ وصل جو ہوئے ہم سے
ہے گا سادہ مزاج جم جم سے"
رہی کچھ روز تو یہی تحریر
پھر موافق ہوئی مری تقدیر
ہوئے اُس گل سے وصل کے اقرار
اٹھ گئی درمیاں سے سب تکرار

Shauq Lucknavi

This is what she wrote me back:
"You are courting death, my chap!
How could I such things conceive,
I wrote in jest, to tickle and tease.
To die for you! What a shame!
Am I mad to court my bane?
Even if I had loved you, foe,
I would never have written you so,
I would rather choose to die,
Than my native grain defy.
You who crave for union sweet,
Are a simpleton, indeed!"
She wrote for sometime in this vein,
But then my fate for better changed.
My rose promised me to meet,
No more on this we disagreed.

Phir kiya yeh jawab mein tahrir,
"Kuchh qaza tau nahin hai damangir!
Zikar in baaton ka yahan kya tha?
Chherne ko tire yeh likha tha.
Tum pe marti! kya qayamat thi,
Kya mire dushmanon ki shamat thi?
Tujh pe marte bhi gar mire bad khwah,
Yun na likhti kabhi, maaza-Allah!
Jaan paposh se nikal jaati,
Par tabiat na yun badal jaati.
Taalib-e-wasal jo hue hum se,
Haiga saada mizaj, jam jam se."
Rahi kuchh roz tau yehi tahrir,
Phir mawafiq hui miri taqdir.
Hue us gul se wasal ke iqraar,
Uth gai darmian se sab takraar.

شوقؔ لکھنوی

جو کہا تھا ادا کیا اُس نے
وعدہ اک دن وفا کیا اُس نے
رات بھر میرے گھر میں رہ کے گئی
صبح کے وقت پھر یہ کہہ کے گئی:
"بات اس دم کی یاد رکھیے گا
ایک دن یہ مزا بھی چکھیے گا
بگڑے گی جب نہ کچھ بن آئے گی
آپ کے پیچھے جان جائے گی
لو مری جان! جاتی ہوں اب تو
یاد رکھیے گا میری صحبت کو"
اتفاق ایسا پھر ہوا ناگاہ!
دو مہینے تلک نہ آئی وہ ماہ
قطع سب ہو گئے پیام و سلام
نہ رہی شکلِ راحت و آرام
دل کو تشویش تھی یہ حد سے زیاد
دفعتاً پڑ گئی یہ کیا افتاد

116

Shauq Lucknavi

True she was in word and deed,
She kept her promise, came to meet.

She came one night and stayed till morn,
While departing, thus she warned:

"Remember what I speak to-day,
We'll come to grief one day.

Things will worsen beyond repair,
I'll die before you hear.

Now from you I must depart,
Keep me ever in your thoughts."

It so happened all it once,
She didn't come for full two months;

No word or greeting betwixt us passed,
All doors of joy were suddenly barred.

I was harried by this thought:
What has suddenly come to pass?

Jo kaha tha ada kiya us ne,
Waada ik din wafa kiya us ne.

Raat bhar mere ghar mein rah ke gai,
Subah ke waqt phir yeh kah ke gai:

"Baat is dam ki yaad rakhieye ga,
Ek din yeh maza bhi chakhieye ga.

Bigre gi jab na kuchh ban aaegi,
Aap ke peechhe jaan jaaegi.

Lo miri jaan! jaati hun ab tau,
Yaad rakhieye ga meri suhbat ko."

Ittefaq aisa phir hua nagah,
Do mahine talak na aai woh maah!

Qata sab ho gaye payaam-o-salaam,
Na rahi shakl-e-raahat-o-aaram.

Dil ko tashweesh thi yeh had se zayad,
Dafatan par gai yeh kya uftaad?

شوقؔ لکھنوی

آئی تو چندی اتنے میں ناگاہ
اس بہانے سے آئی وہ درگاہ
بسکہ مرتی تھی نام پر میرے
چھپ کے آئی وہاں سے گھر میرے
پھر لپٹ کر مرے گلے اک بار
حال کرنے لگی وہ یوں اظہار
اقربا میرے ہو گئے آگاہ
تم سے ملنے کی اب نہیں کوئی راہ
مشورے ہو رہے ہیں آپس میں
بھیجتے ہیں مجھے بنارس میں
گو ٹھکانے نہیں ہیں ہوش و حواس
پر یہ کہنے کو آئی ہوں ترے پاس
جائے عبرت سرائے فانی ہے
موردِ مرگ نو جوانی ہے
کل جہاں پر شگوفہ و گل تھے
آج دیکھا تو خار بالکل تھے

Shauq Lucknavi

But when it was Nauchandi time,
She found pretext to visit the shrine.

As for me she lived and died,
She came to meet me on the sly.

Throwing her arms around my neck,
Her heavy heart she thus expressed:

"My relatives our secret know,
How hard it is to meet you now!

On this strategem they are bent,
That to Benares I be sent.

Though I feel bereaved of wits,
I have come to tell you this:

"This mortal world is a chastening place,
Youth the curse of death entails.

Where once the buds and blooms did sway,
Thorns their prickly heads now raise.

Aai nauchandi itne mein nagaah,
Is bahane se aai woh dargaah;

Bas ke marti thi naam par mere,
Chhip ke aai wahan se ghar mere.

Phir lipat kar mire gale ik baar,
Haal karne lagi woh yun izhaar.

Aqarba mere ho gaye aagaah,
Tum se milne ki ab nahin koi raah;

Mashware ho rahe hain aapas mein,
Bhejte hain mujhe Benares mein.

Go thikane nahin hain hosh-o-hawaas,
Par yeh kahne ko aai hun tire paas:

"Jaae ibrat sara-e-fani hai,
Maurad-e-marg naujawani hai.

Kal jahan par shagoofa-o-gul the,
Aaj dekha tau khaar bilkul the.

شوقؔ لکھنوی

جس چمن میں تھا بلبلوں کا ہجوم
آج اُس جا ہے آشیانۂ بُوم
بات کل کی ہے نوجواں تھے جو
صاحبِ نوبت و نشاں تھے جو
آج خود ہیں، نہ ہے مکاں باقی
نام کو بھی نہیں نشاں باقی
غیرتِ حور مہ جبیں نہ رہے
ہیں مکاں مگر تو وہ مکیں نہ رہے
ہر گھڑی منقلب زمانہ ہے
یہی دنیا کا کارخانہ ہے
زندگی بے ثبات ہے اس میں
موت عین حیات ہے اس میں
ہم بھی گر جان دے دیں کھا کر سَم
تم نہ رو دنا ہمارے سر کی قسم
دل کو ہم جو لیوں میں بہلانا
یا مری قبر پر چلے آنا

Shauq Lucknavi

Where nightingales did reign supreme,
You now would hear the owls scream.

Those who once were proud and young,
Counted among the mighty ones,

Forgotten are their glorious names,
Not a trace of them remains.

Where are the moon-like fairy dames?
The owner goes, the house remains.

Change is the changeless lord of laws,
The wheel of Time for ever revolves.

Man is transient, bound to die,
Death represents the truth of life.

If I take cyanide, and die,
Swear by me you shall not cry.

Engage your heart with your mates,
Or, come and sit beside my grave.

Jis chaman mein tha bulbulon ka hajoom,
Aaj us jaa hai aashiana-e-boom.

Baat kal ki hai, naujawan the jo,
Sahib-e-naubat-o-nishan the jo,

Aaj khud hain, na hai makaan baaqi,
Naam ko bhi nahin nishaan baaqi.

Ghairat-e-hur mah jabeen na rahe,
Hain makaan gar tau woh makeen na rahe.

Har ghari munqalib zamana hai,
Yehi duniya ka karkhana hai.

Zindagi be sabat hai is mein,
Maut ain-e-hayat hai is mein.

Hum bhi gar jaan de dein kha kar sam,
Tum na rona hamare sar ki qasam.

Dil ko humjolion mein bahlana,
Ya miri qabar par chale aana.

شوقؔ لکھنوی

روکے رہنا بہت طبیعت کو
یاد رکھنا مری وصیت کو
میرے مرنے کی جب خبر پانا
یوں نہ دوڑے ہوئے چلے آنا
کہے دیتی ہوں جی نہ کھونا تم
ساتھ تابوت کے نہ رونا تم
ہو گئے تم اگر چہ سودائی
دور پہنچے گی میری رسوائی
میری منّت پہ دھیان رکھیئے گا
بند اپنی زبان رکھیئے گا
پھر ملاقات دیکھیں ہو کہ نہ ہو
آج دل کھول کے گلے مل لو
باہمیں دونوں گلے میں ڈال لو آج
جو جو ارمان ہوں نکال لو آج
دیکھ لو آج ہم کو جی بھر کے
کوئی آتا نہیں ہے پھر مر کے

Shauq Lucknavi

Keep yourself in full control,
Do not, I pray, my will ignore.

Getting news of my demise,
Come not rushing to this side,

Lose not heart, keep your cheer,
Shed no tears at my bier.

If you grow insane or wild,
My honour would be stigmatized.

Don't forget my last request,
Keep your mouth forever shut.

This may be our final night,
Love me now with all your might.

Love me now, hug me tight,
Let your passion spend its might.

Watch us now with all your zest,
None returneth after death."

Roke rahna bahut tabiat ko,
Yaad rakhna meri wasiat ko.

Mere marne ki jab khabar pana,
Yun na daure hue chale aana.

Kahe deti hun ji na khona tum,
Saath taaboot ke na rona tum.

Ho gaye tum agarche saudai,
Door pahunchegi meri ruswai.

Meri mannat pe dhayan rakhieye ga,
Band apni zaban rakhieye ga.

Phir mulaqaat dekhen ho ke na ho,
Aaj dil khol ke gale mil lo.

Bahen donon gale mein dal lo aaj,
Jo jo armaan ho nikaal lo aaj.

Dekh lo aaj hum ko ji bhar ke,
Koi aata nahin hai phir mar ke.

شوقؔ لکھنوی

کہہ کے یہ بات ہوگئی وہ سوار
یاں بندھا آنسوؤں کا چشم سے تار
آتی تھی یاد جب وصیّتِ یار
وہم لاتا تھا دل ہزار ہزار
پھر اٹھا ایک سمت سے وہ غل
ہوش جس سے کہ اڑ گئے بالکل
شعلہ اک آگ کا بھڑکنے لگا
مثل بسمل کے دل پھڑکنے لگا
کہا اک دوست سے کہ تم جاکر
جلد اس شور و غل کی لاؤ خبر
دوڑے آخر ادھر مرے احباب
لے کر آئے خبر یہ داں سے شتاب
کیا اس طرح آ کے مجھ سے بیان
کہ یہاں سے ہے اک قریب مکان
باغ کے پاس جو بنا ہے گھر
واں فرودکش تھا ایک سوداگر

Shauq Lucknavi

Thus she said and back she rode,
While tears down my eyes did roll.

Her parting "will" obsessed my breast,
Which was with sundry fears oppressed.

Ah, then I heard a sudden uproar,
Which numbed my sense and left me cold.

A flame in my heart did rise,
Like a half-dead bird I cried.

I asked a friend of mine to go,
And find the cause of this uproar.

My friend returned running fast,
And brought the news that stunned and shocked.

This is what he said in sooth,
"There's a house in the neighbourhood;

That house by the garden-side,
Where a businessman resides;

Kah ke yeh baat ho gai woh sawaar,
Yaan bandha aansuon ka chashm se taar.

Aati thi yaad jab waseeat-e-yaar,
Wahm laata tha dil hazaar hazaar.

Phir utha ek samat se woh ghul,
Hosh jis se ke ur gaya bilkul.

Shola ik aag ka bharakne laga,
Masal bismal ke dil pharakne laga.

Kaha ik dost se ke tum ja kar,
Jald is shor-o-ghul ki laao khabar.

Daure aakhir idhar mire ahbab,
Le kar aae khabar yeh waan se shatab.

Kiya is tarah aake mujh se bayaan,
Ke yahan se hai ik qarib makaan,

Bagh ke paas jo bana hai ghar,
Waan farokash tha ek saudagar.

شوق لکھنوی

یوں تو اک شور راہ بھر میں ہے
پر یہ آفت انہیں کے گھر میں ہے
کہہ گئی تھی جو وہ کہ کھاؤں گی زہر
میں یہ سمجھا کہ ہو گیا وہی قہر
دیکھا برپا ہے ایک حشر کا غُل
بھیڑ سے بند راہ ہے بالکل
نہ رہی تاب رخ کے مارے
لگے تھرّانے دست و پا سارے
بکر الفت نے دل میں مارا جوش
گر پڑا ہو کے خاک پر بے ہوش
دو گھڑی بعد پھر جو آیا ہوش
دیکھا برپا عجب ہے جوش و خروش
آگے آگے ہے کچھ جلوس رواں
سر کھلے کچھ ہیں پیچھے پیر و جواں
سن رسیدہ ہیں عورتیں کچھ ساتھ
سینہ و سر پہ مارتی ہیں ہاتھ

Shauq Lucknavi

Though the noise is wide-dispersed,
It rises from that house accursed."

"Ah, woe-betide!" thus I cried,
"Consuming poison she has died."

A doom-like din filled the air,
Crowds blocked the thoroughfare.

I was overwhelmed with grief,
A tremour gripped my hands and feet.

The sea of love within me roared,
I fell unconscious on the floor.

In a while when I revived,
I heard a noise, loud and wild.

There was a funeral on the road,
And dishevelled heads of young and old.

Some elderly females too were there,
Who beat their breasts and tore their hair.

Yun tau ik shor raah bhar mein hai,
Par yeh aafat unhin ke ghar mein hai.

Kah gai thi jo woh ke khaoongi zahar,
Main yeh samjha ke ho gaya wohi qahar.

Dekha barpa hai ek hashar ka ghul,
Bhir se band raah hai bilkul.

Na rahi taab ranj ke mare,
Lage tharrane dast-o-pa saare.

Bahr-e-ulfat ne dil mein maara josh,
Gir para ho ke khak par be hosh.

Do ghari baad phir jo aaya hosh,
Dekha barpa ajab hai' josh-o-kharosh.

Aage aage hai kuchh jaloos rawan,
Sar khule hain peechhe pir-o-jawan.

San raseeda hain auraten kuchh saath
Seena-o-sar pe maarti hain haath.

شوق لکھنوی

شامیانہ نیا زری کا ہے
نیچے تابوت اُس پری کا ہے
سہرا اس پر بندھا ہے اک زر تار
جیسے گلشن کی آخری ہو بہار
تھی پڑی اس پہ ایک چادرِ گل
جس سے خوش بو وہ راہ تھی بالکل
عود سوز آگے آگے روشن تھے
مرگئے پر بھی لاکھ جوبن تھے
بھیڑ تابوت کے تھی ایسی ساتھ
جیسے آئے کسی دلہن کی برات
پیچھے پیچھے تھا سب کے سوداگر
مُو پریشاں، اداس، خاک بسر
سب کے پیچھے پنس میں تھی مادر
کہتی جاتی تھی اس طرح رو کر
تیری میت پہ ہوگئی میں نثار
کم سخن ہائے میری غیرت دار

128

Shauq Lucknavi

Beneath an awning golden-laced,
The fairy coffin lay in state.

A wreath of gold glittered above,
Like the spring's parting blush.

A floral sheet covered the bier,
Which lent its fragrance to the air.

Burning censers led the way,
Though dead, she breathed the spirit of May.

The crowds that with the hearse did walk,
Made it like the bridal march.

Behind them all the trader trudged,
Dishevelled, dusty, deep-depressed.

In the palanquin at the end,
Rode the mother, tear-drenched.

'Hail to thee, my daughter dead,
Honour-sensitive, coyness-fed;

Shamiana naya zari ka hai,
Neeche taaboot us pari ka hai.

Sehra is par bandha hai ik zar taar,
Jaise gulshan ki aakhiri ho bahar.

Thi pari is pe ek chadar-e-gul,
Jis se khush boo woh raah thi bilkul.

Ood soz aage aage roshan the,
Mar gaye par bhi laakh joban the.

Bhir taaboot ke thi aisi saath,
Jaise aae kisi dulhan ki baraat.

Peechhe peechhe tha sab ke saudagar,
Moo pareshan, udaas, khak basar.

Sab ke peechhe pins mein thi maadar,
Kahti jaati thi is tarah ro kar;

"Teri mayyat pe ho gai main nisar,
Kam sakhun haae! meri ghairat dar!

شوق لکھنوی

کچھ نہیں ماں کی اب خبر تم کو
کس کی یہ کھا گئی نظر تم کو
کس مصیبت میں پڑ گئی بیٹا
کوکھ میری اجڑ گئی بیٹا
دیکھا آنکھوں سے تھا جو ایسا قہر
کھا گیا میں بھی گھر میں آ کر زہر
تین دن تک رہی وہ بے ہوشی
ہو گئی جس سے خود فراموشی
عین غفلت میں پھر یہ دیکھا خواب
کہ یہ کہتی ہے وہ بہ چشمِ عتاب
سُن تو رے تو نے زہر کیوں کھایا
کچھ وصیّت کا بھی نہ پاس آیا
کہہ کے یہ جب وہ ہو گئی رُوپوش
کھل گئی آنکھ آ گیا مجھے ہوش
حاصل اتنا تھا کچھ کہانی سے
ہم رہے جیتے سخت جانی سے

130

Shauq Lucknavi

"Whose evil eye on you did stare?
You know not how your mamma fares.

What a tragic fate I own,
Devastated lies my womb."

Shattered by the traumatic sight,
Reaching home I took cyanide.

I lay unconscious for three days,
Oblivious all of time and place.

In this state I saw in dream,
My love with angry eyes agleam.

"Why did you poison yourself?" she asked,
My dying will you heeded not."

Thus much and she vanished sore,
I woke and found my sense restored.

Such, in sum, has been my tale,
My life has been a hard travail.

Kuchh nahin maan ki ab khabar tum ko,
Kis ki yeh kha gai nazar tum ko.

Kis museebat mein par gai beta,
Kokh meri ujar gai beta.

Dekha aankhon se tha jo aisa qahar,
Kha gaya main bhi ghar mein aa kar zahr.

Teen din tak rahi woh be hoshi,
Ho gai jis se khud faramoshi.

Ain ghaflat mein phir yeh dekha khwab,
Ke yeh kahti hai woh ba chashm-e-itaab.

"Sun tau re tu ne zahr kyon khaya,
Kuchh waseeat ka bhi na paas aaya."

Kah ke yeh jab woh ho gai rooposh,
Khul gai aankh, aa gaya mujhe hosh.

Haasil itna tha kuchh kahani se,
Hum rahe jeete sakht jaani se.

Abridged

Salamat Ali Dabir
(1803-1875)

SALAMAT ALI DABIR
(1803-1875)

The name of Salamat Ali Dabir is bracketed with that of Babar Ali Anees in any mention of Urdu poetry, more specifically, in the context of the *Marsia*. The *marsia*, strictly speaking, is an elegiac poem written to commemorate the martyrdom and valour of Hazrat Imam Hussain and his comrades of the Karbala fame. In its form the *marsia* generally consists of six-line units, with a rhyming quatrain, and a couplet on a different rhyme. This form found a specially congenial soil in Lucknow, chiefly because it was the centre of Shia Muslim community, which regarded it an act of piety and religious duty to eulogise and bemoan the martyrs of the battle of Karbala. Both Dabir and Anees, who were almost exact contemporaries, were the masters of this genre, and both expended their poetic talent and devotional fervour in refining the form and quality of the *marsia*. Both of them were good friends, respecting each other's poetic ability, yet they were strong poetic rivals chiefly because of the difference in their individual styles of writing and their treatment of this art form. While Dabir tried to impress his audience with the force and flourish of his style, embellished with Persian words and phrases, and a rich wealth of innovative metaphors and imagery, made to look all the more ponderous with occasional scriptural quotation and allusion, Anees followed a simple, natural style, artistic and adequate to his needs, but not affected. Both of them had their bands of admirers who called themselves "dabirias" and "aneesias", depending upon their allegiance to Dabir or Anees. This poetic rivalry between two distinguished masters of the same genre tended to improve the quality not only of the *marsia*, but also of Urdu poetry in general, which acquired a new dimension of realistic writing and natural description.

Dabir was born in Delhi in 1803, a year before the birth of Anees. Right in his childhood Dabir's parents moved to Lucknow which was to become the poet's permanent home. Unlike Anees, who came from a family of reputed poets, Dabir had to depend upon his own inner instincts and abilities, which, however, he developed with utmost diligence and care, under the guidance of his poetic mentor, Mir Muzaffar Ali Zameer. Dabir soon acquired a high position in the field of learning and literature, and as a poet of the *marsia*, to which form he gave all his energy and attention, and in which form he easily surpassed even his master, Zameer. He not only wrote and read his *marsias*, but also recited them in public in an impressive, musical way. Dabir did not write *ghazals*, though he was, like Anees, a specialist of the *rubai*, a four-lined stanza in the special "rajaz" metre, rhyming aaba. Dabir died in 1875 on Muharram, a day traditionally associated with the martyrdom of Imam Hussain, when the bands of the "faithfuls" indulge in heart-rending *marsia khwaani*.

The excerpt chosen for this book describes how tremulously yet tactfully, Hazrat Imam Hussain approaches the enemy camp with a request for water for his infant son, Asghar, half-dead with thirst. The last little detail which shows the infant moving his tongue on his parched lips is a master-stroke of the poet, proving his ability both as a poet and a psychologist.

سلامت علی دبیر

حضرت امامِ حسین کا پانی مانگنا

ہر اک قدم پہ سوچتے تھے سبطِ مصطفیٰ
لے تو چلا ہوں فوجِ عمر سے کہوں گا کیا
نہ مانگنا ہی آتا ہے مجھ کو، نہ التجا
منّت بھی گر کروں گا تو کیا دیں گے وہ بھلا
پانی کے واسطے نہ سنیں گے عدوُ مری
پیاسے کی جان جائے گی اور آبرو مری

پہنچے قریب فوج تو گھبرا کے رہ گئے
چاہا کریں سوال، پہ شرما کے رہ گئے
غیرت سے رنگ فق ہوا تھرّا کے رہ گئے
چا در پسر کے چہرے سے سرکا کے رہ گئے
آنکھیں جھکا کے بولے کہ یہ ہم کو لائے ہیں
اصغر تمہارے پاس غرض لے کے آئے ہیں

گر میں بقولِ عمر و شمر، ہوں گناہ گار
یہ تو نہیں کسی کے بھی آگے قصور وار
ششّ ماہہ، بے زبان، نبی زادہ، شیر خوار
ہفتم سے سب کے ساتھ پیاسا ہے بے قرار

136

Salamat Ali Dabir
Hazrat Hussain Asks for Water for Ali Asghar

The Prophet's grandson, moved along, debating in his mind:
How to plead and argue with the foe unkind,
Begging and beseeching are alien to my mind,
And, will they give me water, if I beg and whine?

The enemy will not hear me, I'll plead in vain,
The thirsty child will lose his life, I'll lose my name.

As he neared the enemy's camp, he stood confused,
Sense of honour forebade him to supplicate or sue;
He was pale with inner fears, trembling in his shoes,
Falteringly, from the child's face the sheet he half-withdrew,

"He it is who brought me here," he said, with downward
    gaze,
"Asghar has, in sooth, brought me to this place."

As alleged by Omar and Shimar, I'm a sinner, agreed,
But this child who comes with me is innocent, indeed;
Six-month old, Nabi's seed, voiceless and unweaned,
Hasn't had a drop of water since we came afield.

Har ik qadam pe sochte the sibt-e-Mustafa;
Le tau chala hoon, fauj-e-Omar se kahunga kya,
Na maangna hi aata hai mujhko, na ilteja,
Minnat bhi gar karunga tau kya dengen woh bhala;

Paani ke waaste na sunenge adoo miri,
Payaase ki jaan jaaegi, aur aabroo miri.

Pahunche qarib-e-fauj tau ghabra ke rah gaye,
Chaaha karen sawaal, pe sharma ke rah gaye,
Ghairat se rang faq hua, tharra ke rah gaye,
Chaadar pisar ke chehre se sarka ke rah gaye.

Aankhen jhuka ke bole ke yeh hum ko laae hain,
Asghar tumhaare paas gharz le ke aae hain.

Gar main baqaul-e-Omar-o-Shimar, hoon gunahgaar,
Yeh tau nahin kisi ke bhi aage qasurwaar;
Shash maha, be zaban, Nabi zada, sheer khwaar,
Haftam se sab ke saath payasaa hai be qaraar.

دبیر

رسن ہے جو کم، تو پیاس کا صدمہ زیادہ ہے
مظلوم خود ہے اور یہ مظلوم زادہ ہے

یہ کون بے زباں ہے، تمہیں کچھ خیال ہے
دُرِّ نجف ہے، بانوے بے کس کا لال ہے
لو مان لو، تمہیں قسم ذوالجلال ہے

یثرب کے شاہ زادے کا پہلا سوال ہے
پوتا علیؑ کا تم سے طلب گارِ آب ہے
دے دو کہ اس میں ناموری ہے ثواب ہے

پھر ہونٹ بے زباں کے چومے جھکا کے سر
رو کر کہا، جو کہنا تھا وہ کہہ چکا پدر
باقی رہی نہ بات کوئی اے میرے پسر
سوکھی زبان تم بھی دکھا دو نکال کر

پھیری زباں لبوں پہ جو اُس نورِ عین نے
تھرّا کے آسمان کو دیکھا حسینؓ نے

(اقتباس)

Salamat Ali Dabir

Because of tender age he finds the shock acute,
Oppressed son of oppressed father now craves your ruth.
Who's this voiceless child, do you know at all?
He's Najaf's priceless pearl, Bano's sole prop.
Prithee, accept my plea in the name of God,
Do respond, O kind sir, to Asghar's maiden call.
Ali's grandson comes to you in his dire need,
God will reward you for this generous deed!
Then he kissed his innocent babe, and threw down his gaze;
Whatever has been said is more than adequate,
There's nothing more to add, nothing more to state,
Put on your tongue, my son, so they know your state.
When the apple of his eye moved his tongue on his lips,
Hussain looked heaven-ward, shaking every bit.

Sin hai jo kam, tau payaas ka sadma zayaada hai,
Mazloom khud hai aur yeh mazloom zaada hai.

Yeh kaun be zaban hai, tumhen kuchh khayaal hai?
Durr-e-Najaf hai, Banoo-e-be kas ka laal hai.
Lo, maan lo tumhen qasam zuljalaal ki,
Yasrab ke shahzaade ka pehla sawaal hai.

Pota Ali ka tum se talabgaar-e-aab hai,
De do ke is mein naamwari hai, sawaab hai.

Phir hont be zaban ke choome, jhuka ke sar,
Ro kar kaha, jo kahna tha woh kah chuka pidar,
Baaqi rahi na baat koi ai mire pisar,
Sookhi zabaan tum bhi dikha do nikaal kar.

Pheri zabaan labon pe us noor-e-ain ne,
Tharra ke aasmaan ko dekha Hussain ne.

Babar Ali Anees
(1804-1874)

BABAR ALI ANEES
(1804-1874)

Anees was born at Faizabad (U.P.) in 1804, but he spent the best part of his life at Lucknow, where his parents had migrated in their old age. Poetry came to him as ancestral heritage, for his forbears, going back to his great grandfather, were eminent poets and men of letters. Anees was the grandson of Mir Hasan who is remembered for his immortal *masnavi*, "Sehir-ul-Bayaan." Anees's father, Mir Khaliq who was a famous poet and litterateur, took personal interest in the education and upbringing of his son, and entrusted him to the care of reputed contemporary teachers, Mir Najaf Ali Faizabadi and Maulvi Hyder Ali Lucknavi. In addition, Anees's mother who was an educated and pious lady, played a significant role in shaping the personality of the boy poet. But above all, it was the boy's own instinctive urge for learning and literature that made him an accomplished poet, proficient in Arabic, Persian and Islamic scriptures, and well-versed in logic, philosophy and prosody.

Anees had started writing poetry quite early in his life right at Faizabad, though he perfected his art in Lucknow under the supervision of Nasikh. In keeping with the popular trend, he first tried his hand at the *ghazal*, but failing to make much headway in this direction, he changed over, under the advice of his father, to the writing of *marsias*, in which domain he soon established a high reputation, equalled (sometimes) by his poetic compere, Salamat Ali Dabir. Anees broadened the scope of this genre by including in its body, in addition to the customary lamentation and mourning, realistic scenes of the battlefield, graphic delineations of the hero's face and figure, lively portrayals of the emotional states of the combatants, accurate descriptions of the lanscape, and occasional interludes of moral edification.

The excerpt from one of his *marsias* included in this book is specially notable for its exact and evocative description, for it enables us not only to see, but also to smell and feel the heat of the day and its impact on the several worlds of men, birds and beasts. It is a piece of fine artistry, reminiscent of Tennyson, the poet of the "Lotos-Eaters" and "The Lady of Shalott." Anees was the master of simple, natural utterance, with a superb command on the language, which was always adequate to express a large variety of moods, scenes, characters and situations. He is specially notable for presenting the same scene or situation, over and over again, in different words or phrases, without letting it sound monotonous. Shibli Numani, a famous Urdu scholar and critic, has emphasized the appropriateness and naturalness of Anees's musical lines, where every word is harmoniously adjusted with its neighbours, resulting in a fine rhythmical pattern, rich in meaning and music. It may also be mentioned that Anees was not only a writer, but also (like Dabir) a singer of *marsias*, gifted as he was with a highly mellifluous voice.

Besides being a master of the *marsia*, Anees was also a specialist of the *rubai*, the shortest complete poem in Urdu, containing only four lines, rhyming aaba.

Anees died in 1874 at the age of 70.

ببر علی انیس

گرمئ دشتِ کربلا

گرمی کا روزِ جنگ کی کیوں کر کروں بیاں
ڈر ہے کہ مثلِ شمع نہ جلنے لگے زباں
وہ لُوں کہ الحَذر وہ حرارت کہ الاَماں
رن کی زمیں تو سُرخ تھی اور زرد آسماں
آبِ خُنک کو خلق ترستی تھی خاک پر
گویا ہوا سے آگ برستی تھی خاک پر

وہ لُوں وہ آفتاب کی حِدّت وہ تاب و تب
کالا تھا رنگ دھوپ سے دن کا مثالِ شب
خود نہرِ علقمہ کے بھی سوکھے ہوئے تھے لب
نیچے جو تھے حبابوں کے تپتے تھے سب کے سب
اُڑتی تھی خاک خشک تھا چشمۂ حیات کا
کھولا ہوا تھا دھوپ سے پانی فرات کا

جھیلوں سے چارپائے نہ اُٹھتے تھے تا بہ شام
مسکن میں مچھلیوں کے سمندر کا تھا مقام
آہو جو کاہلے تھے تو چیتے سیاہ فام
پتھر پگھل کے رہ گئے تھے مثلِ مومِ خام

Babar Ali Anees
The Burning Plain of Karbala (Excerpt)

How to describe the heat intense of the battle day,
It might set my own tongue, taper-like, ablaze.
Oh, the sun and burning winds! save us, God, O save!
Flaming red was the earth, the sky was deadly pale.

People yearned and pined for a drop of water cold,
The sky was hurling fire-balls on the earth below.

The burning winds and the sun, dazzling hot and bright,
The day under the ferocious sun blackened like the night!
Even the lips of the stream had gone sere and dry,
The parasoles of water-bubbles were smouldering day and night.

Dust-storms swept the field, the fount of life had ebbed,
The water on the river Faraat boiled hot and red.

The animals wouldn't leave their lairs till the day declined,
The sea too, in the slimy creeks, loved to lie reclined.
The tigers' skins were burnt black, sluggish grew the hind,
The stones, too, like waxen blocks, seemed to melt and pine.

Garmi ka roz-e-jang ki kyonkar karoon bayaan,
Dar hai ke masl-e-shama na jalne lage zabaan.
Woh loo, ke alhazar! woh hararat, ke alamaan!
Ran ki zameen tau surkh thi aur zard aasman.

Aab-e-khunak ko khalaq tarasti thi khaak par,
Goya hawa se aag barasti thi khaak par.

Woh loo, woh aaftaab ki hiddat, woh tab-o-taab,
Kaala tha rang dhoop se din ka misaal-e-shab;
Khud nahr-e-alqama ke bhi sookhe hue the lab,
Khaime jo the habaabon ke tapte the sab ke sab.

Urti thi khaak, khushk tha chashma hayaat ka,
Khaula hua tha dhoop se paani Faraat ka.

Jheelon se chaarpaae na uthte the ta ba shaam,
Maskin mein machhlion ke samandar ka tha maqaam,
Aahu jo kaahile the, tau cheete seaah faam,
Paththar pighal ke rah gaye the masl-e-mom khaam.

ببر علی انیس

سُرخی اُڑی تھی پھولوں سے سبزی گیاؤں سے
پانی کنوؤں میں اترا تھا سائے کی چاہ سے
کوسوں کسی شجر میں نہ گل تھے نہ برگ و بار
ایک ایک نخل جل رہا تھا صورتِ چنار
ہنستا تھا کوئی گل نہ لہکتا تھا سبزہ زار
کانٹا ہوئی تھی سوکھ کے ہر شاخِ باردار
گرمی یہ تھی کہ زیست سے دل سب کے سرد تھے
پتّے بھی مثلِ چہرۂ مدقوق زرد تھے

اَب رواں سے منھ نہ اُٹھاتے تھے جانور
جنگل میں چھپتے پھرتے تھے طائر اِدھر اُدھر
مَرْدُم تھے سات پردوں کے اندر عَرق میں تر
خَس خانۂ مِژہ سے نکلتی نہ تھی نظر
مگر چشم سے نکل کے ٹھہر جائے راہ میں
پڑ جائیں لاکھ آبلے پائے نگاہ میں
شیر اُٹھتے تھے نہ دھوپ کے مارے کچھار سے
آہو نہ منھ نکالتے تھے سبزہ زار سے

Anees

The grass had lost its green, the flowers hung dismayed,
The water sank down in wells, seeking deeper shade.

Not a plant was there for miles bearing leaf or bloom,
Chinar-like shone the trees, blazoned by the simoom.
Not a single smiling rose, meadows lay in gloom,
Every branch was turned to a thorn, in the scorching noon.

People were despaired of life, so intense was heat,
Like the dropping faces pale, leaves felt bereaved.

With their mouths dipped in water, the beasts stood unmoved,
The birds flapped their wings in vain in search of cool refuge;
The pupils, securely curtained, deep inside did ooze,
Lurking behind the eyelash, the glance refused to move.

If perchance the glance could travel, and stand a while in heat,
It would get blistered feet, and beat a quick retreat.

The lions, fearing raging heat, refused to leave their lairs,
The deer hid in meadows, by the heat scared.

Surkhi uri thi phoolon se, sabzi gayah se,
Paani kooen mein utra tha saae ki chaah se.

Koson kisi shajar mein na gul the na barg-o-baar,
Ek ek nakhal jal raha tha soorat-e-chinaar.
Hansta tha koi gul na lahkta tha sabzazaar,
Kaanta hui thi sookh ke har shaakh-e-baar daar.

Garmi yeh thi ke zeest se dil sab ke sard the,
Patte bhi masl-e-chehra-e-madqooq zard the.

Aab-e-rawaan se munh na uthaate the janwar,
Jungle mein chhipte phirte the taair idhar udhar.
Mardam the saat pardon ke andar araq se tar,
Khaskhana-e-mizha se nikalti na thi nazar.

Gar chashm se nikal kar thahr jaae rah mein,
Par jaaen laakh aable paae nigah mein.

Sher uthte the na dhoop ke maare kachhaar se,
Aahoo na munh nikalte the sabza zaar se.

ببر علی انیس

آئینہ مہر کا تھا مکدّرِ غبار سے
گردوں کو تپ چڑھی تھی زمیں کے بخار سے
گرمی سے مضطرب تھا زمانہ زمین پر
بھُن جاتا تھا جو گرتا تھا دانہ زمین پر
گِرد آب پر تھا شعلۂ جوّالہ کا گماں
انگارے تھے حُباب تو پانی شرر فشاں
منھ سے نکل پڑی تھی ہر اِک موج کی زباں
تہ پر تھے سب نہنگ مگر تھی لبوں پہ جاں
پانی تھا آگ گرمیِ روزِ حساب تھی
ماہی جو سیخ موج تک آئی کباب تھی
آئینۂ فلک کو نہ تھی تاب و تب کی تاب
چھپنے کو برق چاہتی تھی دامنِ سحاب
سب سے سوا تھا گرم مزاجوں کو اضطراب
کافورِ صبح ڈھونڈتا پھرتا تھا آفتاب
بھٹک کی تھی آگ گنبدِ چرخِ اثیر میں
بادل چھپے تھے سب کُرۂ زمہریر میں

(اقتباس)

Anees

Hazily shone the radiant sun smothered by the dusty air,
The fevered earth created shivers in the atmosphere.
Restless felt the world at large, by the heat oppressed,
The sun would roast all at once the grain spilt on earth.
The flames whirled with all their might, the heat was at its height,
The bubbles glowed like livid coals, water volcano-like.
The waves lolled out their tongues, parched and stark dry,
The crocodiles, though submerged, felt despaired of life.
Water was a sea of fire, it was hot as Judgment Day,
The fish would change to roasted meat, if it dared its head to raise.
The shimmering skies didn't have the strength to bear the heat,
The lightning tried to hide itself in some cloudy creek.
But the fiery tempers were specially hit by heat,
The sun implored the morning for a cool retreat.
A wild conflagration raged in the skiey dome,
The clouds looked for covert in the coldest zone.

Aaeena mehar ka tha mukaddar ghubaar se,
Gardoon ko tap charhi thi zameen ke bukhaar se.

Garmi se muztarib tha zamana zameen par,
Bhun jaata tha jo girta tha dana zameen par.

Girdaab par tha shola-e-jawaala ka gumaan,
Angaare the habab, tau paani sharar fishaan.
Munh se nikal pari thi har ik mauj ki zabaan,
Teh par the sab nihang, magar thi labon pe jaan.

Paani tha aag, garmi-e-roz-e-hisaab thi,
Maahi jo seekh-e-mauj tak aai kabaab thi.

Aaeena-e-falak ko na thi taab-o-tab ki taab,
Chhipne ko barq chaahti thi daaman-e-sahaab.
Sab se siwa tha garm mizaajaon ko izteraab,
Kaafoor-e-subah dhoondhta phirta tha aaftaab.

Bharki thi aag gumbad-e-charkh-e-aseer mein,
Baadal chhipe the sab kurrah-e-zamharir mein.

Khawaja Altaf Hussain Hali
(1837-1914)

KHWAJA ALTAF HUSSAIN HALI
(1837-1914)

Hali occupies a special position in the history of Urdu literature. Though he is not as great a lyricist as Ghalib, Momin, or Mir, he is more versatile than all of them. He is a poet, a critic, a teacher, a reformer and an impressive prose-writer. Circumstances did not permit him to attain formal education in a school or college, yet he had acquired, through sustained self-effort, a perfect command of Urdu, Persian and Arabic, and a good working knowledge of English. As a poet he did not confine himself within the narrow bounds of the *ghazal*, but successfully exploited the other poetic forms such as the *nazm*, the *rubai*, and the elegy. More particularly, he harnessed his poetic abilities to the higher aims of social and moral edification. Art for him was a handmaid to life. His famous long poem, *Musaddas-e-Hali*, examines the state of social and moral degradation prevalent in the contemporary Muslim society. His prose treatise, *Muqaddama-e-Shair-o-Shairi*, is a pioneering work of literary criticism. It dwells on the limitations of the traditional *ghazal*, and points to the hollowness of its hackneyed themes and imagery, especially when the form is handled by inferior poets and versifiers. He has also written memorable biographies of Ghalib, Saadi Sheerazi, and Sir Sayed Ahmed Khan, entitled respectively, *Yaadgar-e-Ghalib*, *Hayat-e-Saadi*, and *Hayat-e-Javed*. His poem Barkha Rut," describes the beauties of nature in the rainy season; "Hub-e-Watan," underscores the virtues of patriotism; while "Bewa ki Manajaat" focuses on the plight of widows in Indian society. Hali's interests were wide-ranging, and his literary abilities were commensurate with his humanitarian aims.

Both in his poetry and prose, Hali prefers a simple, natural, matter-of-fact style, which makes him easily acessible to all kinds of readers. He has had the privilege of receiving the partonage and guidance of some of the most illustrious men of his age: Mirza Ghalib, Nawab Mustafa Ali Khan Shefta, and Sir Sayed Ahmed Khan, all of whom contributed to the flowering of his genius.

"Chup ki daad" (here translated as "Patience Rewarded" and presented in an abridged from), contains a moving account of the plight of women, who for ages, have suffered the domination of man, and have led a life of self-suppression and self-sacrifice. Man has kept her debarred from the benefits of education and enlightenment, and has generally used her for purposes of procreation, recreation, and household drudgery. But there are welcome signs of change. Her long and patient suffering is slowly getting recognised and rewarded, and the doors of schools and colleges, so far the exclusive preserves of the male, have now been thrown open to women also. The poem is a feminist document, strongly sympathetic to the cause of women, and a characteristic work of Hali.

خواجہ الطاف حسین حالی

چپ کی داد

اے ماؤ، بہنو، بیٹیو، دنیا کی زینت تم سے ہے
ملکوں کی بستی ہو تمہی، قوموں کی عزت تم سے ہے
نیکی کی تم تصویر ہو، عفت کی تم تدبیر ہو
ہو دین کی تم پاسباں، ایماں سلامت تم سے ہے
فطرت تمہاری ہے حیا، طینت میں ہے مہر و وفا
گھٹی میں ہے صبر و رضا، اِنسان عبارت تم سے ہے
آتی ہو اکثر بے طلب دنیا میں جب آتی ہو تم
پر موہنی سے اپنی یاں گھر بھر پہ چھا جاتی ہو تم
میکے میں سارے گھر کی تھیں گو مالک و مختار تم
پر سارے کٹنے کی رہیں بچپن سے خدمت گار تم
ماں باپ کے حکموں پہ پتلی کی طرح پھرتی رہیں
غم خوار بابوں کی رہیں ماؤں کی تابعدار تم
دن بھر پکانا رِیندھنا، سِینا، پِرونا، ٹانکنا
بیٹھیں نہ گھر پر باپ کے خالی کبھی زنہار تم
راتوں کو چھوٹے بھائی بہنوں کی خبر اٹھ اٹھ کے لی
پہ کوئی سوتے میں رویا اور ہوئیں بیدار تم

Khwaja Altaf Hussain Hali
Chup ki Daad (Patience Rewarded)

O mothers, daughters and sisters, you're our wealth and pride,
You are the nation's honour, the source of bustling life.

You're the models of goodness, a promise of self-esteem,
Guardian of religious faith, preserver of spiritual beam.

Modesty is your native trait, you embody love and faith,
You're patience concretized, humanity's charm and grace.

You often arrive in this world, unwanted, unsought,
But with your attractive grace, you conquer every heart.

Though in your parental home, unquestioned was your sway,
Yet you served one and all right from childhood days.

At the beck and call of parents, puppet-like you danced,
Showing deference to your father, obeying the mother's glance.

All day long you were busy cooking, baking, sewing, stitching,
Never at your father's home did we find you idle sitting.

Tending your brothers and sisters, robbed you of your nightly sleep,
If your charge woke or wept, up you rose on your feet.

Ai maao, behno, betio, duniya ki zeenat tum se hai,
Mulkon ki basti ho tumhi, qaumon ki izzat tum se hai.

Neki ki tum tasvir ho, iffat ki tum tadbir ho,
Ho deen ki tum paasbaan, eemaan salaamat tum se hai.

Fitrat tumhari hai haya, teenat mein hai mehar-o-wafa,
Ghutti mein hai sabar-o-raza, insaan abaarat tum se hai.

Aati ho aksar be talab duniya mein jab aati ho tum,
Par mohni se apni yaan ghar bhar pe chha jaati ho tum.

Maike mein saare ghar ki thin go maalik-o-mukhtar tum,
Par saare kunbe ki rahin, bachpan se taabidaar tum.

Maan baap ke hukmon pe putli ki tarah phirti rahin,
Ghamkhwar baapon ki rahin, maaon ki taabidaar tum.

Din bhar pakana, reendhna, seena, parona, tankna,
Baithein na ghar par baap ke khaali kabhi zinhaar tum.

Raaton ko chhote bhai behnon ki khabar uth uth ke li,
Bachcha koi sote mein roya aur huin bedaar tum.

حالی

سسرال میں پہنچیں تو واں اک دوسرا دیکھا جہاں
جا اُتریں گویا دیس سے پردیس میں اک بار تم
واں فکر تھی ہر دم یہاں ناخوش نہ ہو تم سے کوئی
اپنے سے رنجش کے کبھی پاؤ نہ واں آثار تم
پالا بروں سے گر پڑے بدخوہوں سب چھوٹے بڑے
جیتون پہ میل آنے نہ دو گو دل میں ہو بیزار تم
دردوں کے دُکھ تم نے سہے بڑھاپے کی جھیلیں سختیاں
جب موت کا چکھا مزا تب تم کو یہ دولت ملی
میکے میں اور سسرال میں سب کے ہوئے دل باغ باغ
گھر میں اُجالا تو ہُوا پر تم یہ بپتا پڑ گئی
کھانا پہننا اوڑھنا اپنا گئیں سب بھول تم
بچوں کے دھندے میں تھیں اپنی نہ کچھ سدھ بدھ رہی
سُولی پہ دن کٹنے لگے، راتوں کی نیندیں اُڑ گئیں
اِک اِک برس کی ہو گئی اِک ایک پل اِک اِک گھڑی
کی ہے مہم جو تم نے سر، مردوں کو اس کی کیا خبر
جانے پرائی پیڑ وہ جس کی بوائی ہو چھٹی

156

Hali

As you enter your in-laws' house, you find your world entirely changed,
Sundered from your native home, you inhabit a house strange.

There you are but concerned to please and gladden all,
Taking care that no offence is by you ever caused.

Even if you deal with folks, ill-tempered and mean,
Not a trace of inner grief on your face is seen.

You bear countless pains, including pangs of childbirth,
At a heavy cost, at last, you become a mother blest.

Though this event gives delight to your parents and in-laws,
Yet if makes your own life all the more involved.

You forget to eat and dress, ever with your brood obsessed,
Losing sight of personal comfort, by the daily cares oppressed.

On tenterhooks you spend your days, sleepless spend your nights,
The minutes and hours crawl like years, life becomes a weary strife.

Men are not at all aware of the battles you have fought,
Only he can know the pain who on blistered feet has walked.

Susraal mein pahunchin tau waan ik doosra dekha jahan,
Jaa utrin goya des se pardes mein ik baar tum.

Waan fikar thi har dam yahan naakhush na ho tum se koi,
Apne se ranjish ke kabhi paao na waan aasar tum.

Paala buron se gar pare, bad-khoo hon sab chhote bare,
Chitwan pe mail aane na do, go dil mein ho bezaar tum.

Dardon ke dukh tum ne sahe, jaape ki jhelin sakhtian,
Jab maut ka chakha maza tab tum ko yeh daulat mili.

Maike mein aur susraal mein sab ke hue dil baagh baagh,
Ghar mein ujala tau hua, par tum pe bipta par gai.

Khana, pehan-na, orhna apna gaien sab bhool tum,
Bachchon ke dhande mein tumhen apni na kuchh sudh budh rahi.

Sooli pe din katne lage, raaton ki neenden ur gaien,
Ik ik baras ki ho gai ik ek pal, ik ik ghari.

Ki hai muhim jo tum ne sar, mardon ko us ki kya khabar,
Jaane paraai pir woh jis ki buaai ho phati.

157

حالی

بے خبر اولاد کی مائیں نہ گر چھٹپن میں یاں
خالی کبھی کا سلسلہ سے آدم کی ہو جاتا یہاں
یہ گو شت کا اک لوتھڑا پر وان چڑھتا کس طرح
چھاتی سے لپٹائے نہ ہر دم رکھتی گر بچے کو ماں
وہ دین اور دنیا کے مصلح جن کے وعظ اور پند سے
ظلمت میں باطل کی ہوا دنیا میں نورِ حق عیاں
وہ علم اور حکمت کے بانی جن کی تحقیقات سے
ظاہر ہوئے عالم میں اسرارِ زمین و آسماں
وہ شاہِ کشور گیر، اسکندر کہ جس کی دھاک سے
تھے بید کی مانند لرزاں تاج دارانِ جہاں
وہ فخرِ شاہانِ عجم، کسریٰ کہ جس کے عدل کی
مشرق سے تا مغرب زبانوں پر ہے جاری داستاں
کیا پھول پھل یہ سب ابھی کمزور پودوں کے نہ تھے
سینچا تھا ماؤں نے جنہیں خونِ جگر سے اپنے یاں
کیا صوفیانِ با صفا، کیا عارفانِ با خدا
کیا اولیا کیا انبیا، کیا غوث کیا قطبِ زماں

Hali

Had the mothers not been there to tend their tender breed,
Long ago would have perished human life, stalk and seed.

How could it develop and grow, a mere chunk of flesh,
If the mother with tender care her infant had not nursed?

The world's wise reformers whose enlightening talk
Dispelled the mist of falsehood, removed the pall of dark,

Those scholars and scientists whose research unveiled,
Secrets of the earth and heaven lying beyond our pale,

That mighty conqueror, Alexander the great,
Whose very name was enough to shake the potentates,

Those Persian emperors for love of justice famed,
Whose tales, from East to West, travelled like a flame,

Were they not the fruits and flowers of those tender shrubs,
Which were nurtured by their mothers with their vital blood?

Be they sufis pious-hearted, seers with divining eyes,
Be they high-priests of God or the prophets wise,

Lein khabar aulaad ki maaen na gar chhutpan mein yaan,
Khaali kabhi ka nasal se aadam ki ho jaata jahan.

Yeh gosht ka ik lothra parwaan charhta kistarah,
Chhati se liptaae na har dam rakhti gar bachche ko maan.

Woh deen aur duniya ke muslih jin ke waaz aur pand se,
Zulmat mein baatil ki hua duniya mein noor-e-haq ayaan,

Woh ilm-o-hikmat ke baani jin ki tahqiqaat se,
Zaahir hue aalam mein asrar-e-zameen-o-aasmaan,

Woh shah-e-kishwar gir, Sikander, ke jis ki dhaak se,
The baid ki maanind larzaan taj daraan-e-jahan,

Woh fakhr-e-shahaan-e-ajam, kisra ke jis ke adal ki,
Mashriq se ta maghrib zabaanon par hai jaari daastaan,

Kya phool phal yeh sab unhi kamzor paudon ke na the,
Seencha the maaon ne jinhen khoon-e-jigar se apne yaan?

Kya sufiaan-e-ba safa, kya aarfaan-e-ba khuda,
Kya aulia, kya anbia, kya ghaus, kya qutab-e-zaman,

حالی

سرکار سے مالک کی جتنے پاک بندے ہیں بڑھے
وہ ماؤں کی گودوں کے زینے سے ہیں سب اوپر چڑھے
افسوس! دنیا میں بہت تم پر ہوئے جور و جفا
حق تلفیاں تم نے سہیں، بے مہریاں جھیلیں سدا
گاڑی گئیں تم مدّتوں مٹی میں جیتی جاگتی
حامی تمہارا تھا مگر کوئی نہ جز ذاتِ خدا
زندہ سدا جلتی رہیں تم مردہ خاوندوں کے ساتھ
اندر ہی اندر چین سے عالم رہا یہ سب تماشے دیکھتا
بیاہی گئیں اس وقت تم جب بیاہ سے واقف نہ تھیں
جو عمر بھر کا عہد تھا وہ کچّے دھاگے سے بندھا
گزری امید و بیم میں جب تک رہا باقی سہاگ
بیوہ ہوئیں تو عمر بھر پھر چین قسمت میں نہ تھا
گو صبر کا اپنے نہ کچھ تم کو بلا انعام یاں
پر جو فرشتے سے نہ ہو وہ کر گئیں تم کام یاں
کی تم نے اس دارالمحن میں جس تحمّل سے گزر
زیبا ہے گر کہیے تمہیں فخرِ بنی نوعِ بشر

160

Hali

All the men of holy worth who have risen on this earth,
Propped by the mothers' arms, have climbed to the highest berth.

You, alas, were made to suffer atrocities untold,
Robbed of your basic rights, left out in the cold.

For long were you buried alive in the narrow grave,
None was there to help you, except God the great.

For long were you burnt alive on your husbands' pyre,
And the world stood unmoved, watching flames of fire.

At a tender, unripe age you were pushed to marriage bed,
The binding knot of marriage vows was tied with a flimsy thread.

You spent your married life tossing betwixt hope and fear,
If widowed by cruel chance, none was there your grief to share.

Though your patient sufferance went without reward,
Your deeds eclipse the angels and their fabled tasks.

With a rare fortitude you trod the path of life,
You are worthy to be called the humanity's crown and pride!

Sarkaar se maalik ki jitne paak bande hain barhe,
Woh maaon ki godon ke zeene se hain sab oopar charhe.

Afsos! duniya mein bahut tum par hue jaur-o-jafa,
Haq talfiaan tum ne sahin, be mehariaan jheileen sada.

Gaari gaien tum mudatton mitti mein jeeti jaagti,
Haami tumhaara tha magar koi na juz zaat-e-khuda.

Zinda sada jalti rahin tum murda khaawindon ke saath,
Aur chain se aalam raha yeh sab tamashe dekhta.

Beaahi gaien us waqt tum jab beaah se waaqif na theen,
Jo umar bhar ka ahd tha woh kachche dhaage se bandha.

Guzri umeed-o-beem mein jab tak raha baaqi suhaag,
Bewa huin tau umar bhar phir chain qismat mein na tha.

Go sabr ka apne na kuchh tum ko mila inaam yaan,
Par jo farishte se na ho woh kar gaien tum kaam yaan.

Ki tum ne is daar-ul-mahin mein jis tahammul se guzar,
Zeba hai gar kahieye tumhen fakhr-e-bani nau-e-bashar.

حالی

الفت تمہاری کر گئی گھر دل میں جس بے دید کے
وہ بدگماں تم سے رہا، اے بدنصیبو، عمر بھر
جب تک جیو تم علم و دانش سے رہو محروم یاں
آئی ہو جیسی بے خبر، ویسی ہی جاؤ بے خبر
جو علم مَردوں کے لیے سمجھا گیا آبِ حیات
ٹھہرا تمہارے حق میں وہ زہر، ہلاہل سر بسر
آتا ہے وقت الفاف کا نزدیک ہے یوم الحساب
دنیا کو دینا ہوگا ان حق تلفیوں کا واں جواب
دنیا کے دانا اور حکیم اس خوف سے لرزاں تھے سب
تم پر مبادا علم کی پڑ جائے پرچھائیں کہیں
ایسا نہ ہو مرد اور عورت میں رہے باقی نہ فرق
تعلیم پا کر آدمی بننا تمہیں زیبا نہیں
جو ذلتیں لازم ہیں دنیا میں جہالت کے لیے
وہ ذلتیں سب نفس پر اپنے گوارا تم نے کیں
سمجھا نہ تم کو ایک دن مَردوں نے قابلِ بات کے
تم بے وفا کہلائیں لیکن لونڈیاں بن کر رہیں

Hali

On whomsoever you bestowed your tender love and faith,
Treated you with deep suspicion, O unfortunate!

Closed to you is the book of knowledge, banned the higher lore,
Ignorant you come on earth, ignorant you go.

Knowledge which is deemed a nectar for the race of men,
When drunk by females, becomes pernicious poison.

The time of justice draws near, the judgment day arrives,
When the cruel world of men shall be judged and tried.

The wise and learned of the world tremble at the thought,
That a dose of knowledge might liberate your heart.

That you may not vie with men, knowledge should be banned,
A woman should remain a woman, not become a man.

All ignominy and insult which ignorance entails,
You had to bear with patience, without succour or aid.

Men didn't consider you fit for any serious talk,
Though you lived a bonded slave, "faithless" were you called.

Ulfat tumhari kar gai ghar dil mein jis be-deed ke,
Woh bad gumaan tum se raha, ai bad naseebo, umr bhar.

Jab tak jeeo tum ilm-o-daanish se raho mehroom yaan,
Aai ho jaisi bekhabar, waisi hi jaao be khabar.

Jo ilm mardon ke lieye samjha gaya aab-e-hayaat,
Thahra tumhare haq mein woh zahr-e-halahal sar basar.

Aata hai waqt insaaf ka, nazdik hai yom-ul-hisaab,
Duniya ko dena hoga in haq talfion ka waan jawaab.

Duniya ke daana aur hakim is khauf se larzan the sab,
Tum par mubada ilm ki par jaae parchhaaien kahin.

Aisa na ho mard aur aruat mein rahe baqi na farq,
Taaleem paa kar aadmi ban-na tujhe zeba nahin.

Jo zillaten laazim hain duniya mein jahalat ke lieye,
Woh zillaten sab nafs par apne gawaara tum ne keen.

Samjha na tum ko ek din mardon ne qaabil baat ke,
Tum be wafa kahlaaien lekin laundian ban kar rahin.

حالی

آخر تمہاری چُپ دِلوں میں اہلِ دل کے چُبھ گئی
سچ ہے کہ چُپ کی داد آخر بے ملے رہتی نہیں
بارے زمانہ نیند کے ماروں کو لایا ہوش میں
آیا تمہارے صبر پر دریائے رحمت جوش میں
نوبت تمہاری حق رسی کی بعد مُدّت آئی ہے
انصاف نے دُھندلی سی اِک اپنی جھلک دِکھلائی ہے
اٹکے ہیں روڑے چلتی گاڑی میں سدا سچائی کی
پر فتح جب پائی ہے سچائی نے آخر پائی ہے
اے بے زبانوں کی زبانو، بے نصیبوں کے بازو
تعلیمِ نسواں کی مُہم جو تم کو اب پیش آئی ہے
یہ مرحلہ آیا ہے تم سے پہلے جن قوموں کو پیش
منزل پہ گاڑی ان کی اِستقلال نے پہنچائی ہے
ہے رائی بھی پربت اگر دل میں نہیں عزم درست
پر ٹھان لی جب جی میں پھر پربت بھی ہو تو رائی ہے
یہ جیت بھی کیا کم ہے خود حق ہے تمہاری پُشت پر
جو حق پہ منہ آیا ہے آخر اُس نے منہ کی کھائی ہے

Hali

Your silence has, at last, moved the feeling hearts,
True it is that silent suffering has its own reward.
Rejoice, the time has roused from sleep the folks slumbering fast,
The river of mercy is in spate stirred by your suffering lot.
You are now about to get justice long-denied,
A glimmer of hope in deepening dark has now sprung to sight.
Uphill is the path of truth, strewn with rocks and stones,
But the final triumph would come to the truth alone.
O voice of the voiceless folks, arms of the defenceless ones,
The task of educating women should now be your concern.
The nations which were faced with such a task before,
On the strength of perseverance have achieved their goal.
A mole-hill looks a mountain if you lack strength,
A mountain seems a mole-hill to men of strong intent.
Isn't it a triumph, indeed, truth is on your side,
Those who dare oppose the truth have to eat humble pie!

Aakhir tumhari chup dilon mein ahl-e-dil ke chubh gai,
Sach hai ke chup ki daad aakhir be mile rahti nahin.

Baare zamaana neend ke maaron ko laaya hosh mein,
Aaya tumhare sabar par dariyaa-e-rahmat josh mein.

Naubat tumhaari haq rasi ki baad muddat aai hai,
Insaaf ne dhundli si ik apni jhalak dikhlaai hai.

Atke hain rore chalti gaari mein sada sachaai ki,
Par fateh jab paai hai sachaai ne aakhir paai hai.

Ai be zabaanon ki zabaanon, be bason ke baazuo,
Taaleem-e-naswaan ki muhim jo tum ko ab pesh aai hai,

Yeh marhala aaya hai tum se pehle jin qaumon ko pesh,
Manzil pe gaari unki istaqlaal ne pahunchaai hai.

Hai raai bhi parbat agar dil mein nahin azm-e-darust,
Par thaan li jab ji mein phir parbat bhi ho tau raai hai.

Yeh jeet bhi kya kam hai khud haq hai tumhari pusht par,
Jo haq pe munh aaya hai, aakhir us ne munh ki khaai hai.

Abridged

Akbar Hussain Akbar Allahabadi
(1846-1921)

AKBAR HUSSAIN AKBAR ALLAHABADI
(1846-1921)

Akbar was born in 1846 in a respectable family at Bara, near Allahabad. In keeping with the prevalent custom, Akbar received his early education at home at the hands of his father, Sayed Tafazzul Hussain, who was a man of considerable learning. At about the age of 10 Akbar joined the Mission School at Allahabad. He was married at the age of 15 to a girl who was two or three years his senior. It was an unhappy marriage which didn't last long, and Akbar was forced to marry for the second time. He had two sons from each of these two unions. Akbar was an intelligent, persevering boy who always did well in his examinations. With an eye on his future career he studied law, and worked for a while as a practising lawyer. Later he got into government service, and rose to the high rank of a Sessions Judge. He sought premature retirement for reasons of health, and led a quiet, sequestered life in his old age.

Akbar was a brilliant, ready-witted, affable man, with a marked sense of humour, which, incidentally, is also the hallmark of his poetry—be it *ghazal*, *nazm*, *rubai*, or *qita*. He treats even the serious themes of love and politics with a touch of humour. He is a social reformer, and his reformist zeal works through the medium of wit and humour. There is hardly any aspect of life with escapes his satirical gaze. A champion of Eastern values, Akbar is specially opposed to a mindless imitation of the Western ways of life, which he found morally and spiritually sterile. In his approach to life and religion, he gives preference, like the mystic saints, to love over reason, to faith over knowledge. In one of his *rubaies*, he stresses his affinity with Spenser the poet, as against Mill the philosopher. He is distinctly original in his style too, for he can use any popular word or phrase of English which can convey his meaning, or increase the humorous impact of his verse. This intermingling of Urdu with English vocabulary was a thing unknown to his predecessors, nor was his practice adopted by the younger generation of writers and poets.

Although Akbar is essentially a lively, optimistic poet, his vision of things got clouded in his later life by his experience of tragedy at home. One of his sons, and a grandson, whom he dearly loved, died young. This caused him great shock and despair. Consequently towards the end of his life he got considerably subdued, and became increasingly pensive and religious. He died in 1921 at the age of 75.

The two poems included in this selection, "Miss Seemein Badan", and the "Dialogue of Majnun with Laila's Mother", show the quality of Akbar's humour, and its use for serious, reformative purposes. While the first poem underscores the inevitable consequences of aping Western modes of life and culture, the second points to the Muslims' lamentable apathy to education and intellectual exertion.

اکبر الہ آبادی

مِس سیمیں بدن

اِک مِس سیمیں بدن سے کر لیا لندن میں عقد
اِس خطا پر سُن رہا ہوں طعنہ ہائے دل خراش
کوئی کہتا ہے کہ بس اس نے لگا دی نسلِ قوم
کوئی کہتا ہے کہ یہ ہے بدخصال و بدمعاش
دل میں کچھ انصاف کرتا ہی نہیں کوئی بزرگ
ہو کے اب مجبور خود اس راز کو کرتا ہوں فاش
ہوتی تھی تاکید لندن جاؤ انگریزی پڑھو
قومِ انگلش سے مِلو سیکھو وہی وضع تراش
جگمگاتے ہوٹلوں کا جا کے نظارہ کر و
سوپ و کاری کے مزے لو چھوڑ کر خِنی و آش
لیڈیوں سے مل کے دیکھو اُن کے انداز و طریق
ہال میں ناچو کلب میں جا کے کھیلو اُن سے تاش
بادۂ تہذیبِ یورپ کے چڑھاؤ خُم کے خُم
ایشیا کے شیشۂ تقویٰ کو کر دو پاش پاش
جب عمل اس پر کیا پریوں کا سایہ ہو گیا
جس سے تھا دل کی حرارت کو سراسر انتقاش

170

Akbar Hussain Akbar Allahabadi
Miss Seemein Badan

In London I had married a silver-bodied dame,
For which fault I've to bear taunts unrestrained.
Someone says I've debased my ancient noble race,
Another calls me a rogue, a villain degenerate.
No wise man treats me in a manner just and fair,
This is what compels me to lay the secret bare.
"Go to London, learn English," I was told by every one,
"Emulate the English ways, mix with English men,
Visit the glittering hotels, enjoy delicious treats,
Adopt curry and soup, abandon dal and meat.
Meet the English ladies, watch them walk and talk,
Dance in the night clubs, join them at the game of cards.
Drink the wine of Western culture, drain away the bowl,
Break the glass of Asian piety, reject the moral code."
When I did what I was bid, I fell a prey to fairy charms,
Which fanned the fire within, unleashed the storm.

Ik miss seemein badan se kar liya London mein aqd,
Is khata par sun raha hun taana haae-e-dil khiraash.
Koi kahta hai ke bas is ne bigari nasl-e-qaum,
Koi kahta hai ke yeh hai bad khisal-o-bad maash.
Dil mein kuchh insaaf karta hi nahin koi bazurg,
Ho ke ab majbur is raaz ko karta hun faash.
Hui thi taakeed, London jaao, angrezi parho,
Qaum-e-English se milo, seekho wohi waza-o-tarash;
Jagmagate hotelon ka ja ke nazzara karo,
Soup-o-kaari ke maze lo, chhor kar yakhni-o-aash.
Ladion se mil ke dekho un ke andaaz-o-tariq,
Hall mein naacho, club mein ja ke khelo un se taash.
Baada-e-tehzib-e-Europe ke charhaao khum ke khum,
Asia ke sheesha-e-taqwa ko kar do paash paash.
Jab amal is par kiya, pariyon ka saya ho gaya,
Jis se tha dil ki hararat ko sara sar inte-aash.

اکبر الہ آبادی

سامنے تھیں لیڈیاں زہرہ وش و جادو نظر
یاں جوانی کی امنگ اور ان کو عاشق کی تلاش
اس کی چتون سحر آگیں اس کی باتیں دل رُبا
چال اس کی فتنہ خیز اس کی نگاہیں برق پاش
وہ فروغِ آتش رُخ جس کے آگے آفتاب
اس طرح جیسے کہ پیشِ شمع پروانے کی لاش
جب یہ صورت تھی تو ممکن تھا کہ اک برقِ بلا
دستِ سیمیں کو بڑھا دیتی اور میں کہتا دور باش؟
دونوں جانب بتھارگوں میں جوشِ خون فتنہ زا
دل ہی تھا آخر نہیں تھی برف کی یہ کوئی قاش
بار بار آتا ہے اکبر میرے دل میں یہ خیال
حضرتِ سید سے جا کر عرض کرتا کوئی کاش
"درمیانِ قعرِ دریا تختہ بندم کردہ ٔ
باز میگوئی کہ دامن تر مکن ہُشیار باش"

172

Akbar Allahabadi

I stood surrounded by starry-browed, bewitching maids,
I was young and dashing, they needed a mate;
This one had enchanting eyebrows, that possessed winsome ways,
One could vanquish by her speech, the other ravish by her gait.
One was a dazzling beauty, before whom the sun
Looked like a shrivelled moth by candle flame undone.
Circumstanced as I was, could I say, "Be damned!"
When some beauty, lightning-charged, held out her hand?
Youthful blood warmed our bodies, in our veins did rise,
After all I had a heart, and not a slice of ice.
I'm struck by a thought, Akbar, again and again,
Someone should go to Sayed, and thus to him explain;
"First you push me into the river, bound in hands and feet,
Then you say, beware, beware, waters are too deep."

Saamne thi ladian zuhra wash-o-jadoo nazar,
Yaan jawani ki umang aur unko aashiq ki talash,
Is ki chitwan sehar aageen, us ki baaten dil ruba,
Chaal iski fitna khez, us ki nigahen barq paash;
Woh farogh-e-aatish-e-rukh, jis ke aage aaftaab,
Is tarah jaise ke pesh-e-shama parwane ki laash.
Jab yeh surat thi tau mumkin tha ke ik barq-e-bala,
Dast-e-seemein ko barhati, aur main kahta dur baash?
Donon jaanib tha ragon mein josh-e-khoon-e-fitna za,
Dil hi tha aakhir nahin thi barf ki yeh koi kaash.
Bar bar aata hai Akbar, mere dil mein yeh khayal,
Hazrat-e-sayed se ja kar arz karta koi kaash:
"Darmian-e-qaar-e-dariya takhta bandam kardai,
Baaz mei goi ke daaman tar makun, hushiar baash."

اکبر الہ آبادی
لطیفہ

کہا مجنوں سے یہ لیلیٰ کی ماں نے
کہ بیٹا تو اگر کرلے ایم ۔ اے پاس
تو فوراً بیاہ دوں لیلیٰ کو تجھ سے
بلا دقّت میں بن جاؤں تری ساس
کہا مجنوں نے یہ اچھی سنائی
گجا عاشق، گجا کالج کی بکواس
گجا یہ فطرتی جوشِ طبیعت
گجا گھُسنی ہوئی چیزوں کا احساس
بڑی بی آپ کو کیا ہوگیا ہے
ہرن پر لادی جاتی ہے کہیں گھاس
یہ اچھی قدر دانی آپ نے کی
مجھے سمجھا ہے کوئی ہر چرن داس
دل اپنا خون کرنے کو ہوں موجود
نہیں منظور مغزِ سر کا آماس
یہی ٹھہری جو شرطِ وصلِ لیلیٰ
تو استعفیٰ مرا با حسرت و یاس

Akbar Allahabadi
Majnun's Reply to Laila's Mother

Thus spoke Laila's mother to Majnun one day.
"If, my son, you can somehow obtain a Master of Arts,
I'll at once marry Laila with you,
And be you mother-in-law withal."

"What a thing to say!" Majnun exclaimed,
"Love and the college nonsense stand poles apart!

On one hand is the spontaneous overflow,
On the other, learning stuffed and stocked.

Reverend ma'am, what's wrong with you!
Do we load a deer with grass?

What a way to judge my worth!
Mistake me not for Harcharan Dass.

I can shed my heart's blood,
But to cudgel my brain is beyond my thought.

If this be your condition for my love's fruition,
Here's my resignation, with regret and a sense of loss."

Kaha Majnun se yeh Laila ki maan ne,
Ke beta tu agar kar le M.A. pass,

Tau fauran beaah dun Laila ko tujh se,
Bila diqqat main ban jaaoun teri saas.

Kaha Majnun ne yeh achhi sunaai,
Kuja aashiq, kuja college ki bakwaas?

Kuja yeh fitrati josh-e-tabi-at,
Kuja thaunsi hui cheezon ka ahsaas!

Bari bi apko kya ho gaya hai?
Hiran mein laadi jaati hai kahin ghaas?

Yeh achhi qadardani aapne ki,
Mujhe samjha hai koi Harcharan Dass?

Dil apna khoon karne ko hoon maujood,
Nahin manzoor maghz-e-sar ka aamaas.

Yehi thahri jo shart-e-wasal-e-Laila,
Tau istifa mira ba hasrat-o-yaas.

Sir Mohammed Iqbal
(1873-1938)

SIR MOHAMMED IQBAL
(1873-1938)

Dr. Sir Mohammed Iqbal was a highly educated poet—M.A. in Philosophy from Punjab, Ph. D. from Germany, Bar-at-law, and a recipient of several honours, including an honorary D. Litt from Allahabad University. He was born in Sialkot (now in Pakistan), and stayed for the greater part of his life at Lahore. He also spent three years, from 1905 to 1908, in England and Germany where he had gone for higher studies. While at school Iqbal had shown a great interest in the study of Persian and Arabic, and had also displayed an uncommon gift for poetry. He cultivated these interests under the guidance of a distinguished teacher, Maulvi Mir Hassan of Sialkot. Professor Thomas Arnold of Government College Lahore sharpened his interest in philosophy, and Nawab Mirza Khan Dagh of Delhi advised him on the art of poetic composition. Iqbal was an instinctive writer. In his inspired moments verses flowed from him as naturally as water from the mountain springs. He possessed a phenomenal memory and had no need to commit his verses to paper immediately. In addition, he was endowed with a deep, resonant voice, which won him special acclaim at "mushairas" and cultural meets. More than the music of his verse, it was his subject matter—patriotic, philosophic, humanistic, or Islamic—which made a strong appeal to his audience. He is an eloquent champion of selfhood, and a singer of the greatness of man. Some of his famous Urdu *nazms* include the Indian national song: "Sare jahan se achcha", "Saqi Nama", "Shikwa", and "Jawab-e-Shikwa"—all of which are included (the last three in abridged form) in this selection. His poetry has a tonic, invigorating effect on the readers; it inspires them to live courageously and realise their inner potential. Consequently, some of his couplets have become popular quotations.

In poetry, Iqbal is the inheritor of the tradition of Ghalib, and not of Dagh Dehalvi, who though, was his mentor through correspondence. His poetry, like that of Ghalib, is a blend of deep thoughts and intense feelings, which he expresses in a forceful, Persianised style. This is not to deny that he is also capable of expressing himself in simple, everyday language, as in his famous poem, "Naya Shivala". Though Iqbal is an indisputable master of the *ghazal*, a bulk of his poetry is in the form of *nazm*,—a poem with a single, central theme, logically evolved and developed. Because of his predilection for the *nazm*, some of his *ghazals* too display a *nazm*-like continuity and consistency of thought.

Iqbal's European visit broadened his vision and exposed him to the Western thought and culture, highlighting, by contrast, the strength and weaknesses of the Eastern approach to life. His repeated accent on selfhood and self-realisation as against the Eastern insistence on self-suppression and renunciation, may also be seen as a fruit of his Western visit. The breadth and range of his vision is also reflected in the broad spectrum of his subjects; for he has written poems not only on Indian and Islamic themes, but also on world figures as varied as Lenin, Mussolini, Karl Marx, Napoleon and Shakespeare. However, Iqbal was not particularly enamoured of Western culture and civilisation. He returned to India with a sense of mission, and a determination to use his poetry as a vehicle of social and political revolution. In his later poetry he projects himself as a voice of the East and a crusader of Islam. He was the first to propound the idea of Pakistan as a separate Muslim state. Those who hold that poetry should eschew moral or political sentiment for the sake of artistic purity will perhaps be disappointed in Iqbal who is essentially a poet with a message—a message fit to be given in poetry for which he had an unusual talent. As he wanted his message to go beyond the boundaries of the Indian subcontinent he switched over, in his later life, to writing poetry in Persian language in preference to Urdu, which, however, he did not altogether abandon. His Urdu poems are collected in four volumes: *Bang-e-Dara*, (1924), *Bal-e-Jabreel*, (1935), *Zarb-e-Kalim* (1936) and *Armaghan-e-Hejaz* (1938).

"Shikwa" and "Jawab-e-Shikwa" are among the best known poems of Iqbal. While "Shikwa" is a poem of protest, where the poet, speaking on behalf of the Muslim race complains to God about the undeserved sufferings of the Muslims, guardians of the faith, and warriors of Islam, its companion piece, "Jawab-e-Shikwa" contains God's reply to this plaint, which justifies the ways of God to Muslims, and castigates the speaker for his irreverent arraignment of the Almighty. Both the poems are remarkable for their strength of logic and force of rhetoric, and demonstrate the poet's ability to build and demolish a case.

سر محمّد اقبال
شکوہ

کیوں زیاں کار بنوں سود فراموش رہوں؟
فکرِ فردا نہ کروں، محوِ غم دوش رہوں
نالے بلبل کے سنوں، اور ہمہ تن گوش رہوں
ہمنوا! میں بھی کوئی گل ہوں کہ خاموش رہوں
جرأت آموز مری تابِ سخن ہے مجھ کو
شکوہ اللہ سے خاکم بدہن، ہے مجھ کو

اے خدا! شکوۂ اربابِ وفا بھی سن لے
خوگرِ حمد سے تھوڑا سا گلہ بھی سن لے
تھی تو موجود ازل سے ہی تری ذاتِ قدیم
پھول تھا زیبِ چمن، پر نہ پریشاں تھی شمیم
شرطِ انصاف ہے اے صاحبِ الطافِ عمیم
بوئے گل پھیلتی کس طرح جو ہوتی نہ نسیم؟
ہم سے پہلے تھا عجب تیرے جہاں کا منظر
کہیں مسجود تھے پتھر، کہیں معبود شجر
خوگرِ پیکرِ محسوس تھی انساں کی نظر
مانتا پھر کوئی اَن دیکھے خدا کو کیونکر؟

180

Iqbal
Shikwa

Why should I abet the loss, why forget the gain,
Why forfeit the future, bemoan the past in vain?

Hear the wail of nightingale, and remain unstirred,
Am I a flower insensate that will not say a word?

The power of speech emboldens me to speak out my heart,
I'll sure be damned, I know, if I fault my God.

Hear, O Lord, from the faithful ones this sad lament,
From those used to hymn a praise, a word of discontent.

Eternally were you present, Lord, eternally omniscent,
The flower hung upon the tree, but without incense.

Be Thou fair, tell us true, O fountainhead of grace,
How could the scent spread without the breeze apace?

The world presented a queer sight ere we took the stage,
Stones and plants in your stead were worshipped in that age.

Man, being inured to senses, couldn't accept a thing unseen,
How could a formless God impress his senses keen?

Kyon ziaan kaar banun, sood framosh rahoon?
Fikr-e-farda na karun, mahw-e-ghum-e-dosh rahoon,

Naale bulbul ke sunoon, aur hama tan gosh rahoon,
Hamnawa main bhi koi gul hoon ke khamosh rahoon?

Jurrat aamoz miri taab-e-sakhun hai mujhko,
Shikwa Allah se khakam badahan hai mujhko.

Ai Khuda shikwa-e-arbab-e-wafa bhi sun le,
Khu gar-e-hamd se thora sa gila bhi sun le.

Thi tau maujood azal se hi tiri zaat-e-qadim,
Phool tha zeb-e-chaman, par na pareshan thi shamim;

Shart insaaf hai, ai, sahib-e-altaf-e-amim,
Boo-e-gul phailti kis tarah jo hoti na nasim?

Hum se pahle tha ajab tere jahan ka manzir,
Kahin masjood the pathar, kahin maabood shajar,

Khugar-e-paikar-e-mahsoos thi insaan ki nazar,
Maanta phir koi un-dekhe Khuda ko kyonkar?

محمد اقبال

تجھ کو معلوم ہے لیتا تھا کوئی نام ترا؟
قوتِ بازوئے مسلم نے کیا کام ترا!
بس رہے تھے یہیں سلجوقی بھی، تورانی بھی
اہلِ چین چین میں، ایران میں ساسانی بھی
اسی معمورے میں آباد تھے یونانی بھی
اسی دنیا میں یہودی بھی تھے نصرانی بھی
پر ترے نام پہ تلوار اٹھائی کس نے؟
بات جو بگڑی ہوئی تھی، وہ بنائی کس نے؟
تھے ہمیں ایک ترے معرکہ آراؤں میں!
خشکیوں میں کبھی لڑتے، کبھی دریاؤں میں
دیں اذانیں کبھی یورپ کے کلیساؤں میں
کبھی افریقہ کے تپتے ہوئے صحراؤں میں
تھی نہ کچھ تیغ زنی اپنی حکومت کے لئے
سر بکف پھرتے تھے کیا دہر میں دولت کیلئے؟
قوم اپنی جو زر و مالِ جہاں پر مرتی
بت فروشی کے عوض بت شکنی کیوں کرتی؟

182

Iqbal

Tell me, Lord, if anyone ever invoked Thy name,
The strength of Muslim arm alone restored Thy fame.

There was no dearth of peoples on this earth before,
Turkish tribes and Persian clans lived in days of yore;

The Greeks and the Chinese both bred and throve,
Christians as well as the Jews on this planet roved.

But who in Thy holy name raised his valiant sword,
Who set the things right, resolved the rigmarole?

We were the warrior bands battling for Thy cause,
Now on land, now on water, we the crusades fought.

Now in Europe's synods did we loudly pray,
Now in African deserts made a bold foray.

Not for territorial greed did we wield the sword,
Not for pelf and power did we suffer the blows.

Had we been tempted by the greed of glittering gold,
Instead of breaking idols, would have idols sold.

Tujhko maalum hai leta tha koi naam tira?
Quwwat-e-baazoo-e-Muslim ne kiya Kaam tira!

Bas rahe the yahin saljuq bhi, toorani bhi,
Ahl-e-chin cheen mein, Iran mein sasaani bhi,

Isi maamoore mein aabad the Yunaani bhi,
Isi duniya mein Yahudi bhi the, Nusraani bhi,

Par tire naam pe talwar uthai kis ne,
Baat jo bigri hui thi woh banaai kis ne?

The hameen ek tire maarka aaraaon mein!
Khushkion mein kabhi larte, kabhi dariyaon mein,

Di azaanen kabhi Europe ke kaleesaaon mein,
Kabhi Africa ke tapte hue sahraaon mein.

Thi na kuchh teg zani apni hakumat ke lieye,
Sar ba-kaf phirte the kya dahar mein daulat ke lieye?

Qaum apni jo zar-o-maal-e-jahan par marti,
But faroshi ke iwaz but shikni kyon karti?

محمد اقبال

نقشِ توحید کا ہر دل پہ بٹھایا ہم نے
زیرِ خنجر بھی یہ پیغام سنایا ہم نے
تو ہی کہہ دے کہ اکھاڑا درِ خیبر کس نے؟
شہرِ قیصر کا جو نقشہ تھا اس کو کیا پاش کس نے؟
توڑے مخلوقِ خداوندوں کے پیکر کس نے؟
کاٹ کر رکھ دئیے کفار کے لشکر کس نے؟
آ گیا عین لڑائی میں اگر وقتِ نماز
قبلہ رو ہو کے زمیں بوس ہوئی قومِ حجاز
ایک ہی صف میں کھڑے ہو گئے محمود و ایاز
نہ کوئی بندہ رہا اور نہ کوئی بندہ نواز
بندہ و صاحب و محتاج و غنی ایک ہوئے!
تیری سرکار میں پہنچے تو سبھی ایک ہوئے!
محفلِ کون و مکاں میں سحر و شام پھرے
مئے توحید کو لے کر صفتِ جام پھرے
دشت تو دشت ہیں، دریا بھی نہ چھوڑے ہم نے
بحرِ ظلمات میں دوڑا دئیے گھوڑے ہم نے

184

Iqbal

We impressed on every heart the oneness of our mighty Lord,
Even under the threat of sword, bold and clever was our call.

Who conquered, tell us Thou, the fearful Khyber pass?
Who vanquished the Imperial Rome, who made it fall?

Who broke the idols of the primitive folks?
Who fought the kafirs, massacred their hordes?

If the prayer time arrived right amid the war,
With their faces turned to Kaaba, knelt down the brave Hejaz.

Mahmud and Ayaz stood together in the same flank,
The ruler and the ruled forgot the difference in their rank.

The rich and poor, lord and slave, all were levelled down,
All became brethern in love, with Thy grace crowned.

We roamed the world through, visited every place,
Did our rounds like the cup, serving sacred ale.

Forget about the forests, we spared not the seas
Into the dark, unfathomed ocean, we pushed our steeds.

Naqsh tauheed ka har dil pe bithaya hum ne,
Zer-e-khanjar bhi yeh paigham sunaya hum ne.

Tu hi kah de ke ukhara dar-e-Khyber kis ne,
Shaher qaiser ka jo tha us ko kiya sar kis ne?

Tore makhluq khudawandon ke paikar kis ne?
Kaat kar rakh diye kaffaar ke lashkar kis ne?

Aa gaya ain laraai mein agar waqt-e-namaz,
Qibla roo ho ke zamin bos hui qaum-e-Hejaz,

Ek hi saf mein khare ho gaye mahmud-o-Ayaz,
No koi banda raha aur no koi banda nawaz.

Banda-o-sahib-o-muhtaaj-o-ghani ek hue,
Teri sarkar mein pahunche tau sabhi ek hue.

Mehfil-e-kaun-o-makaan mein sahr-o-shaam phire,
Mai-e-tauheed ko lekar sift-e-jam phire.

Dasht tau dasht hain, darya bhi na chhore hum ne,
Bahr-e-zulmaat mein daura diye ghore hum ne.

محمد اقبال

صفحۂ دہر سے باطل کو مٹایا ہم نے
نوعِ انساں کو غلامی سے چھڑایا ہم نے
تیرے کعبے کو جبینوں سے بسایا ہم نے
تیرے قرآن کو سینوں سے لگایا ہم نے
پھر بھی ہم سے یہ گلہ ہے کہ وفادار نہیں
ہم وفادار نہیں، تو بھی تو دلدار نہیں!
رحمتیں ہیں تری اغیار کے کاشانوں پر
برق گرتی ہے تو بیچارے مسلمانوں پر!
یہ شکایت نہیں، ہیں ان کے خزانے معمور
نہیں محفل میں جنھیں بات بھی کرنے کا شعور
قہر تو یہ ہے کہ کافر کو ملیں حور و قصور
اور بیچارے مسلماں کو فقط وعدۂ حور!
طعنِ اغیار ہے، رسوائی ہے، ناداری ہے
کیا ترے نام پہ مرنے کا عوض خواری ہے؟
ہم تو جیتے ہیں کہ دنیا میں ترا نام رہے
کہیں ممکن ہے کہ ساقی نہ رہے جام رہے؟

Iqbal

We removed falsehood from the earth's face,
We broke the shackles of the human race.

We reclaimed your Kaaba with our kneeling brows,
We pressed the sacred Quran to our heart and soul.

Even then you grumble, we are false, untrue,
If you call us faithless, tell us what are you?

You reserve your favours for men of other shades,
While you hurl your bolts on the Muslim race.

This is not our complaint that such alone are blessed,
Who do not know the etiquette, nor even can converse.

The tragedy is while kafirs are with houries actually blest,
On vague hopes of houries in heaven the Muslim race is made to rest!

Poverty, taunts, ignominy stare us in the face,
Is humiliation the sole reward of our suffering race?

To perpetuate Thy name is our sole concern,
Deprived of the saqi's aid can the cup revolve and turn?

Safah-e-dahar se baatil ko mitaya hum ne,
Nau-e-insaan ko ghulami se chhuraya hum ne,

Tere kaabe ko jabeenon se basaya hum ne,
Tere Quraan ko seenon se lagaya hum ne.

Phir bhi hum se yeh gila hai, ke wafadar nahin,
Hum wafadar nahin, tu bhi tau dildar nahin!

Rahmaten hain tiri aghiyar ke kashaanon par,
Barq girti hai tau bechare Musalmaanon par!

Yeh shikait nahin, hain un ke khazane maamur,
Nahin mehfil mein jinhen baat bhi karne ka shaoor,

Qahar tau yeh hai ke kafir ko milen hoor-o-qasoor,
Aur bechaare Musalmaan ko faqt waada-e-hoor!

Taan-e-aghiyaar hai, ruswai hai, nadaari hai,
Kya tere nam pe marne ka iwaz khwari hai?

Hum tau jeete hain ke duniya mein tira naam rahe,
Kahin mumkin hai ke saqi na rahe, jaam rahe?

محمد اقبال

تیری محفل بھی گئی، چاہنے والے بھی گئے
شب کی آہیں بھی گئیں، صبح کے نالے بھی گئے
دل تجھے دے بھی گئے، اپنا صلہ لے بھی گئے
آ کے بیٹھے بھی نہ تھے اور نکالے بھی گئے
آئے عشاق، گئے وعدۂ فردا لے کر
اب انھیں ڈھونڈ چراغِ رخِ زیبا لے کر!
درد لیلیٰ بھی وہی، قیس کا پہلو بھی وہی
نجد کے دشت و جبل میں رمِ آہو بھی وہی
عشق کا دل بھی وہی، حسن کا جادو بھی وہی
امتِ احمدِ مرسل بھی وہی، تو بھی وہی
پھر یہ آزردگیٔ غیرِ سببب کیا معنی؟
اپنے شیداؤں پہ یہ چشمِ غضب کیا معنی؟
عشق کی خیر، وہ پہلی سی ادا بھی نہ سہی
جادہ پیمائیٔ تسلیم و رضا بھی نہ سہی
کبھی ہم سے، کبھی غیروں سے شناسائی ہے
بات کہنے کی نہیں تو بھی تو ہرجائی ہے

Iqbal

Gone is your assemblage, off your lovers have sailed,
The midnight sighs are no more heard, nor the morning wails;

They pledged their hearts to you, what is their return?
Hardly had they stepped inside, when they were externed.

Thy lovers came and went away, fed on hopes of future grace,
Search them now with the lamp of your glowing face.

Unassuaged is Laila's ache, unquenched is Qais's thirst,
In the wilderness of Nejd, the wild deer are still berserk.

The same passion thrills the hearts, enchanting still is beauty's gaze,
You are the same as before, same too is the Prophet's race.

Why then this indifference, without a cause or fault?
Why with your threatening looks dost thou break our heart?

Accepted that the flame of love burneth low and dim,
We do not, as in yore, dance attendance on your whims;

But you too, pardon us, possess a coquettish heart,
Now on us, now on others, alight your amorous darts.

Teri mehfil bhi gai, chahne wale bhi gaye,
Shab ki aahen bhi gaien, subah ke nale bhi gaye,

Dil tujhe de bhi gaye, apna sila le bhi gaye,
Aa ke baithe bhi na the, ke nikaale bhi gaye.

Aae ushaaq, gaye waada-e-farda lekar,
Ab unhen dhoond chirag-e-rukh-e-zeba lekar!

Dard-e-Laila bhi wohi, Qais ka pahlu bhi wohi,
Nejd ke dasht-o-jabal mein ram-e-aahoo bhi wohi,

Ishq ka dil bhi wohi, husn ka jaadoo bhi wohi,
Ummat-e-Ahmed-e-Mursil bhi wohi, tu bhi wohi,

Phir yeh aazurdagi-e-ghair-sabab kya maani,
Apne shaidaaon pe yeh chashm-e-ghazab kya maani?

Ishq ki khair, woh pehli si ada bhi na sahi,
Jaada paimaai taslim-o-raza bhi na sahi,

Kabhi hum se, kabhi ghairon se shanasaai hai,
Baat kahne ki nahin, tu bhi tau harjaai hai.

محمد اقبال

عہدِ گل ختم ہوا، ٹوٹ گیا سازِ چمن
اڑ گئے ڈالیوں سے زمزمہ پردازِ چمن
ایک بلبل ہے کہ ہے محوِ ترنّم اب تک
اس کے سینے میں ہے نغموں کا تلاطم اب تک
قمریاں شاخِ صنوبر سے گریزاں بھی ہوئیں
پتیاں پھول کی جھڑ جھڑ کے پریشاں بھی ہوئیں
وہ پرانی روشیں باغ کی ویراں بھی ہوئیں
ڈالیاں پیرہنِ برگ سے عریاں بھی ہوئیں
قیدِ موسم سے طبیعت رہی آزاد اس کی
کاش گلشن میں سمجھتا کوئی فریاد اس کی!
چاک اس بلبلِ تنہا کی نوا سے دل ہوں
جاگنے والے اسی بانگِ درا سے دل ہوں
یعنی پھر زندہ نئے عہدِ وفا سے دل ہوں
پھر اسی بادۂ دیرینہ کے پیاسے دل ہوں
عجمی خم ہے تو کیا ہے تو حجازی ہے مری
نغمہ ہندی ہے تو کیا ہے لے حجازی ہے مری

190

Iqbal

The spring has now taken leave, broken lies the lyre string,
The birds that chirped among the leaves have also taken wing;
A single nightingale is left singing on the tree,
A flood of song in her breast is longing for release.
From atop the firs and pines the doves have flown away,
The floral petals lie scattered all along the way.
Desolate lie the garden paths, once dressed and neat,
Leafless hang the branches on the naked trees.
The nightingale is unconcerned with the season's rage,
Would that someone in the grove appreciates her wail.
May the nightingale's wail pierce the listeners' hearts,
May the clinking caravan awaken slumbering thoughts!
Let the hearts pledge anew their faith to you, O Lord,
Let's re-charge our cups from the taverns of the past.
Though I hold a Persian cup, the wine is pure Hejaz,
Though I sing an Indian song, the tune is of the Arabian cast.

Ahd-e-gul khatam hua, tut gaya saaz-e-chaman,
Ur gaye dalion se zamzama pardaaz-e-chaman.

Ek bulbul hai ke hai mahw-e-tarannum ab tak,
Us ke seene mein hai naghmon ka talatam ab tak.

Qumrian shaakh-e-sanober se gurezaan bhi huin,
Pattian phool ki jhar jhar ke pareshan bhi huin;

Woh purani ravishen bagh ki weeran bhi huin,
Daalian parahan-e-barg se uriaan bhi huin.

Qaid-e-mausim se tabiat rahi aazad uski,
Kaash gulshan mein samjhta koi faryaad uski.

Chaak is bulbul-e-tanha ki nawa se dil hon,
Jaagne wale isi baang-e-dara se dil hon.

Yaani phir zinda naye ahd-e-wafa se dil hon,
Phir isi bada-e-deereena ke pyaase dil hon.

Ajmy khum hai tau kya, mai tau Hejaazi hai miri,
Naghma Hindi hai tau kya, lai tau Hejaazi hai miri.

Abridged

محمد اقبال
جوابِ شکوہ

دل سے جو بات نکلتی ہے اثر رکھتی ہے
پر نہیں، طاقتِ پرواز مگر رکھتی ہے
قدسی الاصل ہے، رفعت پہ نظر رکھتی ہے
خاک سے اٹھتی ہے، گردوں پہ گزر رکھتی ہے
عشق تھا فتنہ گر و سرکش و چالاک مرا
آسماں چیر گیا نالۂ بیباک مرا

پیر گردوں نے کہا سن کے، کہیں ہے کوئی!
بولے سیارے، سرِ عرشِ بریں ہے کوئی!
چاند کہتا تھا، نہیں۔ اہلِ زمیں ہے کوئی!
کہکشاں کہتی تھی، پوشیدہ یہیں ہے کوئی!
کچھ جو سمجھا مرے شکوے کو تو رضواں سمجھا
مجھے جنّت سے نکالا ہوا انساں سمجھا!

تھی فرشتوں کو بھی حیرت کہ یہ آواز ہے کیا!
عرش والوں پہ بھی کھلتا نہیں یہ راز ہے کیا!
تا سرِ عرش بھی انساں کی تگ و تاز ہے کیا!
آ گئی خاک کی چٹکی کو بھی پرواز ہے کیا؟

Iqbal
Jawab-e-Shikwa

The word springing from the heart surely carries weight,
Though not endowed with wings, it yet can fly in space.

Pure and spiritual in its essence, it pegs its gaze on high,
Rising from the lowly dust, grazes past the skies.

Keen, defiant, and querulous was my passion crazed,
It pierced through the skies, my audacious wail.

"Someone is there," thus spoke the heaven's warder old,
The planets said, "From above proceeds this voice so bold."

"No, no," the moon said, " 'tis someone on the earth below,"
Butted in the milky way: "The voice is hereabouts, I trow."

Ruzwan alone, if at all, understood aright,
He knew it was the man, from heaven once exiled.

Even the angels wondered who raised this cry,
All the celestial denizens looked about surprised.

Does man possess the might to scale empyreal heights?
Has this mere pinch of dust learnt the knack to fly?

Dil se jo baat nikalti hai, asar rakhti hai,
Par nahin, taaqat-e-parwaaz magar rakhti hai.

Qudsi-ul-asal hai, rif-at pe nazar rakhti hai,
Khaak se uthti hai, gardoon pe guzar rakhti hai.

Ishq tha fitna gar-o-sarkash-o-chalaak mira,
Aasman cheer gaya nala-e-bebaak mira.

Pir-e-gardoon ne kaha sun ke, kahin hai koi!
Bole sayyaare, sar-e-arsh-e-barin hai koi!

Chaand kahta tha, nahin, ahl-e-zamin hai koi!
Kahkashaan kahti thi, poshida yahin hai koi!

Kuchh jo samjha tau mere shikwe ko Ruzwan samjha,
Mujhe jannat se nikala hua insaan samjha.

Thi farishton ko bhi hairat, ke yeh aawaaz hai kya!
Arsh waalon pe bhi khulta nahin yeh raaz hai kya!

Taa sar-e-arsh bhi insaan ki tag-o-taaz hai kya?
Aa gai khak ki chutki ko bhi parwaaz hai kya?

محمد اقبال

غافل آدابِ سے سُکّانِ زمیں کیسے ہیں!
شوخ و گستاخ یہ پستی کے مکیں کیسے ہیں!
اس قدر شوخ کہ اللہ سے بھی برہم ہے
تھا جو مسجودِ ملائک یہ وہی آدم ہے؟
عالمِ کیف ہے، دانائے رموز کم ہے
ہاں، مگر عجز کے اسرار سے نامحرم ہے
ناز ہے طاقتِ گفتار پہ انسانوں کو
بات کرنے کا سلیقہ نہیں نادانوں کو!
آئی آوازِ غم انگیز ہے افسانہ ترا
اشکِ بے تاب سے لبریز ہے پیمانہ ترا
شکر شکوے کو کیا حسنِ ادا سے تُو نے
ہم سخن کر دیا بندوں کو خدا سے تُو نے
ہم تو مائل بہ کرم ہیں، کوئی سائل ہی نہیں
راہ دکھلائیں کسے؟ رہرو و منزل ہی نہیں
تربیت عام تو ہے، جوہرِ قابل ہی نہیں
جس سے تعمیر ہو آدم کی یہ وہ گِل ہی نہیں

Iqbal

What are these earthly folks? Careless of all respect,
How bold and impudent, the lowly dwellers of the earth!

Extremely rude and insolent, cross even with God,
Is it the same Adam whom angels once did laud?

Steeped in bliss, man is of wisdom's lore possessed,
Nonetheless, he's alien to humility's sterling worth.

Man feels proud of the power of his speech,
But the fool doesn't know how and what to speak.

You narrate a woeful tale, thus the voice arose,
Your heart is boiling over with tears uncontrolled.

You have delivered your plaint with perfect skill and art,
You have brought the humans in contact with God.

We are inclined to grant, but none deserves our grace,
None treads the righteous path, whom to show the way?

Our school is open to all, but talent there is none,
Where is that soil fertile to breed the human gems?

Ghaafil aadaab se yeh sukkaan-e-zamin kaise hain,
Shokh-o-gustaakh yeh pasti ke makin kaise hain.

Is qadar shokh ke Allah se bhi barham hai,
Tha jo masjud-e-malaik yeh wohi Aadam hai?

Aalam-e kaif hai, dana-e-ramuz-e-kam hai,
Haan, magar ijaz ke asrar se namahram hai.

Naaz hai taaqat-e-guftaar pe insaanon ko,
Baat karne ka saliqa nahin nadaanon ko!

Aai aawaaz ghum-angez hai afsana tira,
Ashk-e-betaab se labrez hai paimana tira.

Shukr shikwe ko kiya husn-e-ada se tu ne,
Hum sakhun kar diya bandon ko khuda se tu ne.

Hum tau mayal ba-karam hain, koi sayal hi nahin,
Rah dikhlain kise rahraw-e-manzil hi nahin.

Tarbiat aam tau hai, jauhar-e-qabil hi nahin,
Jis se taamir ho aadam ki yeh woh gil hi nahin.

محمد اقبال

کوئی قابل ہو تو ہم شانِ کئی دیتے ہیں
ڈھونڈنے والوں کو دنیا بھی نئی دیتے ہیں!
ہاتھ بے زور ہیں، الحاد سے دل خوگر ہیں
امتی باعثِ رسوائی پیغمبرؐ ہیں
بت شکن اٹھ گئے، باقی جو ہے بت گر ہیں
تھا براہیمؑ پدر، اور پسر آذر ہیں
بادہ آشام نئے، بادہ نیا، خم بھی نئے
حرمِ کعبہ نیا، بت بھی نئے، تم بھی نئے
وہ بھی دن تھے کہ یہی مایۂ رعنائی تھا!
نازشِ موسمِ گل لالۂ صحرائی تھا!
جو مسلمان تھا اللہ کا سودائی تھا
کبھی محبوب تمہارا یہی ہرجائی تھا
صفحۂ دہر سے باطل کو مٹایا کس نے؟
نوعِ انساں کو غلامی سے چھڑایا کس نے؟
میرے کعبے کو جبینوں سے بسایا کس نے؟
میرے قرآن کو سینوں سے لگایا کس نے؟

Iqbal

We reward the deserving folks with splendid meed,
We grant newer worlds to those who strive and seek.

Arms have been drained of strength, hearts have gone astray,
The Muslim race is a blot on the Prophet's face.

Idol-breakers have left the scene, idol-makers remain,
Aazar has inherited Abraham's glorious name.

Wine, flask, and drinkers—all are new and changed,
A different Kaaba, different idols now your worship claim.

There was a time when you were respected far and wide,
Once this desert bloom was the season's wealth and pride.

Every Muslim then was a lover profound of God,
Your sole beloved once was the all-embracing Lord.

Who removed falsehood from the earth's face?
Who broke the shackles of the human race?

Who reclaimed our Kaaba with their kneeling brows?
Who pressed the sacred Quran to their heart and soul?

Koi qabil ho tau hum shan-e-kai dete hain,
Dhoondne waalon ko duniya bhi nai dete hain!

Haath be-zor hain, ilhaad se dil khoo-gar hain,
Ummati baais-e-ruswai-e-paighamber hain.

But-shikan uth gaye, baaqi jo rahe but-gar hain,
Tha Brahim pidar, aur pisar Aazar hain.

Bada aasham naye baada naya khum bhi naye,
Harm-e-Kaaba naya, but bhi naye, tum bhi naye.

Woh bhi din the ke yehi maya-e-raanai tha,
Naazish-e-mausim-e-gul lala-e-sahraai tha!

Jo Musalmaan tha Allah ka saudai tha,
Kabhi mehboob tumhara yehi harjaai tha.

Safah-e-dahar se baatil ko mitaya kis ne?
Nau-e-insaan ko ghulami se chhuraya kis ne?

Mere Kaabe ko jabeenon se basaya kis ne?
Mere Quran ko seenon se lagaya kis ne?

محمد اقبال

تھے تو آباء وہ تمہارے ہی، مگر تم کیا ہو؟
ہاتھ پر ہاتھ دھرے منتظرِ فردا ہو؟
کیا کہا؟ بہرِ مسلماں ہے فقط وعدۂ حور
شکوہ بیجا بھی کرے کوئی تو لازم ہے شعور!
عدل ہے فاطرِ ہستی کا ازل سے دستور
مسلم آئیں ہوا کافر تو ملے حور و قصور
تم میں حوروں کا کوئی چاہنے والا ہی نہیں
جلوۂ طور تو موجود ہے موسیٰؑ ہی نہیں
منفعت ایک ہے اس قوم کی، نقصان بھی ایک
ایک ہی سب کا نبی، دین بھی، ایمان بھی ایک
حرمِ پاک بھی، اللہ بھی، قرآن بھی ایک
کچھ بڑی بات تھی ہوتے جو مسلمان بھی ایک
فرقہ بندی ہے کہیں، اور کہیں ذاتیں ہیں!
کیا زمانے میں پنپنے کی یہی باتیں ہیں!
جا کے ہوتے ہیں مساجد میں صف آرا، تو غریب
زحمتِ روزہ جو کرتے ہیں گوارا، تو غریب

198

Iqbal

True, they were your forbears, but what are you, I say?
Idle sitting, statue-like you dream away your days.

What did you say? Muslims are with hopes of houries consoled,
Even if your plaint is false, your words should be controlled.

Justice is the law supreme, operative on this globe,
Muslims can't expect the houries, if they follow the kafir's code.

None of you is, in fact, deserving of the "hoor",
A Moses is but hard to find, burneth still the Tur.

Common to the race entire is their gain or loss,
Common is their faith and creed, common too the Rasul of God;

One Kaaba, one Allah, and one Quran inspire their heart,
Why can't the Muslims then behave like a single lot?

Cast, creed and factions have disjointed this race,
Is this way to forge ahead, to flourish in the present age?

It's the poor who visit the mosque, join the kneeling rows,
The poor alone observe the fasts, practise self-control.

The tau aaba woh tumhaare hi, magar tum kya ho?
Haath par haath dhare muntezır-e-farda ho!

Kya kaha? "bahr-e-musalmaan hai faqt waade-e-hur,"
Shikwa beja bhi kare koi tau laazim hai shaoor!

Adal hai faatir-e-hasti ka azal se dastur,
Muslim aaeen hua kafir tau mile hur-o-qasur;

Tum mein hooron ka koi chahne wala hi nahin,
Jalwa-e-Tur tau maujood hai, Moosa hi nahin.

Munfait ek hai is qaum ki, nuqsaan bhi ek,
Ek hi sab ka nabi, din bhi, imaan bhi ek,

Harm-e-paak bhi, Allah bhi, Quran bhi ek,
Kuchh bari baat thi hote jo musalmaan bhi ek!

Firqa bandi hai kahin, aur kahin zaaten hain.
Kya zamane mein panpane ki yehi baaten hain?

Jaa ke hote hain masaajid mein saf-aara tau gharib,
Zahmat-e-roza jo karte hain gawara tau gharib.

محمد اقبال

نام لیتا ہے اگر کوئی ہمارا، تو عزیز
پردہ رکھتا ہے اگر کوئی تمہارا، تو عزیز
امراءِ نشۂ دولت میں ہیں غافل ہم سے
زندہ ہے ملّتِ بیضا غرباء کے دم سے
شور ہے ہو گئے دنیا سے مسلماں نابود
ہم یہ کہتے ہیں کہ تھے بھی کہیں مسلم موجود؟
وضع میں تم ہو نصاریٰ، تو تمدّن میں ہنود
یہ مسلماں ہیں! جنہیں دیکھ کے شرمائیں یہود
باپ کا علم نہ بیٹے کو اگر از بر ہو
پھر پسر قابلِ میراثِ پدر کیونکر ہو!
ہر کوئی مستِ مۓ ذوقِ تن آسانی ہے
تم مسلماں ہو؟ یہ اندازِ مسلمانی ہے!
چاہتے سب ہیں کہ ہوں اوجِ ثریّا پہ مقیم
پہلے ویسا کوئی پیدا تو کرے قلبِ سلیم!
عہدِ نو برق ہے، آتش زن ہر خرمن ہے
ایمن اس سے کوئی صحرا نہ کوئی گلشن ہے

Iqbal

If someone repeats our name, it's the poor again,
The devout poor hide your sins, preserve your vaunted name.

Drunk with the wine of wealth, the rich are unconcerned with God,
The Muslim race owes its life to the poor, indigent lot.

"Muslims have vanished from earth," this is what we hear,
But we ask, "Were the Muslims ever present here?"

You are Nisars by your looks, but Hindus by conduct,
Your culture puts to shame even the Jewish sects.

If the son is alien to his learned father's traits,
How can he then claim his father's heritage?

All of you love to lead a soft, luxurious life,
Are you a Muslim indeed? Is this the Muslim style?

All of you desire to be invested with the crown,
You should first produce a heart worthy of renown.

The new age is the lightning blast, it will set your barns on fire,
It can't produce in groves or deserts the Old Sinai's burning spire.

Naam leta hai agar koi hamara, tau gharib,
Pardah rakhta hao agar koi tumhara, tau gharib.

Umra nasha-e-daulat mein hain ghafil hum se,
Zinda hai millat-e-baiza ghurba ke dam se.

Shor hai ho gaye duniya se musalmaan naabood,
Hum yeh kahte hain ke the bhi kahin Muslim maujood?

Waza mein tum ho nisari, tau tamuddan mein Hanood,
Yeh musalmaan hain! jinhen dekh ke sharmain Yahud?

Baap ka ilm na bete ko agar azbar ho,
Phir pisar qabil-e-miraas-e-pidar kyonkar ho!

Har koi mast-e-mai-e-zauq-e-tan aasaani hai,
Tum musalmaan ho? yeh andaaz-e-musalmaani hai?

Chaahte sab hain ke hon auj-e-surayya pe muqeem,
Pahle waisa koi paida tau kare qalb-e-salim!

Ahd-e-nau barq hai, aatish zan-e-har khirman hai,
Aiman is se koi sahra no koi gulshan hai.

محمد اقبال

اس نئی آگ کا اقوامِ کہن ایندھن ہے
ملّتِ ختمِ رُسل شعلہ بہ پیراہن ہے
دیکھ کر رنگِ چمن ہو نہ پریشاں مالی
کوکبِ غنچے سے شاخیں ہیں چمکنے والی
خس و خاشاک سے ہوتا ہے گلستاں خالی
گل برانداز ہے خونِ شہدا کی لالی
رنگ گردوں کا ذرا دیکھ تو عنّابی ہے
یہ نکلتے ہوئے سورج کی افق تابی ہے
نخلِ اسلام نمونہ ہے برومندی کا
پھل ہے یہ سینکڑوں صدیوں کی چمن بندی کا
قافلہ ہو نہ سکے گا کبھی ویراں تیرا
غیرِ یک بانگِ درا کچھ نہیں ساماں تیرا
نخلِ شمع استی و در شعلہ دو درا ریشہ تو
عاقبت سوز بود سایہ اندیشۂ تو
کی محمدؐ سے وفا تو نے تو ہم تیرے ہیں
یہ جہاں چیز ہے کیا لوح و قلم تیرے ہیں

Iqbal

The new fire consumes for fuel the blood of nations old,
The clothes of the Prophet's race are incinerated in its folds.

Don't be depressed, gardener, by the present scene,
The starry buds are about to burst with a brilliant sheen.

The garden will soon be rid of its thorns and weeds,
The martyr's blood will bring to bloom all the dormant seeds.

Mark how the sky reflects its orange purple hues,
The rising sun will flush the sky with its rays anew.

Islamic tree exemplifies cultivation long and hard,
A fruit of arduous gardening over centuries past.

Your caravan needn't fear the perils of the path,
But for the call of bells you own no wealth at all.

You are the plant of light, the burning wick that never fails,
With the power of your thought you can incinerate the veil.

We'll love you as our own, if you follow the Prophet's ways,
The world is but a paltry thing, you'll command the pen and page.

Is nai aag ka aqwaam-e-kuhan eendhan hai,
Millat-e-khatam-e-rasal shoula ba parahan hai.

Dekh kar rang-e-chaman ho na pareshan maali,
Kookab-e-ghuncha se shaakhen hain chamakne wali.

Khas-o-khashaak se hota hai gulistan khaali,
Gul bar andaaz hai khun-e-shuhda ki laali.

Rang gardoon ka zara dekh tau unnabi hai,
Yeh nikalte hue suraj ki ufaq taabi hai.

Nakhl-e-Islam namoona hai bro-mandi ka,
Phal hai yeh sainkron saalon ki chaman bandi ka.

Qaafila ho na sakega kabhi weeran tera,
Ghair yak baang-e-dara kuchh nahin samaan tera.

Nakhl-e-shama asti-o-dar shoula dood resha-e-tu,
Aaqbat soz bood saya-e-andesha-e-tu.

Ki Mohammed se wafa tu ne tau hum tere hain,
Yeh jahan cheez hai kya, lauh-eo-qalam tere hain.

Abridged

محمد اقبال

ساقی نامہ

ہوا خیمہ زن کاروانِ بہار
ارم بن گیا دامنِ کوہسار
گل و نرگس و سوسن و نسترن
شہیدِ ازل لالہ خونیں کفن
جہاں چھپ گیا پردۂ رنگ میں
لہو کی ہے گردش رگِ سنگ میں
فضا نیلی نیلی ہوا میں سرور
ٹھہرتے نہیں آشیاں میں طیور
وہ جوئے کہستاں اچکتی ہوئی
اٹکتی لپکتی سرکتی ہوئی
اچھلتی، پھسلتی، سنبھلتی ہوئی
بڑے پیچ کھا کر نکلتی ہوئی
رکے جب تو سل چیر دیتی ہے یہ
پہاڑوں کے دل چیر دیتی ہے یہ
ذرا دیکھ اے ساقیِ لالہ فام
سناتی ہے یہ زندگی کا پیام

Iqbal
Saqi Naama (Excerpts)

The cavalcade of spring arrives,
The hill-side looks a Paradise!

Narcissus, lily, jasmine, rose,
Martyred tulips ruddy-robed,

A riot of colours, the earth adorns,
Blood pulsates in veins of stones.

Intoxicating is the air, light-blue the sky,
Birds restive in their nests are raring for a flight.

The sinuous rill is bubbling, boiling,
Pausing, foaming, sliding, falling;

Pushing on with cautious steps,
Meandering through the rocky tracts.

Breaking stones that block its path,
Splitting the mountain's heart apart.

Mark, O saqi, crimson-dyed,
The stream breathes the spirit of life!

Hua khaima zan carvaan-e-bahaar,
Aram ban gaya daaman-e-kohsaar.

Gul-o-nargis-o-sosan-o-nastran,
Shahid-e-azal, laala khunin-kafan.

Jahan chhup gaya parda-e-rang mein,
Lahu ki hai gardish rag-e-sang mein.

Faza neeli neeli, hawa mein saroor,
Thahrte nahin aashian mein tayyoor.

Woh joo-e-kuhstaan uchakti hui,
Atkati, lachakti, sarakti hui,

Uchhalti, phisalti, sambhalti hui,
Bare pech kha kar nikalti hui.

Ruke jab tau sil chir deti hai yeh,
Paharon ke dil chir deti hai yeh.

Zara dekh ai saqi-e-laala faam,
Sunaati hai yeh zindagi ka payaam.

محمد اقبال

پلا دے ساقی مجھے وہ مے پردہ سوز
کہ آتی نہیں فصلِ گل روز روز
وہ مے جس سے روشن ضمیرِ حیات
وہ مے جس سے ہے مستیِٔ کائنات
وہ مے جس میں ہے سوز و سازِ ازل
وہ مے جس سے کھلتا ہے رازِ ازل
اٹھا ساقیا پردہ اس راز سے
لڑا دے مموٗلے کو شہباز سے
زمانے کے انداز بدلے گئے
نیا راگ ہے ساز بدلے گئے
ہوا اس طرح فاش رازِ فرنگ
کہ حیرت میں ہے شیشہ بازِ فرنگ
پرانی سیاست گری خوار ہے
زمیں میر و سلطاں سے بیزار ہے
گیا دورِ سرمایہ داری گیا
تماشا دکھا کر مداری گیا

Iqbal

Bring the wine that melts the veil,
Spring cometh not every day.

Bring the conscience-kindling wine,
Which fills the world with bliss divine;

With eternal moan and music charged,
The wine unlocking souls and hearts.

Let the secret stand unveiled,
The sparrow o'er the hawk prevail!

Times have changed their form and style,
Different songs and lutes preside.

Europe's secret lies betrayed,
The crystal-gazers stand amazed.

Shameful is the political game,
The world is tired of dukes and dames.

Capitalism is gone and dead,
The show is over, the juggler fled.

Pila de mujhe woh mai-e-parda soz,
Ke aati nahin fasl-e-gul roz roz.

Woh mai jis se roshan zamir-e-hayaat,
Woh mai jis se hai masti-e-kaainaat.

Woh mai jis mein hai soz-o-saaz-e-azal,
Woh mai jis se khulta hai raaz-e-azal.

Utha saqia parda is raaz se,
Lara de mamole ko shahbaaz se.

Zamaane ke andaaz badle gaye,
Naya raag hai, saaz badley gaye;

Hua is tarah faash raaz-e-farang,
Ke hairat mein hai sheesha baaz-e-farang.

Purani siassat gari khwaar hai,
Zamin mir-o-sultan se bezaar hai.

Gaya daur-e-sarmaya dari gaya,
Tamasha dikha kar madari gaya

محمد اقبال

شرابِ کہن پھر پلا ساقیا
وہی جام گردش میں لا ساقیا
مجھے عشق کے پر لگا کر اڑا
مری خاک جگنو بنا کر اڑا
خرد کو غلامی سے آزاد کر
جوانوں کو پیروں کا استاد کر
ترے آسمانوں کے تاروں کی خیر
زمینوں کے شب زندہ داروں کی خیر
جوانوں کو سوزِ جگر بخش دے
مرا عشق میری نظر بخش دے
مری ناؤ گرداب سے پار کر
یہ ثابت ہے تو اس کو سیّار کر
بتا مجھ کو اسرارِ مرگِ حیات
کہ تیری نگاہوں میں ہے کائنات
امنگیں مری آرزوئیں مری!
امیدیں مری جستجوئیں مری!

Iqbal

Saqi, serve the ancient ale,
Again with globets old regale.

On wings of love, let me be flown,
Like glow-worm let my dust be blown,

Let reason reject the servile yoke,
The young guide the older folks!

May your stars glimmer and glow!
Your wakeful hermits thrive and grow!

Enthuse the young with passionate hearts,
To me the wealth of love impart.

Save my boat in tempest caught,
If its stuck, push it hard.

Reveal the truth of death and life,
You control the universe wide!

Ah, my longings, yearnings deep!
The endless urge to strive and seek!

Sharab-e-kuhan phir pila saqia,
Wohi jaam gardish mein la saqia.

Mujhe ishq ke par laga kar ura,
Miri khak jugnu bana kar ura.

Khirad ko ghulami se aazad kar,
Jawaanon ko peeron ka ustaad kar.

Tire aasmaanon ke taaron ki khair!
Zameenon ke shab zinda daron ki khair!

Jawanon ko soz-e-jigar bakhsh de,
Mira ishq meri nazar bakhsh de.

Miri naao girdaab se paar kar,
Yeh saabit hai tau isko sayyaar kar.

Bata mujhko asraar-e-marg-o-hayaat,
Ke teri nigaahon mein hai kaainaat.

Umangen miri, aarzooen miri!
Umeeden miri, justjooen miri!

محمد اقبال

سمجھتا ہے تو راز ہے زندگی
فقط ذوقِ پرواز ہے زندگی
سفر زندگی کے لئے برگ و ساز
سفر ہے حقیقت حضر ہے مجاز
سمجھتے ہیں ناداں اسے بے ثبات
ابھرتا ہے مٹ مٹ کے نقشِ حیات
بڑی تیز جولاں بڑی زود رس
ازل سے ابد تک رمِ یک نفس
یہ موجِ نفس کیا ہے تلوار ہے
خودی کیا ہے تلوار کی دھار ہے
خودی کیا ہے رازِ درون حیات
خودی کیا ہے بیداریِ کائنات
اندھیرے میں اجالے ہیں تابناک
من و تو میں پیدا من و تو سے پاک
ازل اس کے پیچھے ابد سامنے
نہ حد اس کے پیچھے نہ حد سامنے

Iqbal

A mystery seems to you this life,
In essence 'tis the urge to fly.

Travel is the grace of life,
Travel is truth, the rest a lie.

Life is mortal, the fools opine,
The image of life now fades, now shines.

The flow of breath till life doth last,
Is extremely subtle, extremely fast.

The breath that flows is but a sword,
Self-respect is the edge of the sword.

Self is the secret source of life,
Awakening of the universe wide.

A beam of light in deepening dark,
A part of us, and yet apart.

Eternity lies before it, eternity lies behind,
Self accepts no limits, rejects all confines.

Samajhta hai tu raaz hai zindagi,
Faqt zauq-e-parwaaz hai zindagi.

Safar zindagi ke lieye barg-o-saaz,
Safar hai haqiqat hazar hai majaaz.

Samjhte hain nadaan ise be-sabaat,
Ubharta hai mit mit ke naqsh-e-hayaat.

Bari tez jaulaan bari tez ras,
Azal se abad tak ram-e-yak nafas.

Yeh mauj-e-nafas kya hai talwaar hai,
Khudi kya hai? talwaar ki dhaar hai.

Khudi kya hai raaz-e-daroon-e-hyaat,
Khudi kya hai bedaari-e-kaainaat.

Andhere mein ujaale hain taabnaak,
Man-o-tu mein paida, man-o-tu se paak.

Azal is ke peechhe abad saamne,
Na had is ke peechhe, na had saamne.

محمد اقبال

خودی کا نشیمن ترے دل میں ہے
فلک جس طرح آنکھ کے تل میں ہے
وہی سجدہ ہے لائقِ اہتمام
کہ ہو جس سے ہر سجدہ تجھ پر حرام
یہ عالم یہ ہنگامہُ رنگ و صوت
یہ عالم کہ ہے زیرِ فرمانِ موت
یہ عالم، یہ بت خانہُ چشم و گوش
جہاں زندگی ہے فقط خورد و نوش
خودی کی ہے یہ منزلِ اوّلیں
مسافر یہ تیرا نشیمن نہیں
تری آگ اس خاکداں سے نہیں
جہاں تجھ سے ہو تو جہاں سے نہیں
یہ ہے مقصدِ گردشِ روزگار
کہ تیری خودی تجھ پہ ہو آشکار
تو ہے فاتحِ عالمِ خوب و زشت
تجھے کیا بتاؤں تری سرنوشت

Iqbal

In your heart doth self reside,
As in the iris lives the sky.

There alone your head should bow,
Where your self-respect may grow.

This world, a feast of sound and sight,
The world where death o'er life presides,

The idol house of ear and eye,
The place to eat and drink and die,

Is not your home, O traveller wise,
But a stage where self springs to sight.

Your fire is not an earthy spark,
You own the earth, she owns you not.

The purpose of diurnal round,
Is to rouse the self from slumber sound.

O, conqueror of the good and ill,
Your tale defies our strength and skill.

Khudi ka nasheman tire dil mein hai,
Falak jis tarah aankh ke til mein hai.

Wohi sijda hai laaiq-e-ihtemaam,
Ke ho jis se har sijda tujh par haraam.

Yeh aalam, yeh hangama-e-rang-o-saut,
Yeh aalam ke hai zer-e-farman-e-maut,

Yeh aalam, yeh but khana-e-chashm-o-gosh,
Jahan zindagi hai faqt khurd-o-nosh,

Khudi ki hai yeh manzil-e-awaleen,
Musafir yeh tera nasheman nahin.

Tiri aag is khakdaan se nahin,
Jahaan tujh se hai, tu jahaan se nahin.

Yeh hai maqsad-e-gardish-e-rozgaar,
Ke teri khudi tujh pe ho aashkaar.

Tu hai fateh-e-aalam-e-khub-o-zisht,
Tujhe kya bataaun tiri sar nawisht.

محمد اقبال

ترانۂ ہندی

سارے جہاں سے اچھا ہندوستاں ہمارا
ہم بلبلیں ہیں اس کی یہ گلستاں ہمارا

غربت میں ہوں اگر ہم رہتا ہے دل وطن میں
سمجھو وہیں ہمیں بھی دل ہو جہاں ہمارا

پربت وہ سب سے اونچا ہمسایہ آسماں کا
وہ سنتری ہمارا، وہ پاسباں ہمارا

گودی میں کھیلتی ہیں اس کی ہزاروں ندیاں
گلشن ہے جن کے دم سے رشکِ جناں ہمارا

اے آبِ رودِ گنگا! وہ دن ہیں یاد تجھ کو
اترا تیرے کنارے جب کارواں ہمارا

مذہب نہیں سکھاتا آپس میں بیر رکھنا
ہندی ہیں ہم وطن ہے ہندوستاں ہمارا

یونان و مصر و روما سب مٹ گئے جہاں سے
اب تک مگر ہے باقی نام و نشاں ہمارا

کچھ بات ہے کہ ہستی مٹتی نہیں ہماری
صدیوں رہا ہے دشمن دورِ زماں ہمارا

اقبالؔ کوئی محرم اپنا نہیں جہاں میں
معلوم کیا کسی کو دردِ نہاں ہمارا

214

Iqbal
Tarana-e-Hind (Song of Hindustan)

Nothing like our Hindustan in the world entire,
She is o'r garden, we her warbling choir.
We may wander far from home, home resides in our thoughts,
We too live at that place where lies our heart.
The highest mountain of the world, a neighbour of the skies,
That tough and tall watchman guards us day and night.
A thousand rivulets criss-cross through her plains and wilds,
Because of which our garden vies with Paradise.
O Ganges, flowing past thy banks, remember thou that time,
When we landed on thy shore, in this sacred clime.
Religion does not teach us to harbour mutual spite,
We are Indians, one and all, Hindustan our land of pride.
Greece, Egypt and Rome, have vanished out of sight,
But our name lives on in spite of time and tide.
Something must be there to keep our name alive,
Though the world for centuries has been to us hostile.
We do not have a confidant in the world, Iqbal,
None knows what sorrows lurk within our heart.

Saare jahaan se achha Hindustan hamaara,
Hum bulbulen hain iski, yeh gulistan hamaara.
Ghurbat mein hon agar hum, rahta hai dil watan mein,
Samjho wahin hamen bhi dil ho jahaan hamaara.
Parbat woh sab se ooncha, hamsaaya aasman ka,
Woh santary hamaara, woh passbaan hamaara.
Godi mein khelti hain iski hazaaron naddian,
Gulshan hai jinke dam se rashk-e-janaan hamaara.
Ai aab-e-rod-e-Ganga, woh din hain yaad tujhko,
Utra tere kinaare jab caarvan hamaara.
Mazhab nahin sikhaata aapas min ber rakhna,
Hindi hain hum, watan hai Hindustan hamaara.
Unaan-o-Misr-o-Roma sab mit gaye jahaan se
Ab tak magar hai baaqi naam-o-nishaan hamaara.
Kuchh baat hai ke hasti mit-ti nahin hamaari,
Sadion raha hai dushman daur-e-zamaan hamaara.
Iqbal, koi mahram apna nahin jahaan mein,
Maalum kya kisi ko dard-e-nihaan hamaara.

محمد اقبال

نیا شوالہ

سچ کہ دوں اے برہمن گر تو برا نہ مانے
تیرے صنم کدوں کے بت ہو گئے پرانے
اپنوں سے بیر رکھنا تونے بتوں سے سیکھا
جنگ و جدل سکھایا واعظ کو بھی خدا نے
تنگ آ کے میں نے آخر دیر و حرم کو چھوڑا
واعظ کا وعظ چھوڑا، چھوڑے ترے فسانے
پتھر کی مورتوں میں سمجھا ہے تو خدا ہے
خاکِ وطن کا مجھ کو ہر ذرّہ دیوتا ہے
آ غیریت کے پردے اک بار پھر اٹھا دیں
بچھڑوں کو پھر ملا دیں نقشِ دوئی مٹا دیں
سونی پڑی ہوئی ہے مدت سے دل کی بستی
آ، اک نیا شوالہ اس دیس میں بنا دیں
دنیا کے تیرتھوں سے اونچا ہو اپنا تیرتھ
دامانِ آسمان سے اس کا کلس ملا دیں
ہر صبح اٹھ کے گائیں منتر وہ میٹھے میٹھے
سارے پجاریوں کو مے پیت کی پلا دیں
شکتی بھی شانتی بھی بھگتوں کے گیت میں ہے
دھرتی کے باسیوں کی مکتی پریت میں ہے

216

Iqbal
Naya Shivala

Mind ye not, O Brahman, if I tell the truth:
The idols of your temple have outlived their use.

These idols have taught you hatred and ill-will,
The mullah too has learnt from them how to fight and kill.

In disgust I renounce both the mosque and shrine,
The sheikh's sermonizing, your tales divine.

You think that God lives in images carved of stone,
Every grain of my land is to me the deity's home.

Let's remove the marks of otherness, dividing lines erase,
Let's unite the severed selves, lift the falling veil.

For long has the land of heart remained unreclaimed,
Let's build at this place a new, superior fane.

Higher than all the shrines should be our holy place,
With its spire in the skies, its head proudly raised.

Let's sing every morn hymns with love replete,
Let's with the wine of love fete the holy priests.

The devotees' hymns are a source of both strength and peace,
In love alone the sons of earth can find release.

Sach kah doon, ai Brahaman, gar tu bura na maane,
Tere sanam kadon ke but ho gaye purane,

Apnon se ber rakhna tu ne buton se seekha,
Jango-o-jadal sikhaaya waaiz ko bhi Khuda ne.

Tang aa ke aakhir main ne der-o-haram ko chhora,
Waaiz ka waaz chhora, chhore tere fasaane.

Pathar ki moorton mein samjha hai tu Khuda hai,
Khaak-e-watan ka mujhko har zarra devta hai.

Aa, ghairiat ke parde ik baar phir utha den,
Bichhron ko phir mila den, naqsh-e-dui mita den.

Sooni pari hui hai muddat se dil ki basti,
Aa, ik naya shivala is des mein bana den.

Duniya ke teerathon se ooncha ho apna teerath,
Damaan-e-aasman se iska kalas mila den.

Har subah mil ke gaaen mantar woh meethe, meethe,
Saare pujaarion ko mai peet ki pila den.

Shakti bhi shanti bhi bhakton ke geet mein hai,
Dharti ke baasion ki mukti preet mein hai.

محمد اقبال
رام

لبریز ہے شرابِ حقیقت سے جامِ ہند
سب فلسفی ہیں خطۂ مغرب کے رامِ ہند
یہ ہندیوں کے فکرِ فلک رس کا ہے اثر
رفعت میں آسماں سے بھی اونچا ہے بامِ ہند
اس دیس میں ہوئے ہیں ہزاروں ملک سرشت
مشہور جن کے دم سے ہے دنیا میں نامِ ہند
ہے رام کے وجود پہ ہندوستاں کو ناز
اہلِ نظر سمجھتے ہیں اس کو امامِ ہند
اعجاز اس چراغِ ہدایت کا ہے یہی
روشن تر از سحر ہے زمانے میں شامِ ہند
تلوار کا دھنی تھا، شجاعت میں فرد تھا
پاکیزگی میں، جوشِ محبت میں فرد تھا

Iqbal
Ram

Brimful with the wine of Truth is the cup of Indian thought,
Western thinkers feel enraptured when they drink this spiritual draught.

Thanks to the skiey flights of the Indian mind,
Far above the heavens high shines the Indian star.

This land has given birth to men of angelic worth,
Who have glorified this land with their deeds and thoughts.

India is mighty proud of Rama's sacred name,
Discerning minds respect him as the voice of God.

The Indian evening outshines the morning in the other climes,
What a great miracle this beacon light has wrought!

Ram was a warrior great, a man of courage supreme,
A reservoir of love abounding, a fount of virtuous thought.

Labrez hai sharab-e-haqiqat se jaam-e-Hind,
Sab falsafi hain khitta-e-maghrib ke raam-e-Hind;

Yeh Hindion ke fikr-e-falak-ras ka hai asar,
Rifaat mein aasmaan se bhi ooncha hai baam-e-Hind.

Is des mein hue hain hazaaron malik sarisht,
Mashhur jin ke dam se hai duniya mein naam-e-Hind.

Hai Ram ke wajud pe Hindustan ko naaz,
Ahl-e-nazar samajhte hain usko amaam-e-Hind;

Aijaaz is chiragh-e-hadaait ka hai yehi,
Roshan tar az sahr hai zamane mein shaam-e-Hind.

Talwaar ka dhani tha, shujaat mein fard tha,
Paakizgi mein, josh-e-mahabbat mein fard tha.

Brij Narain Chakbast
(1882-1926)

BRIJ NARAIN CHAKBAST
(1882-1926)

Chakbast's ancestors hailed from Kashmir and had settled in Delhi, U.P. and Bihar in 15th century A.D. His father, Udit Narain Chakbast, was born at Lucknow in, probably, 1843. Brij Narain was born at Faizabad in 1882. After the death of his father in 1887 the family shifted to Lucknow. It was here that the boy poet received his education which included, apart from a thorough grounding in Urdu and Persian, an LL.B. degree also. Chakbast married in 1905, but lost his wife and first child in 1906. He married again in 1907, and settled down as a practising lawyer at Lucknow. He was also actively involved in social and political affairs, and was an ardent champion of the Home Rule. He lived for just 44 years and died of a paralytic stroke in 1926.

Chakbast is primarily a poet of the *nazm*. He began his poetic career with a *nazm* in 1894, and ended, in 1925, with a *nazm* again. His famous poems are: "Khak-e-Hind", "Ramayan ka Ek Scene", "Nala-e-Dard", and "Nala-e-Yaas". He also wrote a *Masnavi* entitled: "Gulzar-e-Naseem", and a play named "Kamla". He wrote no more than 50 *ghazals*, but most of them are remarkable for the beauty of their thought and the lucidity and urbanity of his style. Much of his verse is didactic, patriotic and aphoristic. He uses impressive, Persianised diction, in the manner of Ghalib and Aatish, by whose poetry he was deeply influenced. Chakabast is among the few early Urdu poets who had the benefit of a university degree. He is also distinctive for not having used his "takhallus", his poetic name, in the conclusions of his *ghazals*—which perhaps shows the humility and modesty of his temperament.

Chakbast's collected works are available under the title: *Subah-e-Watan*, which title, incidentally, correctly reflects the central concern of his mind and art, for many of the poems included in this volume are inspired by the feeling of patriotism. Lines like: "Hamara watan, dil se piara watan," and "Watan ko hum, watan hum ko mubarak," have by now made a permanent place in the minds and memories of the educated Indians. Similarly, his poems, "Khak-e-Hind"and "Aawaaza-e-Qaum" bear testimony to the poet's love for his motherland, and respect for her ancient glory. He has also written a memorable poem on the cow, whom Hindus hold in reverence. It contains such beautiful lines as: "Doodh se tire larakpan mein zaban dhoi hai," (With your milk in childhood we have washed our tongues.) The poem selected for translation describes a scene from the *Ramayana*, when Ram goes to his mother to seek her blessings, and her permission to go on his epic 14-year exile. The dialogue of the mother and son is deeply moving, appropriately expressive of the character and situation. The poem is written in the poet's favourite measure: "musaddas", a six-line stanza, composed of a quatrain and a couplet.

برج نارائن چکبست

رامائن کا ایک سین

رُخصت ہوا وہ باپ سے لے کر خدا کا نام
راہِ وفا کی منزلِ اوّل ہوئی تمام
منتظر تھا جو ماں کی زیارت کا انتظام
دامن سے اشک پونچھ کے دل سے کیا کلام
اظہارِ بے کسی سے کسی کو ستم ہوگا اور بھی
دیکھا ہمیں اُداس تو غم ہوگا اور بھی
دل کو سنبھالتا ہوا آخر وہ نونہال
خاموش ماں کے پاس گیا صورتِ خیال
دیکھا تو ایک در میں ہے بیٹھی وہ خستہ حال
سکتا سا ہوگیا ہے یہ ہے شدّتِ ملال
تن میں لہو کا نام نہیں زرد رنگ ہے
گویا بشر نہیں کوئی تصویرِ سنگ ہے
کیا جانے کس خیال میں گم تھی وہ بے گناہ
نورِ نظر پہ دیدۂ حسرت سے کی نگاہ
جنبش ہوئی لبوں کو بھری ایک سرد آہ
لی گوشہ ہائے چشم سے اشکوں نے رُخ کی راہ

Brij Narain Chakbast
A Scene from Ramayana

Thus he parted from his sire, calling upon his God,
Thus ended the first stage on his filial path.
As he geared to see his mother and make the farewell call,
Wiping a tear from his eye, thus he reasoned with his heart:
It will aggravate her sorrow if I express my woe,
My grief will break her heart, falling like a blow.
With faltering feet the darling son approached her mother's resort,
Subduing his brimming heart, silent like a thought.
She was sitting at the door, deep-depressed and lost,
Stunned and paralysed by the sudden shock.
Not a trace of blood was there, her face was deadly pale,
Statue-like she sat still, downward was her gaze.
Who knows what fearful thoughts in her mind did creep,
What a longing look she cast at her darling sweet!
Her trembling lips began to move, a cold sigh she heaved,
Tears welling from her eyes rolled down her cheeks.

Rukhsat hua woh baap se le kar khuda ka naam,
Raah-e-wafa ki manzil-e-awwal hui tamaam.
Manzur tha jo maan ki zayarat ka intezaam,
Daaman se ashk poonch ke dil se kiya kalaam:

Izhaar-e-be-kasi se sitam hoga aur bhi,
Dekha hamen udaas tau ghum hoga aur bhi.

Dil ko sambhaltaa hua, aakhir woh naunihaal,
Khaamosh maan ke paas gaya soorat-e-khayal.
Dekha tau ek dar mein hai baithi woh khasta haal,
Sakta sa ho gaya hai yeh hai shiddat-e-malaal.

Tan mein lahu ka naam nahin, zard rang hai,
Goya bashar nahin, koi tasvir-e-sang hai.

Kya jaane kis khayaal mein gum thi woh be-gunaah,
Noor-e-nazar pe deeda-e-hasrat se ki nigaah.
Jumbish hui labon ko, bhari ek sard aah,
Li gosha haae chashm se ashkon ne rukh ki raah.

چکبست

چہرے کا رنگ حالتِ دل کھولنے لگا
ہر موئے تن زباں کی طرح بولنے لگا
روک کر کہا خموش کھڑے کیوں ہو میری جان
میں جانتی ہوں جس لئے آئے ہو تم یہاں
سب کی خوشی یہی ہے تو صحرا کو ہو رواں
لیکن میں اپنے منھ سے نہ ہرگز کہوں گی ہاں
کس طرح بن میں آنکھوں کے تارے کو بھیج دوں
جوگی بنا کے راج دلارے کو بھیج دوں
یہی کسی فقیر کے گھر میں اگر جنم
ہوتے نہ میری جان کو سامان یہ بہم
ڈستا نہ سانپ بن کے مجھے شوکت و حشم
تم میرے لال تھے مجھے کس سلطنت سے کم
میں خوش ہوں پھونک دے کوئی اس تخت و تاج کو
تم ہی نہیں تو آگ لگاؤں گی راج کو
سرزد ہوئے تھے مجھ سے خدا جانے کیا گناہ
منجدھار میں جو یوں مری کشتی ہوئی تباہ

226

Chakbast

The shade of her pallid face her inner state betrayed,
Every pore acquired a tongue, every hair spake.
Overcome by grief she said: Why are you tongue-tied?
I know what brings you here, I know your plight.
Set out, if they all desire, for the distant wilds,
But my lips can never say: "Go my son, good-bye!"
How can I grant exile to the apple of my eye,
How can a darling prince roam the deserts beggar-like?
Oh, I wish I were born in some humble home,
Where such calamities are things quite unknown.
I wouldn't then have been undone by this pomp and show,
Aren't you to me, my son, dearer than this throne?
Let the throne and crown be burnt, I'm not concerned,
What use this kingdom vast without my darling son?
What sins have brought me to this sorry pass?
Why thus in mid-stream my boat is tempest-tossed?

Chehre ka rang halat-e-dil kholne laga,
Har moo-e-tan zaban ki tarah bolne laga.

Ro kar kaha khamosh khare hyon ho meri jaan,
Main jaanti hun jis lieye aae ho tum yahaan.
Sab ki khushi yehi hai tau sahra ko ho rawaan,
Lekin main apne munh se na hargiz kahungi "haan."

Kis tarah ban mein aankh ke taare ko bhej doon,
Jogi bana ke raaj dulaare ko bhej doon.

Leti agar fakir ke ghar mein agar janam,
Hote na meri jaan ko samaan yeh baham.
Dasta na saanp ban ke mujhe shaukat-o-hasham,
Tum mere laal the mujhe kis saltanat se kam?

Main khush hun phoonk de koi is takhat-o-taaj ko,
Tum hi nahin tau aag lagaaun gi raaj ko?

Sarzad hue the mujh se khuda jaane kya gunaah,
Manjhdhaar mein jo yun miri kashti hui tabaah.

چکبست

آتی نظر نہیں کوئی امن و اماں کی راہ
اب یاں سے کوچ ہو تو عدم میں لے پناہ
تقصیر میری خالقِ عالم بخُل کرے
آسان مجھ غریب کی مشکل اجل کرے
سن کر زباں سے ماں کی یہ فریادِ دَرد خیز
اس خستہ جاں کے دل پہ چلی غم کی تیغِ تیز
عالم یہ تھا قریب کہ آنکھیں ہوں اشک ریز
لیکن ہزار ضبط سے رونے کی گریز
سوچا یہی کہ جان سے بیکس گزر نہ جائے
ناشاد ہم کو دیکھ کے ماں اور مر نہ جائے
پھر عرض کی یہ مادرِ ناشاد کے حضور
مایوس کیوں ہیں آپ الم کا ہے کیوں وفور
صدمہ یہ شاقِ عالمِ پیری میں ہے ضرور
لیکن نہ دل سے کیجئے صبر و قرار دور
شاید خزاں سے شکل عیاں ہو بہار کی
کچھ مصلحت اسی میں ہو پروردگار کی

228

Chakbast

I see no ray of light in this deepening dark,
Death alone can give relief to this broken heart.
May God forgive my sins, take a kinder view,
May the kindly hand of death come to my rescue!
When he heard his dear mother thus lament and wail,
Grief, like a dagger sharp, did his heart assail.
He was on the verge of weeping, but with hard assay,
He controlled his tears, stemmed the rising wave.
Lest his mother died of grief, he was so afraid,
Unable to bear the shock, she may faint and fade.
Thus did he console his mother, thus did he implore,
Why are you so down in dumps, why benumbed and cold?
No doubt 'tis a heavy shock, and you're so old,
But you mustn't feel despaired, take heart, be bold.
Who knows the autumn gale may spring breeze presage,
The seeming evil might prove an act of God's grace.

Aaati nazar nahin koi aman-o-amaan ki raah,
Ab yaan se kooch ho tau adam mein mile panah.
Taqsir meri khaaliq-e-aalam ba-hal kare,
Aasaan mujh gharib ki mushkil ajal kare.
Sun kar zaban se maan ki yeh faryaad-e-dard khez,
Is khasta jaan ke dil pe chali ghum ki tegh-e-tez.
Aalam tha yeh qarib ke aankhaen hon ashk rez,
Lekin hazaar zabt se rone se ki gurez.
Socha yehi ke jaan se bekas guzar na jaae,
Nashaad hum ko dekh maan aur mar na jaae.
Phir arz ki maadar-e-nashaad ke hazoor,
Maayoos kyon hain aap, alam ka hai kyon wafoor?
Sadma yeh shaaq aalam-e-piri men hai zaroor,
Lekin na dil se kijieye sabr-o-qarar door.
Shaid khizaan se shakl ayaan ho bahaar ki,
Kuchh maslihat isi mein ho parwurdigaar ki.

چکبست

پڑتا ہے جب عزیب پہ رنج و محن کا بار
کرتا ہے اُس کو صبر عطا آپ کردگار
مایوس ہو کے ہوتے ہیں انساں گناہگار
یہ جانتے نہیں وہ ہے دانائے روزگار

انسان اُس کی راہ میں ثابت قدم رہے
گر دن وہی ہے امرِ رضا میں جو خم رہے
اکثر ریاض کرتے ہیں پھولوں پہ باغباں
ہے دن کی دھوپ رات کی شبنم انھیں گراں

لیکن جو رنگ باغ بدلتا ہے ناگہاں
وہ گُل ہزار پردوں میں جائے ہیں رائگاں
رکھتے ہیں جو عزیز انھیں اپنی جاں کی طرح
کھلتے ہیں دستِ یاس وہ برگِ خزاں کی طرح

لیکن جو پھول کھلتے ہیں صحرا میں بے شمار
موقوف کچھ ریاض پہ اُن کی نہیں بہار
دیکھو یہ قدرتِ چمن آرائے روزگار
وہ ابر و باد و برف میں رہتے ہیں برقرار

Chakbast

Whenever some poor soul is by griefs assailed,
God gives the courage to bear, God shows the way.
'Tis a sin to give up hope and feel dismayed,
We should know that gracious God is wisdom incarnate!

Man should steadfastly tread the path of grace,
He should, without demur, accept His will and ways.

Gardeners toil day and night to protect the flowers frail,
The heat of day and dews of night both turn them pale.
But when the garden suddenly falls a prey to deadly gale,
Even strongly sheltered flowers wither behind the veil.

Those who held them dear as life and tended them with care,
Like the fallen leaves adrift, wring their hands despaired.

But countless flowers in the desert growing unespied,
Untended, unwatered, blossom fresh and bright;
Mark ye the glorious ways of the gardener wise,
Wind, rain or snow, the desert blooms survive!

Parta hai jis gharib pe ranj-o-mehan ka baar,
Karta hai usko sabr itaa aap kirdgaar.
Maaypos ho ke hote hain insaan gunahgaar,
Yeh jaan-te nahin woh hai daanaa-e-rozgaar.

Insaan us ki raah mein saabit qadam rahe,
Gardan wohi hai amar-e-raza mein jo kham rahe.

Aksar rayaaz karte hain phoolon pe baaghbaan,
Hai din ki dhoop, raat ki shabnam unhen giraan;
Lekin jo rang baagh badalta hai naagahaan
Woh gul hazaar pardon mein jaate hain raaegaan.

Rakhte hain jo aziz unhen apni jaan ki tarah,
Malte hain dast-e-yaas woh barg-e-khazan ki tarah.

Lekin jo phool khilte hain sahra mein be-shumaar,
Mauqoof kuchh rayaaz pe un ki nahin bahaar;
Dekho yeh qudarat-e-chaman aaraa-e-rozgaar,
Woh abar-o-baad-o-barf mein rahte hain barqaraar.

چکبست

ہوتا ہے اُن پہ فضل جو ربّ کریم کا
موجِ سموم بنتی ہے جھونکا نسیم کا
اپنی نگاہ ہے کرمِ کارساز پر
صحرا چمن بنے گا وہ ہے مہرباں اگر
جنگل ہو یا پہاڑ سفر ہو کہ ہو حضر
رہتا نہیں وہ حال سے بندے کے بے خبر
اس کا کرم شریک اگر ہے تو غم نہیں
دامانِ دشت دامنِ مادر سے کم نہیں

Chakbast

Shaded by the grace of God they swing and smile at ease,
For them the desert wind blows like the vernal breeze.

We should have faith in God whose grace divine,
Can turn a desert to a grove, rich with fruitful vines.
Out on travel, or at home, amid the peaks or pines,
God is there to help us, He knows our mind.

Assured of the grace of God we have nothing to fear,
Like the mother's lap protects then the desert drear.

Hota hai un pe fazal jo rabb-e-karim ka,
Mauj-e-samoom banti hai jhonka naseem ka.

Apni nigah hai karam-e-kaar saaz par,
Sahra chaman banega woh hai meharbaan agar.
Jungle ho ya pahaar, safar ho ke ho hazar,
Rahta nahin woh haal se bande ke be khabar.

Us ka karam sharik agar hai tau ghum nahin,
Daamaan-e-dasht daaman-e-maadar se kam nahin.

Tilok Chand Mehroom
(1885-1966)

TILOK CHAND MEHROOM
(1885-1966)

Tilok Chand Mehroom was born in 1885 in a village of Mianwali district, West Punjab (now Pakistan). After doing his B.A. he joined, in 1908, the Mission High School at Dera Ismail Khan as a teacher in English. In 1932 he became the headmaster of Cantonment Board Middle school, from where he retired in 1943. After the partition of India, Mehroom came to Delhi where he spent the rest of his life. He had to suffer a number of shocks in his personal life, the greatest being the death of his young wife, a bare five years after her marriage. The sorrow of this tragic event sank deep into his heart and coloured his mind and art. His poem, "Ashk-e-Hasrat", written when his wife was on her death-bed, shows the intensity of the poet's affection for his wife, and the sorrow of losing her. This poem is a part of the collection called *Toofan-e-Ghum*, which contains a series of sad poems such as, "Na-paidaar Rishte", and "Soz-e-Dil", all reflecting his disenchantment with the ephemerality of life and instability of relationships. His poetic name, "Mehroom", appropriately expresses the general sense of deprivation that pervades his mind and art. Even in the midst of spring, he can find a cause for grief.

Mehroom's first major publication, *Ganj-e-Maani*, contains a rich variety of 175 *nazms*, besides *rubaies*, *qasidas*, *sehras*, and *nohas* (elegies). A persistent note of sadness, and a pronounced didactic strain are the two chief characteristics of his work. He has been called the poet and painter of sorrow, "musawar-e-ghum". In one of his *rubaies* Akbar Allahabadi has thus summed up his poetic and human qualities:

ہے دادِ کا مستحق کلامِ محروم
لفظوں کا جمال اور معانی کا ہجوم
ہے ان کا سخن مفید، دانش آموز
ان کی لفظوں کی ہے بجا ملک میں دھوم

The poetry of Mehroom deserves full praise,
It contains deep thoughts in perfect word and phrase,
Beneficent is its content, instructive is its mode,
No wonder, he's admired all over the place.

Appropriateness of language, grace of style and nobility of thought are the chief marks of Mehroom's poetry.

The poem, "Nur Jahan ka Mazaar", is a fine specimen of Mehroom's descriptive skill and pensive frame of mind, seeking inspiration in neglected graves, mouldering mansions, twilight shades, and black bats, symbols all of death and decay. He has also written poems on religious topics, such as "Rawan ka Matam" and "Sita ki Faryaad", but in this domain he is surpassed by Chakbast whose "Scene from Ramayana" sounds more convincing and more powerful. His elegies on the death of Chakbast and Saroor again point to a sensitive heart, easily moved by the spectacle of death.

His famous works include: *Ganj-e-Maani, Rubaiyat-e-Mehroom, Karwan-e-Watan, Nairang-e-Maani, Shola Nawa,* and *Aks-e-Jameel.*

Mehroom died on 6th January, 1966. Jagan Nath Azad, the famous poet and scholar of Urdu, is his son and poetic heir.

تلوک چند محروم

نُورجہاں کا مزار

دن کو بھی یہاں شب کی سیاہی کا سماں ہے
کہتے ہیں یہ آرام گہہِ نورِ جہاں ہے
مدّت ہوئی، وہ شمعِ تہِ خاک نہاں ہے
اُٹھتا مگر اب تک سرِ مرقد سے دھواں ہے
جلووں سے عیاں جن کے ہُوا طُور کا عالم
تُربت پہ ہے اُن کی شبِ دیجور کا عالم
اے حسنِ جہاں سوز! کہاں ہیں وہ شرارے
کس باغ کے گُل ہو گئے؟ کس عرش کے تارے؟
کیا بن گئے اب کرمکِ شب تاب وہ سارے؟
ہر شام چمکتے ہیں جو راوی کے کنارے
یا ہو گئے وہ داغ جہانگیر کے دل کے؟
قابل ہی تو تھے عاشقِ دلگیر کے دل کے!
تُجھ سی مَلِکہ کے لئے یہ بارہ دری ہے
غالیچہ پہ سرِ فرش ہے کوئی، نہ دری ہے
کیا عالَمِ بے چارگی اے تاجوری ہے
دن کو یہیں بسرام، یہیں شب بسری ہے

238

Tilok Chand Mehroom
Nur Jahan ka Mazaar (Tomb of Nurjahan)

Here where even the day reflects the shades of night,
Here, they say, Nur-e-Jahan is resting day and night.

Long ago was buried in dust this taper dazzling bright,
Till to-day from her grave a smoke-streak doth rise.

Once did she glow and glimmer like the Sinai's heights,
To-day, alas, over her grave the dark night presides.

O world-warming beauty, where are your sparkling sparks?
Which garden they now illume, which sky deck with stars?

Have they all been changed to glow-worms glittering bright,
Hopping along the Ravi's bank all eve and night?

Or, are they hid in Jehangir's heart in the form of scars,
Indeed, they were fit to adorn such a passionate heart!

A queen like you, and confined within the many-gated walls,
Without a carpet or a mat your weary heart to prop!

What a state of helplessness, O royalty, armed with might,
Here must you lie reclined, be it day or night!

Din ko bhi yahan shab ki siaahi ka saman hai,
Kahte hain yeh aaraam gah-e-Nur-e-Jahan hai.

Muddat hui woh shama tah-e-khaak nihan hai,
Uthta magar ab tak sar-e-marqad se dhuan hai.

Jalwon se ayaan jin ke hua Tur ka aalam,
Turbat pe hai un ki shab-e-deejoor ka aalam.

Ai husn-e-jahan-soz kahan hain woh sharare,
Kis bagh ke gul ho gaya, kis arsh ke taare,

Kya ban gaye ab kirmak-e-shab taab woh saare?
Har shaam chamakte hain jo Ravi ke kinare?

Ya ho gaye woh dagh Jehangir ke dil ke,
Qabil hi tau the aashiq-e-dilgir ke dil ke!

Tujh si malika ke lieye yeh bara dari hai,
Ghalicha sar-e-farsh hai koi, na dari hai,

Kya aalam-e-bechargi ai, tajwari hai,
Din ko yahin bisram, yahin shab basri hai.

محروم

ایسی کسی بھی جوگن کی کٹیا نہیں ہوتی
ہوتی ہو، مگر یوں سرِ صحرا نہیں ہوتی
تعویذِ لحد ہے زبر و زیر، یہ اندھیر!
یہ دورِ زمانہ کے الٹ پھیر، یہ اندھیر!
آنگن میں پڑے گرد کے ہیں ڈھیر، یہ اندھیر!
اے گردشِ ایام! یہ اندھیر، یہ اندھیر!
ماہِ فلکِ حُسن کو یہ برج بلا ہے
اے چرخ ترے حُسنِ نوازش کا گِلا ہے
حسرت ہے ٹپکتی در و دیوار سے کیا کیا!
ہوتا ہے اثر دل پہ اِن آثار سے کیا کیا!
نالے ہیں نکلتے دلِ افگار سے کیا کیا!
اٹھتے ہیں شرر آہِ شرر بار سے کیا کیا!
یہ عالمِ تنہائی یہ دریا کا کنارا
ہے تجھ سی حسینہ کے لئے ہُو کا نظارا
چوپائے جو گھبراتے ہیں گرمی سے تو اکثر
آرام لیا کرتے ہیں اس روضے میں اکثر

Mehroom

Better far than this place is a hermit's hut,
Even an ascetic doesn't live in such a desert dust.

Topsy-turvy lies, alas, the tablet of the grave,
Ah, the whirl-wheel of Time, ah, the quirks of Fate!

Heaps of dust fill the yard, what a sorry state!
Ah, the revolution of Time, and its fitful ways!

Is this the dome allotted to the beauty's brightest moon?
Is this the way, O heavens, to grant your generous boons?

The doors and walls breathe an air of longings unrealised,
How depressing are the thoughts roused by such a sight!

The wounded heart cannot help raising painful cries,
Burning sparks spring to sight as it sobs and sighs.

Oh, this desolate river bank, and loneliness supreme!
What a horrific sight for such a beauty queen!

Oft do the stray beasts when oppressed with heat,
Seek refuge beneath the dome of your burial seat.

Aisi kisi jogan ki bhi kutiya nahin hoti,
Hoti ho, magar yun sar-e-sahra nahin hoti.

Taawiz-e-lahd hai zer-o-zabar, yeh andher!
Yeh daur-e-zamana ke ulat pher, yeh andher!

Aangan mein pare gard ke hain dher, yeh andher!
Ai gardish-e-ayyam, yeh andher, yeh andher!

Maah-e-falak-e-husn ko yeh burj mila hai,
Ai charkh, tire husn-e-niwazish ka gila hai.

Hasrat hai tapakti dar-o-deewar se kya kya!
Hota hai asar dil pe in aasaar se kya kya!

Naale hain nikalte dil-e-afgaar se kya kya!
Uthte hain sharar aah-e-sharar baar se kya kya!

Yeh aalam-e-tanhaai, yeh dariya ka kinara,
Hai tujh si haseena ke lieye hoo ka nazzara.

Chaupaae jo ghabraate hain garmi se tau aksar,
Aaraam liya karte hain is rauze mein aksar.

محروم

اور شام کو بالائی سیہ خانوں سے شپّر
اڑ اڑ کے لگاتے ہیں درِ بام پہ چکّر
معمور ہے یوں محفلِ جانا نہ کسی کی
آباد رہے گورِ غریباں نہ کسی کا
آراستہ جن کے لئے گلزار و چمن تھے
جو نازکی میں داغِ دہ برگِ سمن تھے
جو گلرخ و گل پیرہن و غنچہ دہن تھے
شاداب گلِ تر سے کہیں جن کے بدن تھے
پژمردہ وہ گل دب کے ہوئے خاک کے نیچے
خوابیدہ ہیں خار و خس و خاشاک کے نیچے
رہنے کے لئے دیدۂ و دلِ جن کے مکاں تھے
جو پیکرِ ہستی کے لئے روحِ رواں تھے
محبوبِ دلِ خلق تھے، جاں بخشِ جہاں تھے
تھے یوسفِ ثانی، کہ مسیحائے زماں تھے
جو کچھ تھے، کبھی تھے، مگر اب کچھ بھی نہیں ہیں
ٹوٹے ہوئے پنجرے سے پڑے زیرِ زمیں ہیں

Mehroom

In the eve the black bats, denizens of the sky,
Flap their wings against these doors, along these roofs fly.

Someone's court of love remains thus imbued with life!
May this poor sovereign's grave always bustle alive!

Those for whom the vernal groves were specially trimmed and shaped,
Those who outdid the flowers in their delicate grace,

Bud-mouthed, blossom-breathing, flower-decked, and robed,
Richer than the rose itself whose bodies once did glow,

Now lie crushed and crumpled, beneath the dust interred,
Locked in eternal sleep, clad in weeds and burrs.

Those who once did lodge in the people's hearts,
Those who were the moving spirits of the world, alas!

Darlings of the folks at large, source of light and life,
Who were called Yousaf's rivals, ranked with Jesus Christ,

Whatsoever they might have been, all is come to naught,
A handful of broken bones now mark the spot.

Aur shaam ko baalaai sayaah khanon se shappar,
Ur ur ke lagate hain dar-o-baam pe chakkar.

Maamoor hai yun mehfil-e-janana kisi ki,
Aabad rahe gor-e-gharibana kisi ki!

Aaraasta jin ke lieye gulzar-o-chaman the,
Jo naazuki mein dagh dah-e-barg-e-saman the,

Jo gulrukho-o-gul-parahan-o-ghuncha dahan the,
Shadab gul-e-tar se kahin jin ke badan the,

Pazhmurda woh gul dab ke hue khak ke neeche,
Khwabeeda hain khar-o-khas-o-khashak ke neeche!

Rahne ke lieye deeda-o-dil jin ke makan the,
Jo paikar-e-hasti ke lieye rooh-e-rawan the,

Mehboob-e-dil-e-khalaq the, jaan bakhsh-e-jahan the,
The yousaf-e-saani, ke masiha-e-zaman the,

Jo kuchh the kabhi the, magar ab kuchh bhi nahin hain,
Tute hue pinjar se pare zer-e-zamin hain.

محروم

دُنیا کا یہ انجام ہے دیکھ اے دلِ ناداں!
ہاں بھول نہ جائے تجھے یہ مدفنِ ویراں
باقی ہیں نہ وُہ باغ، نہ وُہ قصر نہ ایواں
آرام کے اسباب نہ وُہ عیش کے ساماں
ٹوٹا ہوا اِک ساحلِ راوی پہ مکاں ہے
دن کو بھی جہاں شب کی سیاہی کا سماں ہے

Mehroom

This is the end of mortal world, mark, O silly heart,
Let the barren tomb unkempt remind you of your lot!

Palaces, courts, gardens—nothing is now in sight,
Modes of comfort, means of luxury, all have taken flight.

This is all that's left—a mouldering house on Ravi's side,
Where even during the day the shades of night preside!

Duniya ka yeh anjaam hai, dekh ai dil-e-nadaan,
Haan bhul na jaae tujhe yeh madfan-e-weeraan,

Baaqi hain na woh bagh, na woh qasar, na woh aiwaan,
Aaraam ke asbaab, na woh aish ke saamaan,

Tuta hua ik saahil-e-Ravi pe makan hai,
Din ko bhi jahan shab ki siaahi ka samaan hai.

Shabir Hassan Josh Malihabadi
(1898-1982)

SHABIR HASSAN JOSH MALIHABADI
(1898-1982)

Josh Malihabadi was a poet, patriot, and a public figure whose poetry enthused the hearts of millions of people in the pre-Independence days. A friend of the poor and the dispossessed, and a tireless crusader for freedom, Josh exploited to the full the resources of his poetic genius for spreading the message of social and political revolution. In one of his famous couplets he has thus defined his mission as a poet:

کام ہے میرا تغیّر نام ہے میرا شباب
میرا نعرہ انقلاب و انقلاب و انقلاب

I'm youth embodied, revolution is my aim,
"Change, change, and change," is my sole refrain.

Josh has written *ghazals*, *rubaies*, and *nazms*—all in abundance—but he is essentially a poet of the *nazm*, and a specialist of the *rubai*. He had a facile pen and could compose fairly long poems just at one sitting. Some of his famous poems such as, "Kissan", "Baghawat", "Bhooka Hindustan", "Husn aur Mazdoori", "Zawaal-o-Jahanbani", "Zaeefa", etc., are fine specimens of spirited and inspiring verse, written with compassion and conviction, and a matching artistic competence. His *ghazals* are charged with the same passion and power which characterise his *nazms*. A master craftsman and a wizard of words, Josh overwhelms his readers with the sheer force of linguistic opulence and emotional power. He may not be a profound thinker, but he is a firebrand poet capable of mesmerising his audience with his verbal fusillades and poetic eloquence. Both in his ready command of word and rhyme, and in his passionate fight against cant and oppression, Josh reminds us of Lord Byron, the great romantic radical and rebel. In addition, Josh possesses a remarkable gift for describing natural scenes with precision and loving artistry.

Josh was born in Lucknow in December 1898. He inherited his poetic taste from his forbears, for his father, grandfather, and his great grandfather, all were poets of acknowledged merit. He received his schooling at Lucknow, Agra, and Aligarh, and studied up to Senior Cambridge. Due to the death of his father, Bashir Ahmed Khan, in 1916, Josh was debarred from the benefit of college education. He was greatly influenced by Dr Rabindranath Tagore, whom he met during his sojourn at Calcutta in 1921. He then went to Hyderabad and worked for a few years in Osmania University, supervising translation work. However, he spent the best part of his life in Delhi, where he stayed from 1934 till after Independence, with a short stint at Poona and Bombay, where he wrote songs and lyrics for the cinema. He was appointed editor of the Urdu magazine, *Aajkal*, and was honoured with Padma Bhushan by the government of India. Some of his famous publications include: *Shola-o-Shabnam, Harf-o-Hikayat, Janoon-o-Hikmat, Aayaat-o-Naghmaat,* and *Sumbal-o-Salaasal.*

In 1956, Josh migrated to Pakistan, where, in the fag-end of his life he felt sadly alone and alienated. Pakistanis called him a "kafir," while Indians considered him a traitor to the country of his birth. Josh died on 22nd February, 1982.

The three poems selected for this book testify to the poet's artistic competence and radical fervour. Written in the context of the Indian struggle for independence, "Bahgawat" (Rebellion) describes, with realistic detail, the genesis, growth, and the eventual upsurge of rebellion, which, beginning in war and bloodshed, ushers in, ultimately, an era of peace and justice. "Kissan", written in a gentler vein to match with the quiet tenor of its subject, draws our attention to the bane of social injustice that compels the farmer, a procurer of food for all, to live in poverty and hunger. And, in a somewhat similar vein, but with a sensitive appreciation of feminine beauty, "Husn and Mazdoori" shows the plight of young, delicate girls, hard-pressed by poverty to toil and drudge in trying conditions.

جوش ملیح آبادی
بغاوت

ہاں بغاوت! آگ بجلی، موت آندھی میرا نام
میرے گرد و پیش اجل، میری بغلو میں قتلِ عام
زرد ہو جاتا ہے میرے سامنے رودے حیات
کانپ اٹھتی ہے مری چین جبیں سے کائنات
جنگ کی میداں میں میری سیف کی اللہ ری ضو
خاک بن جاتی ہے بجلی برف دے اٹھتی ہے لو
ذکر ہوتا ہے مرا پر ہول پیکاروں کے ساتھ
ذہن میں آتی ہوں تلواروں کی جھنکاروں کے ساتھ
اللہ اللہ کروٹیں میرے دلِ آزاد کی
جن سے گر جاتی ہیں ڈاٹیں قصرِ استبداد کی
میری اک جنبش سے ہوتا ہے جہاں زیر و زبر
میری مستابی ثریا کا جھکا دیتی ہے سر
ایک چنگاری مری جنّت کو کرتی ہے تباہ
مانگتا رہتا ہے میری آگ سے دوزخ پناہ
الحذر! میری کڑک کا زور ہنگامِ مصاف
صاف پڑ جاتا ہے ایوانِ حکومت میں شگاف

Shabir Hassan Josh Malihabadi
Baghawat (Rebellion)

Yeah, Rebellion! fire, tempest, thunder, ruin are my names?
Death is my accompanist, massacre is my game!

Life turns pale with fear seeing me approach,
Universe starts trembling as I ruffle my brows;

My God! in the battlefield, so gleams my sword,
Lightning turns to dust and ash, ice emits a glow.

My name is synonymous with blood-curdling wars,
My thought brings to mind clanging swords and spars.

Oh, the twists and turns of my restless heart!
Arches of the palaces shrink and fall apart!

A single move on my part unsettles the world;
'Fore my might the highest star tumbles down to earth.

A single spark of my flame can burn the Paradise,
Even hell shrinks with fear from my fiery sight.

What a terrible force is hidden in my battle cry!
It can cause in citadels cracks and chasms wide.

Haan baghawat! aag, bijli, maut, aandhi mera naam,
Mere gird-o-pesh ajal, meri jilau mein qatal-e-aam!

Zard ho jaata hai mere saamne roo-e-hayaat,
Kaanp uthti hai miri cheen-e-jabeen se kainaat.

Jang ke maidan mein meri saif ki Allah ri zau,
Khak ban jaati hai bijli, baraf de uthti hai lau.

Zikar hota hai mira pur haul paikaaron ke saath,
Zehan mein aati hun talwaron ki jhankaron ke saath.

Allah Allah, karwaten mere dil-e-aazad ki,
Jin se gir jaati hain daaten qasar-e-istabdad ki.

Meri ik jumbish se hota hai jahan zer-o-zabar,
Meri sartaabi surayya ka jhuka deti hai sar.

Ek chingari miri jannat ko karti hai tabah,
Maangta rahta hai meri aag se dozakh panah!

Alhazar! meri karak ka zor hangam-e-masaaf,
Saaf par jaata hai aiwaan-e-hakoomat mein shigaaf.

جوش ملیح آبادی

اللہ اللہ بزمِ ہستی میں مری گل باریاں
ٹکڑے ٹکڑے دست و بازو ریزہ ریزہ استخواں
الاماں و الحذر۔۔۔ میری کڑک، میرا جلال!
خون، سفاکی، گرج، طوفان، بربادی، قتال!
برچھیاں، بھالے، کمانیں، تیر، تلواریں، کٹار
بیرقیں، پرچم، علم، گھوڑے، پیادے، شہسوار
آندھیوں سے میری اڑ جاتا ہے دنیا کا نظام
رحم کا احساس ہے میری شریعت میں حرام
موت ہے خوراکِ میری، موت پر جیتی ہوں میں
سیر ہو کر گوشت کھاتی ہوں، لہو پیتی ہوں میں
پیاس سے باہر نکل پڑتی ہے جب میری زباں
بہنے لگتی ہیں سرِ میدان لہو کی ندّیاں
جنگ کی صورت سے گو ہنگامہ کرتی ہوں شروع
امن کی صبحیں مرے خنجر سے ہوتی ہیں طلوع
میرا مولد مفلسی کا دل ہے، عسرت کا دماغ
میری پیدائش کے حجرے میں نہیں جلتا چراغ

252

Josh Malihabadi

How I fire sparkling shots on the earth beneath,
Grinding human bones to dust, hacking hands and feet!

Mind-boggling is the might of my dreadful roar,
Murder, ruin, loud alarms, streets filled with gore!

Daggers, swords and bayonets, bows and scimitars,
Barracks, flags, standards, men on foot and horse!

My gale can uproot systems deep-entrenched,
Ruth and pity are unknown to my temperament.

Death is my staple diet, death sustains my breath,
I drink from bowls of blood, feed on chunks of flesh.

When my tongue hangs out with excessive thirst,
On battle front begin to flow streams of blood unchecked.

Though my revolution starts on a note of war,
From my sword itself is born the lasting peace at last.

The poor people's head and heart give me birth and life,
My cell has never seen a lighted lamp at night.

Allah, Allah, bazm-e-hasti mein miri gulbaarian,
Tukre tukre dast-o-baazoo, reza reza ustakhwan;

Alamaan-o-alhazar! meri karak, mera jalal!
Khoon, suffaki, garaj, toofan, barbadi, qataal!

Barchhian, bhale, kamanen, teer, talwaren, katar,
Bairacken, parcham, alam, ghore, payade, shahsawar.

Aandhion se meri ur jaata hai duniya ka nizam,
Raham ka ahsaas hai meri shariat mein haram,

Maut hai khoraak meri, maut par jeeti hun main,
Ser ho kar gosht khati hun, lahu peeti hun main.

Payaas se bahar nikal parti hai jab meri zaban,
Bahne lagti hain sar-e-maidan lahu ki naddian.

Jang ki soorat se go hangama karti hun shuroo,
Aman ki subhen mire khanjar se hoti hain taloo.

Mera maulid muflisi ka dil hai, usrat ka dimagh,
Meri paidaaish ke hujre mein nahin jalta chiragh.

جوشؔ ملیح آبادی

مجھ کو بچپن کے زمانے ہی سے ہر صبح ومسا
پیٹ کی ماری ہوئی مخلوق دیتی ہے غذا
ختم ہو جاتا ہے جب اہلِ جہاں کا غلغلہ
رات کے آغوش میں کھلتا ہے میرا مدرسہ
اوّل اوّل جان دینے کا سبق لیتی ہوں میں
آخر آخر جان لینے کا سبق لیتی ہوں میں
برق کے سانچے میں ڈھل جاتی ہیں گفتاریں مری
میان سے باہر ابل پڑتی ہیں تلواریں مری
موت بن کر زندگی کے سر پہ چھا جاتی ہوں میں
سب سے پہلے بڑھ کے غدّاروں کو کھا جاتی ہوں میں
سلطنت کی سمت پھر بڑھتی ہوں بل کھاتی ہوئی
قید اور قانون کو ذلت سے ٹھکراتی ہوئی
باندھتی ہوں شہر یاروں کے سر پہ یہ کہہ کر کفن!
تم ہو اشجع ، ناوک افگن، صف شکن، شمشیر زن
اے جوانمردو! یہ ذلت کس لئے سہتے ہو تم؟
مرد ہو کر ٹھوکروں کی زد پہ کیوں رہتے ہو تم؟

Josh Malihabadi

Every morn and every eve since my life began,
Famished folks have fed me with the orts at hand.

When at the end of day the noise of life subsides,
My school begins to work in the lap of night.

First of all I'm taught, how to dare and die,
In the end I'm asked to kill the foe at sight.

My words are shaped and rolled in the lightning's mould,
Leaping out from their sheathes, shine forth my swords.

Hovering in the form of death, threatening human life,
First of all I pounce on traiters, kill them in a trice.

Then I surge towards the government like an angry wave,
Spurning every law and limit, uprooting the state.

I dress my men in coffins, inspire them with rhetoric bold;
Brave you are, unerring shots, phalanx-breakers, men of sword.

Why should you, O valiant men, tolerate disgrace?
Why bear rebuffs and kicks, why feel debased?

Mujhko bachpan ke zamaane hi se har subah-o-masa,
Pet ki maari hui makhlooq deti hai ghiza.

Khatam ho jaata hai jab ahl-e-jahan ka ghulghala,
Raat ki aaghosh mein khulta hai mera madrasa.

Awwal awwal jaan dene ka sabaq leti hun main,
Aakhir aakhir jaan lene ka sabaq leti hun main.

Barq ke saanche mein dhal jaati hain guftaaren miri,
Miaan se baahar ubal parti hain talwaaren miri.

Maut ban kar zindagi ke sar pe chha jaati hun main,
Sab se pahle barh ke ghaddaaron ko kha jaati hun main.

Saltanat ki simat phir bharti hun bal khati hui,
Qaid aur qaanoon ko zillat se thukrati hui.

Baandhti hun shahrion ke sar pe yeh kah kar kafan;
Tum ho ashja, nawak-afghan, saf-shikan, shamshir-zan.

Ai, jawanmardo, yeh zillat kis lieye sahte ho tum,
Mard ho kar thokron ki zad pe kyon rahte ho tum?

جوشؔ ملیح آبادی

کپکپاتی ہے زمیں اٹھتا ہے ہلکا سا غبار
دوڑنے لگتے ہیں مرکب بڑھنے لگتے ہیں سوار
طبل کی دُوں دُوں سے جل اٹھتے ہیں آنکھوں میں چراغ
جھنجھناتے ہیں جلاجل سنسناتے ہیں دماغ
کھلنے لگتا ہے مگر جس وقت پرچمِ جنگ کا!
پہلے بڑھ کر میں حکومت کو یہ دیتی ہوں صدا
اے جفا پرور امارت! دیکھ نا دار و نسے بھاگ
بھاگ، دیوانوں کی خوں آشام تلوار و نسے بھاگ
خلق ہے بیتاب تیرا منہ جھلسنے کے لئے!
تیرے سونے پر ہے اب لوہا برسنے کے لئے
تیرا مطبخ مفلسوں کی بھوک کھا جانے کو ہے
تیرے زر کی سرخیوں میں آگ لگ جانے کو ہے
حریّت کی تند لہروں میں ٹھہر سکتا ہے کون؟
جذبۂ خلقِ خدا کو فتح کر سکتا ہے کون؟
اب بھی آنکھیں کھول اے جنِّ خودی، دیو ریا!
جذبۂ خلقِ خدا ہے اصل میں عزمِ خدا

256

Josh Malihabadi

A mild storm begins to brew, earth begins to quake,
Horses begin to gallop, riders march apace.

Eyes begin to glare and glow with the beat of drums,
The sounding bands leave the brains utterly dazed and numb.

But before the battle starts, and the flag unfurls,
I warn the rulers in the following words:

"O, ye Powers, tyranny-based, beware the poor man's lash,
Beware the madman's fury, the sword blood-splashed!"

The masses are all intent to scorch and singe your face,
Your gold will have to face the anger of the iron mace.

Starving men have set their eyes on your sumptuous stores,
A conflagration will consume all your glittering gold.

Who can withstand the fury of Freedom's angry waves,
Who can check the human heart, let loose in spate?

High time you woke, selfish jinn, spirit of fraud!
The will of people is, in fact, the very will of God.

Kapkapati hai zameen, uthta hai halka sa ghubaar,
Daurne lagte hain murakkab, barhne lagte hain sawaar.

Tabal ki doon doon se jal uthte hain aankhon mein chiragh,
Jhunjhunaate hain jalajal, sansanaate hain dimagh.

Khulne lagta hai magar jis waqt parcham jang ka,
Pehle barh kar main hakoomat ko yeh deti hun sada:

Ai jafa parwar amarat! dekh naadaaron se bhaag,
Bhaag, deewaanon ki khoon-aasham talwaaron se bhaag!

Khalq hai betaab tera munh jhulasne ke lieye,
Tere sone par hai ab loha barasne ke lieye.

Tera matbakh muflison ki bhook kha jaane ko hai,
Tere zar ki surkhion mein aag lag jaane ko hai.

Hurriat ki tund lahron mein thahr sakta hai kaun?
Jazba-e-khalq-e-Khuda ko fatah kar sakta hai kaun?

Ab bhi aankhen khol, ai jinn-e-khudi, dev-e-raya,
Jazbe-e-khalq-e-Khuda hai, asal mein azm-e-Khuda.

جوش ملیح آبادی

راہ سے اپنی مشیّت کو ہٹا سکتا ہے کون؟
عظیم خلّاقِ جہاں کا سر جھکا سکتا ہے کون؟
گو نبھے لگتی ہیں جب میری صدائیں مثلِ صور
سر اٹھا کر شکر اتا ہے حکومت کا غرور
مفتیکہ، اور قطرۂ شبنم کا، انگاروں کے ساتھ
پنکھڑی، اور ناز سے پیش آئے تلواروں کے ساتھ
عقل کا دستِ سُبک، رخشِ جنوں کی باگ پر
قہقہہ خس کا کڑکتی بجلیوں کی آگ پر
ایک مٹی کے دیئے کا طنز اور کعبے کا طاق
نرم و نازک آبگینہ اور پتھر سے مذاق
اس تمسخر سے مرے سینے میں لگ جاتی ہے آگ
قلعۂ شاہی کی جانب موڑ دیتی ہوں میں باگ
پھر تو جاتا ہے جدھر میرا جنونِ تند خو!
پُشت پر ہوتی ہیں لاشیں، ہڈیاں، ڈھانچے، لہو
میرے گرد و پیش کی ہنگامہ خیزی الاماں
شور، غوغا، غلغلہ، فریاد، واویلا، فغاں

Josh Malihabadi

Who can ever bypass the writ of fate divine?
Who can bend the neck of mighty humankind?

When my voice reverberates like a bellowing horn,
The empire lifts its head in pride, smiles away in scorn.

How dare a drop of dew deride the burning coals?
How dare a flower-petal strut before the sword?

Can the delicate hand of reason control the horse berserk?
How dare a mere straw with thunderflash flirt?

Can a petty earthen lamp Kaaba's sacred flame bemock?
Can a fickle water bubble make fun of solid rocks?

Such a rude sarcasm sets my heart ablaze,
Straight on the royal fort then I fix my gaze.

Thereafter, wherever goes my frenzy uncontrolled,
Blood, bones and corpses, behind me trail and roll.

All around me you'll find a terrifying furore,
Shouts, wails, cries for help, loud alarm, uproar.

Raah se apni mashiat ko hata sakta hai kaun?
Azm-e-khallaq-e-jahan ka sar jhuka sakta hai kaun?

Goonjne lagti hain jab meri sadaaen masl-e-soor,
Sar utha kar muskarata hai hakoomat ka gharoor.

Mazhika, aur qatra-e-shabnam ka angaaron ke saath!
Pankhari, aur naaz se pesh aae talwaaron ke saath!

Aqal ka dast-e-subak, rakhsh-e-janoon ki bag par,
Qahqaha khas ka karakti bijlion ki aag par!

Ek mitti ke dieye ka tanaz, aur kaabe ka taaq,
Narm-o-naazuk aabgeena, aur paththar se mazaaq!

Is tamaskhar se mere seene mein lag jaati hai aag,
Qila-e-shahi ki jaanib mor deti hun main baag.

Phir tau jaata hai jidhar mera janoon-e-tund-khoo,
Pusht par hoti hain laashen, haddian, dhaanche, lahu.

Mere gird-o-pesh ki hangama khezi alaaman,
Shor, ghaugha, ghulghula, faryaad, wavela, fughan.

جوشؔ ملیح آبادی

اللہ اللہ میرے دہشت ناک خونی ولولے
آندھیاں، طوفان، تلاطم، سیل، صرصر، زلزلے
ابتری، وحشت، ترلزل، طنطنہ، دہشت، فساد
دبدبے، گرمی، کشاکش، دغدغے، ہلچل، جہاد
کنگرے ایوانِ شاہی کے جھکا دیتی ہوں میں
جبروِ استبداد کی چولیس ہلا دیتی ہوں میں
دندناتی گنبدِ زرّیں میں گھس جاتی ہوں میں
چاٹ کر سونے کا پانی آگ برساتی ہوں میں
الاماں! میرا جنوں پر ورِ تمسخّر، الاماں!!
آ سنا دوں میں تجھے دو حرف میں یہ داستاں
جب ازل میں سجدۂ آدمؑ کا اٹھا تھا سوال
ہاں اسی ہلچل کے موقع پر کہ تھا وقتِ جلال
خود خدائے برتر و قہار سے افلاک پر
کی تھی میں نے گفتگو آنکھوں میں آنکھیں ڈال کر
رعبِ سلطانی سے یہ چہرہ اتر سکتا نہیں
جو خدائی سے لڑے، شاہی سے ڈر سکتا نہیں

Josh Malihabadi

Ah, God! my dreadful deeds, my blood-curdling tales,
Storms, tempests, whirlwinds, floods, quakes and gales!

Mayhem, madness, threat and ruin, clash and carnage,
Flurry, flutter, struggle, alarm, and gruesome crusades!

I pull down the battlements of the palace heights,
Shake and break the very being of oppressive might.

Roaring loud and wild, I invade the royal dome,
Licking liquid gold, I spit out fire-stones.

Ah God! my mad defiance, ruthless all the way!
Let me put in nutshell all I have to say.

When in the beginning of Time, Adam defied the fiat of God,
When the supernal might of heaven began to reel under the shock;

Before the God of terrible might in the Elysian hall,
Boldly had I stood my ground, held my head aloft.

Kingly might cannot dilute the colour of my face,
He who has fought with God, is not afraid of potentates.

Allah, Allah, mere dahshat naak khooni walwale,
Aandhian, toofan, talatum, sail, sar sar, zalzale.

Abtari, wahshat, tazalzal, tantana, dahshat, fasaad,
Dabdabe, garmi, kashakash, daghdaghe, halchal, jahad;

Kungre aiwaan-e-shahi ke jhuka deti hun main,
Jabr-o-istabdad ki choolen hila deti hun main,.

Dandanati gumbad-e-zarrin mein ghus juati hun main,
Chaat kaar sone ka paani aag barsati hun main.

Alaaman! mera janoon parwar tamurrad, alaaman!
Aa suna doon main tujhe do harf mein yeh daastaan,

Jab azal mein sijda-e-Adam ka utha tha sawaal,
Haan usi halchal ke mauqe par ke tha waqt-e-jalaal;

Khud khuda-e-bar tar-o-qahhaar se iflaak par,
Ki thi main ne gufatgoo, aankhon mein aankhen dal kar.

Ruab-e-sultani se yeh chehra utar sakta nahin,
Jo khudai se lare, shahi se dar sakta nahin.

Abridged

جوش ملیح آبادی
کسان

جھٹپٹے کا نرم رو دریا، شفق کا اضطراب
کھیتیاں، میدان، خاموشی، غروبِ آفتاب
دشت کے کام و دہن کو، دن کی تلنی سے فراغ
دور، دریا کے کنارے، دھند لے دھندلے سے چراغ
زیرِ لب، ارض و سما میں، باہمی گفت و شنود
مشعلِ گردوں کے بجھ جانے سے اک ہلکا سا دود
وسعتیں میدان کی، سورج کے چھپ جانے سے تنگ
سبزۂ افسردہ پر، خوابِ آفریں ہلکا سا رنگ
خامشی اور خامشی میں سنسناہٹ کی صدا
شام کی خنکی سے گویا دن کی گرمی کا گلا!
اپنے دامن کو برابر قطع سا کرتا ہوا
تیرگی میں کھیتیوں کے دربیاں کا فاصلا!
خار و خس پر ایک درد انگیز افسانے کی شان
بامِ گردوں پر کسی کے روٹھ کر جانے کی شان
دوب کی خوشبو میں شبنم کی نمی سے اک سرور
چرخ پر بادل، زمیں پر تتلیاں، سر پر طیور

262

Josh Malihabadi
Kissan (The Farmer)

In the evening, twilight-tinged, the river gently flows,
Fields and plains, silence-steeped, beneath the sunset glow.

Mouth and palate of the forest feel relieved of day-long heat,
Dimly twinkle rows of lights in the distant mead.

Earth and sky commune together in whispers soft and sweet,
The lamp of heaven, blowing out, leaves behind a smoke-streak.

The sunset makes the level lands suddenly shrink in size,
The withered verdure lies clothed under the dreamy light.

The all-pervasive silence, broken by the rustling leaves,
Makes one feel, the heat of day is grumbling to the cool of eve.

Beneath the spell of deepening dark, the space betwixt the fields
Seems to gather up its hem, and roll up its sleeves.

The thorns and weeds seem to tell a withered, woeful tale,
The sky presents the scene of someone parting in an angry way.

Sweet is the smell of grass, that dew-drunk doth lie,
Clouds in sky, birds above, on the earth the butterflies.

Jhutpate ka narm-rau dariya, shafaq ka izteraab,
Khetian, maidan, khamoshi, gharub-e-aaftaab.

Dasht ke kaam-o-dahan ko din ki talkhi se faragh,
Door dariya ke kinare dhundle dhundle se chiragh;

Zer-e-lab, arz-o-sama mein, baahmi guft-o-shunood,
Mashal-e-gardun ke bujh jaane se ik halka sa dood;

Wus-aten maidan ki suraj ke chhip jaane se tang,
Sabza-e-afsurda par, khwab-aafreen halka sa rang.

Khamshi aur khamshi mein sansanahat ki sada,
Sham ki khunki se goya din ki garmi ka gila!

Apne daman ko barabar qata sa karta hua,
Teeragi mein khetion ke darmian ka fasla!

Khar-o-khas par ek dard-angez afsane ki shaan,
Baam-e-gardun par kisi ke rooth kar jaane ki shaan.

Doob ki khushboo mein shabnam ki nami se ik saroor,
Charkh par badal, zamin par titlian, sar par tayyoor.

جوش ملیح آبادی

پارہ پارہ ابر، سرخی، سرخیوں میں کچھ دھواں
بھولی بھٹکی سی زمیں، کھویا ہوا سا آسماں
پتّیاں مخمور، کلیاں آنکھ جھپکاتی ہوئی
نرم جاں پودوں کو گویا نیند سی آتی ہوئی
یہ سماں، اور اک قوی انسان یعنی کا شٹکار
ارتقا کا پیشوا، تہذیب کا پروردگار
طفلِ باراں، تاجدارِ خاک، امیرِ بوستاں
ماہرِ آئینِ قدرت، ناظمِ بزمِ جہاں
ناظرِ گل، پاسبانِ رنگ و بو، گلشن پناہ
ناز پرور لہلہاتی کھیتیوں کا بادشاہ
وارثِ اسرارِ فطرت، فاتحِ امید و بیم!
محرمِ آثارِ باراں، واقفِ طبعِ نسیم!
صبح کا فرزند، خورشیدِ زر افشاں کا علم
محنتِ پیہم کا "پیماں"، سخت کوشی کی قسم
جلوۂ قدرت کا شاہد، حسنِ فطرت کا گواہ
ماہ کا دل، مہرِ عالم تاب کا نورِ نگاہ

Josh Malihabadi

Crimson glow, smoke-streaked, clouds in broken bits,
The land drunk and drowsy, the sky shorn of wits.
Intoxicated petals, buds winking their eyes,
Tender plants, sleep-infected, yawn beneath the skies.
Such an hour brings to fore a ploughman, stout, erect,
Harbinger of progress, civilisation's architect!
The child of rain, ruler of earth, controller of the gardens wide,
Master of the laws of nature, manager of terrestrial sights!
Lover of flowers, garden's saviour, watchmen of the hue and scent,
Emperor of the waving crops, reared with tireless diligence.
Heir of the nature's lore, nurtured by hope and fear,
Reader of the signs of rain, of the moods of breeze aware.
Standard-bearer of the sun, darling of the morning rays,
A promise of eternal labour, committed to the harder ways.
A witness of the nature's charms, observer of her lovely sights,
Heart and soul of the moon, apple of the sun's eye.

Para para abr, surkhi, surkhion mein kuchh dhuan,
Bhooli bhatki si zamin, khoya hua sa aasmaan;

Pattian makhmoor, kalian aankh jhapkati hui,
Narm-jaan paudon ko goya neend si aati hui.

Yeh saman aur ik qawi insaan, yaani kaashtkaar,
Irtaqa ka peshwa, tehzib ka parwurdigaar,

Tifal-e-baraan, taajdar-e-khak, amir-e-bostaan,
Maahir-e-aaeen-e-qudrat, naazim-e-bazm-e-jahan.

Naazir-e-gul, paasbaan-e-rang-o-boo, gulshan panaah,
Naaz parwar lahlahati khetion ka badshah.

Waaris-e-asraar-e-fitrat, fatah-e-umeed-o-beem,
Mahram-e-aasaar-e-baaran, waaqif-e-taba-e-naseem!

Subah ka farzand, khurshid-e-zar-afshan ka alam,
Mehanat-e-paiham ka paiman, sakht-koshi ki qasam!

Jalwa-e-qudrat ka shahid, husn-e-fitrat ka gawah,
Maah ka dil, mehr-e-aalam taab ka noor-e-nigah!

جوشؔ ملیح آبادی

خونِ حبس کا دوڑتا ہے نبض استقلال میں
لوچ بھر دیتا ہے جوشِ شہزادیوں کی چال میں
جس کے ماتھے کے پسینے سے پئے عزّ و وقار
کرتی ہے دریوزۂ تابشِ کلاہِ تاجدار
جس کے بازو کی صلابت پر نزاکت کا مدار
جس کے کَس بل پر اکڑتا ہے غرورِ شہریار
ٹوکرا سر پر، بغل میں پھاوڑا، تیوری پہ بل
سامنے بیلوں کی جوڑی، دوش پر مضبوط ہل
کون ہل؟ ظلمت شکن قندیلِ بزمِ آب و گل
قصرِ گلشن کا دریچہ، سینۂ گیتی کا دل
دھار پر جس کی چمن پرور شگوفوں کا نظام
شامِ زیرِ ارض کو صبحِ درخشاں کا پیام
جس کے چھو جاتے ہی مثلِ نازنینِ مہ جبیں!
کروٹوں پر کروٹیں لیتی ہے لیلائے زمیں
جس کی تابش میں درخشانی ہلالِ عید کی!
خاک کے مایوس مطلع پر کرن امید کی!

Josh Malihabadi

His blood courses through the Determination's veins,
He lends litheness to the gait of royal dames.

To him, for the gift of gloss, the crowns supplicate,
To him, for the dole of honour, approach the potentates.

To his stout, iron hands, delicate beauty owes its growth,
His erect, unbending head preserves the regal pomp and show.

A shovel in hand, basket on head, furrows on his brow,
A pair of oxen tread in front, his shoulders carry a plough.

A plough? no, a candle bright that lifts the pall of gloom from earth,
A window on the gardens royal, a heart within the world's breast.

On whose sharp edge depends the beauty of the blooms and buds,
A message of approaching dawn to the darkening eve on earth;

At whose touch the beloved earth begins to turn and twist,
Like a dainty moon-like maid, tickled by her lover's kiss;

The plough conceals within its sheen the radiance of the moon of Eid,
Which brings a ray of hope for the famished, withering fields.

Khoon jiska daurta hai nabz-e-istaqlal mein,
Loch bhar deta hai jo shahzadion ki chaal mein.

Jis ke manthe ke paseene se pa-e-izz-o-waqaar,
Karti hai daryooza taabish kullah-e-tajdar.

Jis ke baazoo ki salabat par nazakat ka madaar,
Jis ke kas bal par akarta hai gharoor-e-shahr yaar.

Tokra sar par, baghal mein phaora, teori pe bal,
Saamne bailon ki jori, dosh par mazboot hal.

Kaun hal? Zulmat shikan qandeel-e-bazm-e-aab-o-gil,
Qasr-e-gulshan ka daricha, seena-e-geeti ka dil.

Dhaar par jiski chaman parwar shagoofon ka nizam,
Sham-e-zer-e-arz ko subah-e-darakhshan ka payaam.

Jis ke chhoo jate hi masl-e-naazneen-e-mah jabeen,
Karwaton par karwaten leti hai laila-e-zameen;

Jiski taabish mein darakhshani halal-e-Eid ki,
Khak ke maayoos matla par kiran umeed ki.

جوش ملیح آبادی

اس سیاسی رتھ کے پہیّوں پر جمائے ہے نظر
جس میں آجاتی ہے تیزی کھیتیوں کو روند کر
اپنی دولت کو جگر پر تیرِ غم کھاتے ہوئے
دیکھتا ہے ملکِ دشمن کی طرف جاتے ہوئے
قطع ہوتی ہی نہیں تاریکیٔ حرماں سے راہ
فاقہ کش بچوں کے دہند لے آنسوؤں پر ہے نگاہ
پھر رہا ہے خوں چکاں آنکھوں کے نیچے بار بار
گھر کی نا امید دیوی کا شباب سوگوار
سوچتا جاتا ہے کن آنکھوں سے دیکھا جائیگا
بے ردا بیوی کا سر، بچوں کا منہ اترا ہوا
سیم و زر، نان و نمک، آب و غذا کچھ بھی نہیں
گھر میں اک خاموشی ماتم کے سوا کچھ بھی نہیں
ایک دل، اور یہ ہجومِ سوگواری! ہائے ہائے
یہ ستم، اے سنگدل سرمایہ داری ہائے ہائے

Josh Malihabadi

His mind is riveted on the wheels of that political cart,
Which gains in speed and strength as it mows the crops.

Bearing cruel, painful darts on his tender breast,
He sees the national wealth slipping into the enemy's chest.

He finds it hard to move by deep depression weighed,
Before his eyes vaguely swims his children's famished face.

Before his blood-dripping eyes, persistently do roam,
The weary looks and blighted youth of the queen of home.

This is what he cogitates: "How can I brook,
To see my wife's bare head, my children's hungry look?"

Gold or silver, bread or salt, food or fare—nothing is there,
But for the mournful gloom, the house is stark still and bare.

One poor heart, and a flood of sorrows, alas, alas, O God!
How despotic is your reign, O Capitalism, alas!

Us sayaasi rath ke pathiyon par jamaae hai nazar,
Jis mein aa jaati hai tezi khetion ko raund kar.

Apni daulat ko jigar par teer-e-ghum khate hue,
Dekhta hai mulk-e-dushman ki taraf jaate hue.

Qata hoti hi nahin taariki-e-hirman se rah,
Faqa kash bachchon ke dhundle aansu-on par hai nigah.

Phir raha hai khoon-chukan aankhon ke neeche bar bar,
Ghar ki na umeed devi ka shabab-e-sogwar.

Sochta jaata hai kin aankhon se dekha jaaega,
Berida beewi ka sar, bachchon ka munh utra hua.

Seem-o-zar, nan-o-namak, aab-o-ghiza, kuchh bhi nahin,
Ghar mein ik khamosh matam ke siwa kuchh bhi nahin.

Ek dil, aur yeh hajum-e-sogawari, haae, haae!
Yeh sitam, ai sangdil sarmaya dari, haae, haae!

Abridged

جوش ملیح آبادی
حسن اور مزدوری

ایک دوشیزہ سٹرک پر دھوپ میں ہے بیقرار
چوڑیاں بجتی ہیں کنکر کوٹنے میں بار بار
چوڑیوں کے ساز میں یہ سوز ہے کیسا بھرا
آنکھ میں "آنسو" بنی جاتی ہے جس کی ہر صدا
گرد ہے رخسار پر، ہر قیص اڑی ہیں خاک میں
نازکی بل کھا رہی ہے دیدۂ غمناک میں
ہو رہا ہے جذب مہرِ خونچکاں کے روبرو
کنکروں کی نبض میں اٹھتی جوانی کا لہو
دھوپ میں لہرا رہی ہے کاکلِ عنبر سرشت
ہو رہا ہے کمسنی کا لوچ جزوِ سنگ و خشت
پی رہی ہیں سرخ کرنیں مہرِ آتش بار کی
نرگسی آنکھوں کا رس، مے چپی رخسار کی
غم کے بادل، خاطرِ نازک پہ ہیں چھائے ہوئے
عارضِ رنگیں ہیں، یا دو پھول مرجھائے ہوئے
چیتھڑوں میں دیدنی ہے روئے غمگین شباب
ابر کے آوارہ ٹکڑوں میں ہو جیسے ماہتاب

Josh Malihabadi
Husn aur Mazdoori (The Toiling Beauty)

There she sweats on the road, a beauteous, restless lass,
In scorching sun she breaks the stones, her bangles clink and clash.

A painful moan with the music strangely mixed up lies,
At each stroke drops of tears trickle down her eyes.

Dust-splattered are her cheeks, her locks embroiled in dust,
Her deep depressed eyes a tender grace reflect.

The blood-red sun sucks her blood without a touch of ruth,
Each heavy hammer stroke tells upon her budding youth.

In the sun her fragrant locks are flying about adrift,
Her limber self is getting wrecked amid the stones and bricks.

Ruddy rays of the sun are drinking undefied,
The wine of her jasmine cheeks, nectar of narcissus' eyes.

Clouds of sorrow heavily hang o'er her tender heart,
Are these her cheeks, or roses two which are fading fast?

Through her tatters can be glimpsed her youthful shape, sorrow-gripped,
Like the moon that wanders through bits of clouds adrift.

Ek dosheeza sarak par, dhoop mein hai be-qarar,
Choorian bajti hain kankar kootne mein bar, bar.

Choorian ke saaz mein yeh soz hai kaisa bhara,
Aankh mein "aansu" bani jaati hai jiski har sada.

Gard hai rukhsar par, zulfen ati hain khak mein,
Naazuki bal kha rahi hai deeda-e-ghumnak mein.

Ho raha hai jazb mehar-e-khoon-chukan ke roobaroo,
Kankaron ki nabz mein uthti jawani ka lahu.

Dhoop mein lahra rahi hai kaakul-e-amber sarisht,
Ho raha hai kamsini ka loch juzw-e-sang-o-khisht.

Pi rahi hain surkh kirnen mehar-e-aatish bar ki,
Nargisi aankhon ka ras, mai champai rukhsar ki.

Ghum ke badal khatir-e-naazuk pe hain chhaae hue,
Aaraz-e-rangeen hain ya do phool murjhaae hue.

Cheethron mein deedni hai roo-e-ghumgeen-e-shabab,
Abar ke aawara tukron mein ho jaise mahtaab.

جوشؔ ملیح آبادی

اُف یہ ناداری! مرے سینے سے اٹھتا ہے دھواں
آہ، اے افلاس کے مارے ہوئے ہندوستاں!
حسن ہو مجبور کنکر توڑنے کے واسطے
دستِ نازک اور پتھر توڑنے کے واسطے
فکر سے جھک جائے وہ گردن تُف اے لیل و نہار
جس میں ہونا چاہئے پھولوں کا اک ہلکا سا ہار
آسماں جانِ طرب کو وقفِ رنجوری کرے
صنفِ نازک بھوک سے تنگ آ کے مزدوری کرے
اس جبیں پر، اور پسینہ ہو جھلکنے کے لئے
جو جبینِ ناز ہو افشاں چھڑکنے کے لئے
بھیک میں وہ ہاتھ اٹھیں التجا کے واسطے
جن کو قدرت نے بنایا ہو حنا کے واسطے
نازکی سے جو اٹھا سکتی نہ ہوں کاجل کا بار
ان مُشک پلکوں پہ بیٹھے راہ کا بوجھل غبار
کیوں فلک! مجبور ہوں میں آنسو بہانے کے لئے
انکھڑیاں ہوں جو دل میں ڈوب جانے کے لئے

Josh Malihabadi

Ah, the curse of poverty! my heart wells up in grief!
O, my dear land of birth, sunk in misery deep!

Beauty to be thus engaged in breaking stones and bricks!
Tender hands to ply the hammer, and break the rocks and cliffs!

O evil day that care should bend and bow that delicate neck,
Which with a floral garland should be lightly decked.

The joy of life made to pine in sorrow's ruthless jaws!
The fair-sex thus hunger-pressed to labour long and hard!

Ah, the drops of perspiration that trickle down her brow,
The brow that with perfumes rich deserves to shine and glow;

Those hands in a begging pose thus be humbly raised,
Which were meant with henna paste to be gently laved!

Those eyes to bear the weight of wayside dust and dirt,
The eyes which cannot even bear a light collyrium touch.

Why should those eyes, O God, be thus compelled to weep,
Which are meant to pierce the heart, or into the soul to seep!

Uf, yeh nadari! mire seene se uthta hai dhuan,
Aah, ai iflass ke maare hue Hindustan!

Husn ho majboor kankar torne ke waaste,
Dast-e-naazuk, aur paththar torne ke waaste!

Fikar se jhuk jaae woh gardan, tuf, ai lail-o-nihaar,
Jis mein hona chaahieye phoolon ka ik halka sa haar.

Aasmen jaan-e-tarab ko waqf-e-ranjoori kare,
Sinaf-e-naazuk bhook se tang aa ke mazdoori kare.

Us jabeen par, aur paseena ho jhalakne ke lieye,
Jo jabeen-e-naaz ho afshan chhirakne ke lieye.

Bhik mein woh haath uthen ilteja ke waaste,
Jin ko qudrat ne banaya ho henna ke waaste.

Naazuki se jo utha sakti na hon kaajal ka bar,
Un subak palkon pe baithe raah ka bojhal ghubar.

Kyon falak, majboor hon aansu bahane ke lieye,
Ankharian ho jo dilon mein doob jaane ke lieye.

جوش ملیح آبادی

مفلسی، چھانٹے اسے قہر و غضب کے واسطے
جس کا مکھڑا ہو شبستانِ طرب کے واسطے
فرطِ خشکی سے وہ لب ترسیں تکلّم کے لئے
جن کو قدرت نے تراشا ہو تبسّم کے لئے
نازنینوں کا یہ عالم، مادرِ ہند! آہ، آہ
کس کے جورِ ناروا نے کر دیا تجھ کو تباہ؟
ہن برساتا تھا کبھی دن رات تیری خاک پر
سچ بتا اے ہند! تجھ کو کھا گئی کس کی نظر؟
باغ تیرا، کیوں جہنم کا نمونہ ہو گیا؟
آہ، کیوں تیرا بھرا در بار سونا ہو گیا؟
اے خدا! ہندوستاں پر یہ نحوست تا کجا؟
آخر اس جنّت پہ دوزخ کی حکومت تا کجا؟
سر زمینِ رنگ و بو پر عکسِ گلشن تا کجا؟
پاک سیتا کے لئے زندانِ راون تا کجا؟
دستِ نازک کو رسن سے اب چھڑانا چاہئے
اس کلائی میں تو کنگن جگمگانا چاہئے

Josh Malihabadi

Poverty preys upon her life, cruelly doth she treat,
That lovely face which was meant to grace the nightly meets.

Those lips now crave for water, unslaked, athirst,
Which were by nature carved with joyous smiles to burst.

Beauty trapped in such a plight, O motherland, alas!
Whose curse has brought you to such a sorry pass?

There was a time when hordes of huns for you did lust,
What has caused your ruin, which evil eye accursed?

How has your paradise turned into a hell?
Who has laid waste your court, struck your funeral knell?

How long, O Lord, will this land lie under an evil spell?
How long will this paradise bear the yoke of hell?

How long will the fiery forge burn this verdant vale?
How long will noble Sita rot in Ravana's jail?

These delicate hands should now be rid of fetters fell and cold,
These wrists should now be decked with bracelets of gold.

Muflisi chhaante use qahr-o-ghazab ke waaste,
Jis ka mukhra ho shabastaan-e-tarab ke waaste.

Fart-e-khushki se woh lab tarsen takallum ke lieye,
Jin ko qudrat ne tarasha ho tabassum ke lieye.

Naazneenon ka yeh aalam, maadar-e-Hind, aah, aah!
Kis ke jaur-e-narawane kar diya tujhko tabah?

Hun barasta tha kabhi din raat teri khak par,
Sach bata, ai Hind! tujhko kha gai kis ki nazar?

Bagh tera kyon jahannum ka namoona ho gaya?
Aah, kyon tera bhara darbar soona ho gaya?

Ai Khuda, Hindustan par yeh nahusat ta kuja?
Aakhir is jannat pe dozakh ki hakoomat ta kuja?

Sar zameen-e-rang-o-boo par aks-e-gilkhin ta kuja?
Paak seeta ke lieye zindaan-e-Ravan ta kuja?

Dast-e-naazuk ko rasan se ab chhurana chahieye,
Is kalai mein tau kangan jagmagana chahieye!

Abu-Al-Asar Hafeez Jullundhary
(1900-1982)

ABU-AL-ASAR HAFEEZ JULLUNDHARY
(1900-1982)

Hafeez was born at Jullundhar (Punjab) on January 14, 1900. His ancestors were Hindu Rajputs of the Suraj Bansi Branch, who had embraced Islam some 200 years back. "My family," the poet tells us, "was not even distantly interested in education or literature." But Hafeez had shown great interest in poetry and literature even in his childhood, and had written his first poem at the age of eleven. He made up for the lack of formal education with self-study and hard work. It was under the guidance of his poetic mentor, Maulana Ghulam Qadir Grami, that he developed his faculties, and carved a place for himself in the poetic pantheon. The ruler of Khairpur state (Sindh) appointed him the official poet of his court, but Hafeez gave up this appointment after a short while and preferred to pursue his interests independently. He devoted his time and talent to the writing of the history of Islam, which brought him great national fame. He also worked as director of song publicity during World War II. In recognition of his services to literature and society, the then British government honoured him with the titles of "Khan Sahib" and "Khan Bahadur". After the partition of India Hafeez opted to stay in Pakistan, and lived, for the most part of his life, at Lahore.

Though not a profound thinker like Ghalib, nor a philosophic poet like Iqbal, Hafeez is certainly a popular poet of the "mushairas". He could sway his audiences with the enchanting melody of his voice, and with the lilting rhythms of his songs and lyrics, which generally deal with romantic, religious, patriotic, or natural themes. Some of his famous poems like "Abhi Tau Main Jawan Hun" and "Raqasa"—the poems included in this book—have been set to music by professional composers, and sung by radio artists like Malika Pukhraj. Hafeez has also written *ghazals*, but he is more at home in the medium of the *nazm* and *geet*, especially in short poetical measures. Hafeez's national fame rests on his long poem "Shahnama-e-Islam" which, in the manner of Firdausi's Shahnama, is a record of the glorious history of Islam. Hafeez also wrote the national song of Pakistan, which earned him countrywide reputation. Though he holds Islamic religion and Islamic history in great esteem, he is not a religious fundamentalist, and can, with equal eclat, hymn the praise of Lord Krishna and his sacred flute. He is a pure Indian poet who chooses his themes, his images, and his tunes from the Indian soil, and whose language is a fine blend of Hindi and Urdu diction, reflecting India's composite culture. He is a poet of the Indian seasons and festivals, and a lover of the Indian landscape which he has lovingly described in several of his poems, on Barsaat or Basant or Eid. His famous works include the following titles: "Naghama-e-Zaar", "Soz-o-Saaz", and "Talkhaba-e-Shirin".

Hafeez died in Pakistan on December 21, 1982.

حفیظ جالندھری

رقّاصہ

اٹھی ہے مغرب سے گھٹا
پینے کا موسم آگیا!
ہے رقص میں اک مہ لقا
نازک ادا ناز آفریں
ہاں ناچتی جا گائے جا!
نظروں سے دل برمائے جا
تڑپائے جا تڑپائے جا
او دُشمنِ دنیا و دیں
تیرا تھرکنا خوب ہے
تیری ادائیں دل نشیں
لیکن ٹھہر تُو کون ہے
او نیم عُریاں نازنیں
کیا مشرقی عورت ہے تُو
ہرگز نہیں ہرگز نہیں
تیری ہنسی بے باک ہے
تیری نگہ چالاک ہے

Abu-Al-Asar Hafeez Jullundhary
Raqasa (The Dancing Belle)

Western clouds are gathering fast,
Time to drink the purple draught;

A moon-like face performs the dance,
How exquisite her grace and glance!

Go on with your song and dance,
Leave our hearts and souls entranced!

Let the gazers yearn and pine,
O thou foe of faith divine!

Your gyrations wondrous fine!
Bold overtures tempt the mind.

But wait a little, who are you?
O dancing belle, semi-nude!

Are you a woman of the East?
Not at all, not the least.

Impudent is this your laugh,
Your looks betray a cunning heart.

Uthi hai maghrib se ghata,
Peene ka mausim aa gaya!

Hai raqs mein ik mah laqa,
Nazuk ada, naaz aafreen;

Haan nachti jaae, gaae ja,
Nazron se dil barmaae ja;

Tarpaae ja, tarpaae ja,
O dushman-e-duniya-o-deen.

Tera thirakna khub hai,
Teri adaaen dil nashin,

Lekin thahr tu kaun hai,
O neem urian naazneen?

Kya mashriqi aurat hai tu?
Hargiz nahin, hargiz nahin.

Teri hansi bebaak hai,
Teri nigah chalaak hai;

حفیظ

اُف کِس قدر دل سوز ہے
تقدیر بازاری تری
کتنی ہوس آمیز ہے
یہ سادہ پُرکاری تری

شرم اور عزّت والیاں
ہوتی ہیں عفّت والیاں
وہ حُسن کی شہزادیاں
پردے کی ہیں آبادیاں

چشمِ فلک نے آج تک
دیکھی نہیں اُن کی جھلک
سرمایۂ شرم و حیا
زیور ہے اُن کے حُسن کا

شوہر کے دُکھ سہتی ہیں وہ
منھ سے نہیں کہتی ہیں وہ
کب سامنے آتی ہیں وہ
غیرت سے کٹ جاتی ہیں وہ

Hafeez Jullundhary

Ah, how they stun and shock the heart!
Your vulgar ways and rude remarks!

How bold, how full of lust,
This your artless artfulness!

Those who value honour and name,
Pure of heart, modest dames,

Those virtuous beauty queens,
Observe the veil, live unseen.

The world has never had a glimpse,
Of these pretty, pious mymphs.

They share the sorrows of their men,
Uncomplaining and content;

The wealth of coyness and reserve,
Multiplies their beauty's worth.

They always shun the public gaze,
Sense of honour forbids display.

Uf kisqadar dilsoz hai,
Taqrir bazaari tiri.

Kitni hawas aamez hai,
Yeh saada purkaari tiri.

Sharm aur izzat waalian,
Hoti hain iffat waalian.

Woh husn ki shahzaadian,
Parde ki hain aabaadian.

Chashme-e-falak ne aaj tak,
Dekhi nahin unki jhalak.

Sarmaya-e-sharm-o-haya,
Zewar hai unke husn ka;

Shohar ke dukh sahti hain woh,
Munh se nahin kahti hain woh.

Kab ṣaamne aati hain woh,
Ghairat se kat jaati hain woh.

حفیظؔ

اعزازِ ملّت اُن سے ہے
نام شرافت اُن سے ہے
وہ ایمان پر قائم ہیں
وہ پاکیزہ و صائم ہیں
تجھ میں نہیں شرم و حیا!
تجھ میں نہیں مہر و وفا
سچ سچ بتا تو کون ہے
او بے حیا تو کون ہے
یہ پُر فسُوں غمزے ترے
نا محرموں کے سامنے!
ہٹ سامنے سے دُور ہو
مردُود ہو مقہُور ہو
تقدیر کی ہیٹی ہے تُو
شیطان کی بیٹی ہے تُو
جس قوم کی عورت ہے تُو
اُس قوم پر لعنت ہے تُو

Hafeez Jullundhary

They are the nation's precious pride,
They are goodness personified!

Firm and deep in their belief,
They are faithful to their creed.

You are shameless and debased,
Devoid of love and kindly grace.

Who art thou? tell me true,
O brazen-face, who are you?

These coquettish glances, boldly strewn,
Before a gathering quite unknown.

Vanish, get thee out of sight,
Be thou damned, evil sprite!

You are the Fate's abandoned child,
A daughter of the devil's tribe!

A curse you are upon your race,
That bred and reared a thing so base.

Aizaaz-e-millat un se hai,
Naam-e-sharafat un se hai.

Imaan par qayam hain woh,
Pakeeza-o-sayam hain woh;

Tujh mein nahin sharm-o-haya,
Tujh mein nahin mehr-o-wafa;

Sach sach bata tu kaun hai,
O be-haya tu kaun hai?

Yeh purfasun ghamze tire,
Na mahramon ke samne!

Hat, samne se door ho,
Mardood ho, maqhoor ho,

Taqdir ki heti hai tu,
Shaitan ki beti hai tu,

Jis qaum ki aurat hai tu,
Us qaum par laanat hai tu.

حفیظ

لیکن ٹھہر جانا ذرا
تیری نہیں کوئی خطا
مُردوں میں غیرت ہی نہیں
قومی حمیّت ہی نہیں!
وہ ملّتِ بیضا کہ تھی!
سارے جہاں کی روشنی
جمعیّتِ اسلامیاں!
شاہنشہِ ہندوستاں
اب اس میں دم کچھ بھی نہیں
ہم کیا ہیں ہم کچھ بھی نہیں
ملّی سیاست اُٹھ گئی
بازو کی طاقت اُٹھ گئی
شانِ حجازی اب کہاں
وہ ترکتازی اب کہاں!
اب غزنوی ہمّت گئی
اب بابری شوکت گئی

Hafeez Jullundhary

But wait a little, hold a while,
Why should you be stigmatised?

Men have lost their sense of shame,
Manly pride is crushed and tamed.

That radiant race, divinely bright.
The fountainhead of grace and light,

Islamic force and Muslim might,
Lord of Indian earth and skies,

All is now a hollow boast,
What are we? a spent up force.

The wise statesmanship is gone,
Fled the strength of will and arm;

Where are the glorious days of Hejaz?
Turkish valour is a thing of the past;

Ghazni's strength is a vanished gleam,
Babar's pomp and pride, a dream.

Lekin thahr jana zara,
Teri nahin koi khata.

Mardon mein ghairat hi nahin,
Qaumi hameeat hi nahin;

Woh millat-e-baiza ke thi,
Sare jahan ki roshni.

Jamiat-e-islamian,
Shahnshah-e-Hindustan!

Ab is mein dam kuchh bhi nahin,
Hum kya hain, hum kuchh bhi nahin.

Milli siasat uth gai,
Baazoo ki taqat uth gai;

Shan-e-Hejazi ab kahan?
Woh turktaazi ab kahan?

Ab Ghaznavi himmat gai,
Ab Babari shaukat gai;

حفیظ

لیکن مجھے کیا خبط ہے
تقریر کیوں بے ربط ہے
اتنا شرابی ہوگیا!
عقل و خِرد کو کھوگیا
مجھ کو زمانے سے عرض؟
مٹنے مٹانے سے غرض؟
ہندوستاں سے کام کیا
اندیشۂ اسلام کیا
جینے دو جینے دو مجھے
پینے دو پینے دو مجھے
جب حشر کا دن آئے گا
اُس وقت دیکھا جائے گا
ہاں ناچتی جا گائے جا
نظروں سے دل برماٸے جا
تڑپائے جا تڑپائے جا
او دُشمنِ دنیا و دیں!

Hafeez Jullundhary

But why am I concerned in vain,
Why can't I my tongue restrain?

I am so badly drunk,
I've lost my sober sense.

What care I for the world or times?
Let them prosper or decline;

Islam's future concerns me not,
India doesn't disturb my thoughts.

Let me live as I will,
Let me drink to my fill.

When the day of judgement arrives,
We shall see what Fate decides;

Continue to sing and dance,
Let your looks our hearts entrance!

Make us yearn, make us pine!
O,'thou foe of faith divine!

Lekin mujhe kya khabt hai,
Taqrir kyon be rabt hai?

Itna sharabi ho gaya,
Aql-o-khirad bhi kho gaya.

Mujh ko zamane se gharaz?
Mitne mitane se gharaz?

Hindustan se kam kya?
Andesha-e-islam kya?

Jeene do jeene do mujhe,
Peene do peene do mujhe;

Jab hashar ka din aaega,
Us waqt dekha jaaega.

Haan nachti ja, gaae ja,
Nazron se dil barmaae ja,

Tarpaae ja, tarpaae ja,
O, dushman-e-duniya-o-deen.

حفیظؔ

ابھی تو میں جوان ہوں

ہوا بھی خوشگوار ہے
گلوں پہ بھی نکھار ہے
ترنّم ہزار ہے
بہار پرُ بہار ہے
کہاں چلا ہے ساقیا
ادھر تو لوٹ اِدھر تو آ
ارے یہ دیکھتا ہے کیا؟
اُٹھا سبُو۔ سبُو اُٹھا
سبُو اُٹھا پیالہ بھر
پیالہ بھر کے دے ادھر
چمن کی سمت کر نظر
سماں تو دیکھ بے خبر
وہ کالی کالی بدلیاں
اُفق پہ ہوگئیں عیاں
وہ اک ہجومِ کہکشاں
ہے سُوئے مےکدہ رواں

Hafeez Jullundhary
Abhi Tau Main Jawan Hoon (I am as yet rather Young)

Exhilarating is the air,
Flowers too are fresh and fair;
Melodious is the atmosphere,
Spring displays its bridal wear.
Whither dost thou wend thy way?
Saqi, come and grace this place.
Why demur, why delay?
Pick the flask, serve the ale;
Pick the flask, fill the cup,
Let me drink, and drink it up.
Towards the garden turn your gaze,
What a beauteous scene prevails!
With sable clouds gathering fast,
The sky is getting overcast;
It seems a crowd of revellers bold,
Is marching to the tavern door.

Hawa bhi khushgawar hai,
Gulon pe bhi nikhar hai,
Tarannum-e-hazaar hai,
Bahar pur bahar hai.

Kahan chala hai saqia,
Idhar tau laut, idhar tau aa,
Are yeh dekhta hai kya?
Utha saboo, saboo utha,
Saboo utha, pyaala bhar,
Payaala bhar ke de idhar,
Chaman ki simt kar nazar,
Saman tau dekh, be khabar;

Woh kaali kaali badlian,
Ufaq pe ho gaein ayyan,
Woh ik hajum-e-maikashan,
Hai soo-e-maikada rawan;

حفیظؔ

یہ کیا گماں ہے بدگماں
سمجھ نہ مجھ کو ناتواں
خیالِ زُہد ابھی کہاں
ابھی تو میں جوان ہوں

عبادتوں کا ذکر ہے
نجات کی بھی فکر ہے
جنون ہے ثواب کا
خیال ہے عذاب کا

مگر سنو تو شیخ جی
عجیب شئے ہیں آپ بھی
بھلا شباب و عاشقی
الگ ہوئے بھی ہیں کبھی؟

حسین جلوہ ریز ہوں
اداُئیں فتنہ خیز ہوں!
ہواُئیں عطر بیز ہوں
تو شوق کیوں نہ تیز ہوں

Hafeez Jullundhary

Why this doubt, O doubting man?
Think not I'm weak or wan.

By thought of piety unstung,
I'm as yet rather young!

Prayer and worship form our talk,
Salvation too attracts our heart;
Intent on following godly ways,
Our hearts dread the Judgement Day.

But listen to me, O reverend priest,
A strange thing you are indeed!
Have youth and beauty ever been,
Unrelated, alien things?

When winsome beauties lie in wait,
Tempting in their charm and grace,
When fragrance-fraught is all the place
Passions cannot help but rage.

Yeh kya gumaan hai bad gumaan,
Samajh na mujhko natawaan.

Khayal-e-zuhd abhi kahan,
Abhi tau main jawan hun.

Ibadaton ka zikar hai,
Nijat ki bhi fikr hai,
Janoon hai sawaab ka,
Khayal hai azaab ka;

Magar suno tau sheikh ji,
Ajib shai hain aap bhi,
Bhala shabab-o-aashiqi,
Alag hue bhi hain kabhi?

Haseen jalwa-rez hon
Adaein fitna-khez hon,
Hawain itar-bez hon,
Tau shauq kyon na tez hon?

حفیظؔ

نگاہ ہائے فتنہ گر
کوئی اِدھر کوئی اُدھر
اُبھارتے ہوں عیش پر
تو کیا کرے کوئی بشر؟
چلو جی قصہ مختصر
تمہارا نقطۂ نظر
درست ہے تو ہو مگر
ابھی تو میں جوان ہوں

Hafeez Jullundhary

When lovely, cute and coquettish eyes,
Glance on us from every side,
When sensuous thrills give delight,
Can a man resist or fight?
O.K. let us cut it short,
Your point of view, your kindly thought,
Is sane and wise, but what to do?
I'm as yet rather young.

Nigah-haae fitna gar,
Koi idhar koi udhar,
Ubhaarte hon aish par,
Tau kya kare koi bashar?

Chaloji qissa mukhtasar
Tumhara nukta-e-nazar,
Darust hai tau ho magar,
Abhi tau main jawaan hun.

Abridged

Akhtar Sheerani
(1905-1948)

AKHTAR SHEERANI
(1905-1948)

Mohammed Dawood Khan Akhtar Sheerani was born on 4th May, 1905, in Tonk state (Rajpootana, now Rajasthan). His father Mehmood Khan Sheerani was a professor at Oriental College, Lahore. Akhtar too joined his father's college, but beyond passing his Munshi Fazil and Adib Fazil examinations, he showed no special interest in academic achievements. He spent his time in cultivating his poetic taste, and studying English and Urdu literature on his own. By virtue of his literary and linguistic abilities, Akhtar could secure editorial assignments on several literary journals like *Hamayun* and *Shahkar*. He also tried to run his own journals, *Baharastaan, Khayalastaan*, and *Rooman*, but such attempts proved abortive as Akhtar lacked the steadiness of purpose and mind, so essential to carry such tasks to success. Excessive drinking told on his health, and he died on September 9, 1948, at the comparatively young age of 43. His poetical works include: *Naghma-e-Haram, Shairistaan, Subah-e-Bahar*, and *Tayyur-e-Aawara*.

Akhtar is quintessentially a romantic poet, a singer, like John Keats, of love and beauty, be it the beauty of woman, or of natural landscape. Romanticism gives preference to the individual over the society, to imagination over reason, to beauty over philosophy. Just as the Romantic movement in English literature marks a reaction against the classical poetry of Dryden and Pope, the advocates of reason and precision, and adherents of the heroic couplet, Akhtar's poetry may be seen as a reaction against the overly didactic and ethical verse of Hali, Akbar and Iqbal. All these poets carefully excluded from their poetry any mention of sensuous beauty or romance, and used it mainly as an instrument of social edification. Akhtar tried to reverse this trend by turning away from social and public issues, and by focussing his gaze on the inner world of feeling and imagination, highlighting in the process, the pivotal role of woman in the theatre of human existence. He builds his poetry round the endearing figures of Salma, Azra, Rehana or Cleopatra. Though these women are not real, flesh and blood characters, but creatures of imagination and models of womanhood, Akhtar deserves credit for giving a new direction to poetry, and for tapping the tremendous potential of a hiterto neglected topic.

In the matter of style, Akhtar adheres to the tradition of rhymed verse, along with "radif" and "qafia", and is not generally drawn by the new vogue for free verse or blank-verse. He is the master of the musical line and an adept in describing the beauties of the landscape. He has written several memorable poems on Barsaat or Basant, the two seasons specially adored by a wine-bibber.

Out of the three poems included in this volume "Aurat" dwells on the central role of woman in every sphere of human life, "Ai Ishq Hamen Barbad na Kar" is a plaintive song of a lovelorn lover, while the third poem, "Reehana", centres round a sweet little girl, breathing innocent charm, and dwelling in the lap of nature, strongly recalling Wordsworth's Lucy.

اختر شیرانی

عورت

حیات و حرمت و مہر و وفا کی شان ہے عورت
شباب و حسن و انداز و ادا کی جان ہے عورت
حجاب و عصمت و شرم و حیا کی کان ہے عورت
جو دیکھو غور سے ہر مرد کا ایمان ہے عورت
اگر عورت نہ آئی گل جہاں ماتم کدہ ہوتا!
اگر عورت نہ ہوتی ہر مکاں اک غم کدہ ہوتا!
یدِ قدرت میں اک چلتی ہوئی شمشیر ہے عورت
زمیں پر فطرتِ معصوم کی تصویر ہے عورت
جہاں میں کم کرتی ہے شاہی مگر لشکر نہیں رکھتی
دلوں کو کرتی ہے زخمی مگر خنجر نہیں رکھتی
کہیں معصوم طفلی اس کے نغموں سے بہلتی ہے
کہیں بیتاب جوانی اس کے نوشِ لب سے پھلتی ہے
کہیں مجبور پیری اس کی باتوں سے سنبھلتی ہے
کہیں آرام سے جاں اس کے قدموں پر نکلتی ہے
وہ روتی ہے تو ساری کائنات آنسو بہاتی ہے
وہ ہنستی ہے تو فطرت بے خودی سے مسکراتی ہے

Akhtar Sheerani
Aurat (Woman)

Woman lends a glow to life, love, honour and faith,
She's the pride of youth and beauty, fountainhead of grace.
She's the mine of virtuous honour, of shyness, self-esteem,
A guiding star for every man, a shining spiritual gleam.
Without her presence the world would be a sad and weary place,
But for her every home would seem a barren waste.
Woman is the flaming brand in the Nature's hands,
She's innocence incarnate on this dusty strand.
Without commanding armies she rules over the earth,
Without carrying a sword she can wound and hurt.
Somewhere innocent infants are by her songs cajoled,
Somewhere bubbling youth is feted on her bowl.
Helpless age from her talk somewhere strength receives,
Sometimes someone at her feet finds a quiet release.
When she weeps, the universe brims o'er with tears,
When she smiles, nature too brightens up and cheers.

Hayaat-o-hurmat-o-mehar-o-wafa ki shaan hai aurat,
Shabaab-o-husn-o-andaaz-o-ada ki jaan hai aurat.
Hijaab-o-ismat-o-sharm-o-haya ki kaan hai aurat,
Jo dekho ghaur se har mard ka eemaan hai aurat.
Agar aurat na aati kul jahan maatam kada hota!
Agar aurat na hoti har makaan ik ghum kada hota!
Yad-e-qudrat mein ik chalti hui shamsheer hai aurat,
Zamin par fitrat-e-masoom ki tasvir hai aurat.
Jahan mein karti hai shahi, magar lashkar nahin rakhti,
Dilon ko karti hai zakhmi magar khanjar nahin rakhti.
Kahin maasoom tifli us ke naghmon se bahlti hai,
Kahin bekhud jawani us ke nosh-e-lab se phalti hai;
Kahin majboor peeri us ki baaton se sambhalti hai,
Kahin aaram se jaan us ke qadmon par nikalti hai.
Woh roti hai tau saari kaaenaat aansu bahati hai,
Woh hansti hai tau fitrat bekhudi se muskarati hai.

اخترشیرانی

وہ سوتی ہے تو ساتوں آسماں کو نیند آتی ہے
وہ اُٹھتی ہے تو کل خوابیدہ دُنیا کو اُٹھاتی ہے
وہی ارمانِ ہستی ہے، وہی ایمانِ ہستی ہے
بدن کہیے اگر ہستی کو تو وہ جانِ ہستی ہے
وہ چاہے تو اُلٹ دے پردۂ دُنیائے فانی کو
وہ چاہے تو مٹا دے جوشِ بحرِ زندگانی کو
وہ چاہے تو مٹا دے نخلِ زارِ حکمرانی کو
وہ چاہے تو بدل دے رنگِ بزمِ آسمانی کو
وہ کہہ دے تو بہارِ جلوہ مِٹ جائے نظاروں سے
وہ کہہ دے تو لباسِ نو چھن جائے ستاروں سے
غرض جب تک یہ دُنیا اور اس کی خوشنمائی ہے
ہماری زندگی بھر ہم پہ عورت کی خدائی ہے

Akhtar Sheerani

When she sleeps, the seven skies doze off to sleep,
When she wakes, the earth itself rises out of deep.

She's the object deep-desired, the faith deep-ingrained,
If life be called the body, she should be soul proclaimed.

She can raise the veil of life, if she so decides,
If she likes she can arrest the gushing flow of life.

If she wants she can destroy foundations of the state,
She can, if she feels inclined, mighty heavens shake.

The vernal sights would shed their green if she gives a hint,
The stars themselves would begin to shiver, shrivel away and shrink.

So long as the world doth last and its beauty shines,
So long would she rule our lives like a force divine.

Woh soti hai tau saaton aasmaan ko neend aati hai,
Woh uthti hai tau kul khwabeeda duniya ko uthati hai.

Wohi armaan-e-hasti hai, wohi eemaan-e-hasti hai,
Badan kahieye agar hasti ko tau woh jaan-e-hasti hai.

Woh chaahe tau ulat de parda-e-duniya-e-fani ko,
Woh chaahe tau mita de josh-e-bahr-e-zindagani ko.

Woh chaahe tau mita de nakhl zaar-e-hukamraani ko,
Woh chaahe tau badal de rang-e-bazm-e-aasmaani ko.

Woh kah de tau bahaar-e-jalwa mit jaae nazzaaron se,
Woh kah de tau libaas-e-noor chhin jaae sitaaron se.

Gharz jab tak yeh duniya aur is ki khushnumaai hai,
Hamaari zindagi bhar hum par aurat ki khudaai hai.

اختر شیرانی

اے عشق، ہمیں برباد نہ کر

اے عشق نہ چھیڑ آ کے ہمیں، ہم بھولے ہوؤں کو یاد نہ کر
پہلے ہی بہت ناشاد ہیں ہم تو اور ہمیں ناشاد نہ کر
قسمت کا ستم ہی کم نہیں کچھ، یہ تازہ ستم ایجاد نہ کر
یوں ظلم نہ کر بیداد نہ کر
اے عشق ہمیں برباد نہ کر

جس دن سے ملے ہیں دونوں کا سب چین گیا آرام گیا
چہروں سے بہارِ صبح گئی، آنکھوں سے فروغِ شام گیا
ہاتھوں سے خوشی کا جام چھٹا، ہونٹوں سے ہنسی کا نام گیا
غمگیں نہ بنا، ناشاد نہ کر
اے عشق ہمیں برباد نہ کر

راتوں کو اُٹھ اُٹھ کر روتے ہیں رو رو کے دعائیں کرتے ہیں
آنکھوں میں تصوّرِ دل میں خلشِ سر رکھتے ہیں آہیں بھرتے ہیں
اے عشق یہ کیسا روگ لگا جیتے ہیں نہ ظالم مرتے ہیں
یہ ظلم تو اے جلّاد نہ کر
اے عشق ہمیں برباد نہ کر

304

Akhtar Sheerani
Ai Ishaq Hamen Barbad Na Kar
(Undo us not, O Love)

Why comest thou to tease us love, why arouse the slumbering folks?
Torment us not with more of grief, we're already sorrow-soaked.
Enough are the slings of fate, why invent new fatal strokes?
But not cruel, relent, I say,
Undo us not, O Love, I pray.

Both of us have lost our peace ever since we met,
Cheeks have lost their morning bloom, eyes their evening calm have shed,
Hands have dropped the cup of joy, lips of smiles stand bereft;
Do not with newer aches assail,
Undo us not, O Love, I pray.

We keep awake and weep at night, pray to God with tearful eyes,
With aching hearts, abstracted gaze, we beat our head and loudly sigh,
Oh, what a strange disease is love, we neither live nor die;
O hangman, change your cruel ways,
Undo us not, O Love, I pray.

Ai ishq na chher aa aa ke hamen, hum bhoole huon ko yaad na kar,
Pehle hi bahut naashaad hain hum, tu aur hamen naashaad na kar.
Qismat ka sitam hi kam nahin kuchh, yeh taaza sitam eejaad na kar.
Yoon zulam na kar, bedaad na kar,
Ai ishq hamen barbaad na kar.

Jis din se mile hain donon ka sab chain gaya aaraam gaya,
Chehron se bahar-e-subah gai, aankhon se farogh-e-sham gaya,
Haathon se khushi ka jaam chhuta, honton se hansi ka naam gaya;
Ghumgeen na bana, naashaad na kar,
Ai ishq hamen barbaad na kar.

Raaton ko uth uth rote hain, ro ro kar duaaen karte hain,
Aankhon mein tasawur, dil mein khalish, sar dhunte hain aahen bharte hain,
Ai ishq, yeh kaisa rog laga, jeete hain na zaalim marte hain.
Yeh zulam tau ai jallaad na kar,
Ai ishq hamen barbaad na kar.

اخترشیرانی

یہ روگ لگا ہے جب سے ہمیں، رنجیدہ ہوں میں بیمار ہے وہ
ہر وقت تپش، ہر وقت خلش، بےخواب ہوں میں بیدار ہے وہ
جینے سے اِدھر بیزار ہوں میں، مرنے پہ اُدھر تیار ہے وہ
اور ضبط کیے فریاد نہ کر
اے عشق ہمیں برباد نہ کر

بیدردا درا انصاف تو کر اس عمر میں اور مغموم ہے وہ
پھولوں کی طرح نازک ہے ابھی تاروں کی طرح معصوم ہے وہ
یہ حسنِ ستم! یہ رنج غضب، مجبور ہوں میں مظلوم ہے وہ؟
مظلوم پہ یوں بیداد نہ کر
اے عشق ہمیں برباد نہ کر

اے عشق خدا را دیکھ کہیں، وہ شوخ حزیں بدنام نہ ہو
وہ ماہِ لقا بدنام نہ ہو، وہ زہرہ جبیں بدنام نہ ہو
ناموس کا اس کے پاس رہے، وہ پردہ نشیں بدنام نہ ہو
اس پردہ نشیں کو یاد نہ کر
اے عشق ہمیں برباد نہ کر

Akhtar Sheerani

Since the day we caught this plague, she's sick and I'm sad,
She can't sleep, I can't dream, raging pain has made us mad.
There she sits and craves for death, here my life has gone so drab,
Reason says: "Suppress your wails,"
Undo us not, O Love, I pray.

Be thou just, O despot! A tryst with sorrow at this age!
She's innocent like the stars, like flowers she's frail,
I'm helpless, she oppressed, such beauty, such terrible fate!
Oppress us not, show some grace,
Undo us not, O Love, I pray.

Let not my darling, cute and sad, undergo disgrace,
That moon-like face, starry-browed, may it preserve its native grace!
May she never stain her honour, that veiled, beauteous face!
Why bring to mind that visage veiled?
Undo us not, O Love, I pray.

Yeh rog laga hai jab se hamen, ranjeeda hoon main, beemaar hai woh,
Har waqt tapash, har waqt khalish, be khwab hoon main, bedaar hai woh,
Jeene se idhar bezaar hun main, marne pe udhar tayyaar hai woh;
Aur zabat kahe faryaad na kar,
Ai ishq hamen barbaad na kar.

Be dard zara insaaf tau kar, is umar mein aur maghmoom hai woh,
Phoolon ki tarah naazuk hai abhi, taaron ki tarah maasoom hai woh;
Yeh husn sitam! yeh ranj ghazab, majboor hoon main mazloom hai woh;
Mazloom pe yun bedaad na kar,
Ai ishq hamen barbaad na kar.

Ai ishq khuda ra dekh kahin, woh shokh hazin, badnaam no ho,
Woh maah-e-laqa badnaam na ho, woh zuhra jabeen badnaam na ho;
Naamoos ka usko paas rahe, woh parda nasheen badnaam na ho;
Us parda nasheen ko yaad na kar,
Ai ishq hamen barbaad na kar.

اخترؔ شیرانی

امید کی جھوٹی جنّت کے، رہ رہ کے نہ دکھلا خواب ہمیں
آئندہ کے فرضی عشرت کے وعدے سے نہ کر بیتاب ہمیں
کہتا ہے زمانہ جس کو خوشی، آتی ہے نظر کم یاب ہمیں
چھوڑ ایسی خوشی کو یاد نہ کر
اے عشق ہمیں برباد نہ کر

دو دن ہی میں عہدِ طفلی کے معصوم زمانے بھول گئے
آنکھوں سے وہ خوشیاں مٹ سی گئیں، لب کو وہ ترانے بھول گئے
اُن پاک بہشتی خوابوں کے دلچسپ فسانے بھول گئے
اِن خوابوں سے یوں آزاد نہ کر
اے عشق ہمیں برباد نہ کر

آنکھوں کو یہ کیا آزار ہوا، ہر جذبِ نہاں پر رو دینا
آہنگِ طرب پر جھجک جانا آوازِ فغاں پر رو دینا
بربط کی صدا پر رو دینا، مطرب کے بیاں پر رو دینا
احساس کو غم بنیاد نہ کر
اے عشق ہمیں برباد نہ کر

Akhtar Sheerani

Delude us not with pleasant dreams, with hopes of future bright,
Rob us not of inner peace by promising false delights,
What is commonly known as joy, rarely comes to sight,
Forget the joy's elusive ray,
Undo us not, O Love I pray.

The innocent days of childhood are too soon forgot,
Our lips have forgot to sing, our joys have come to naught,
Those pure heavenly dreams have gone beyond recall;
Let not those dreams fade and fail,
Undo us not, O Love, I pray.

What's wrong with my eyes, they melt at every thought,
They bend at any joyous tune, weep with any wailing heart,
The sound of lyre makes them flow, songs make them swell and start;
Let not this mind be sorrow-based
Undo us not, O Love, I pray.

Umeed ki jhooti jannat ke rah rah ke na dikhla khwab hamen,
Aainda ke farzi ishrat ke waade se na kar betaab hamen,
Kahta hai zamana jisko khushi, aati hai nazar kamyaab hamen,
Chhor aisi khushi ko yaad na kar,
Ai ishq hamen barbaad na kar.

Do din hi mein ahd-e-tifli ke maasoom zamaane bhool gaye,
Ankhon se woh khushian mit si gaien, lab ko woh tarane bhool gaye;
Un paak bahishti khwabon ke, dilchasp fasaane bhool gaye;
Un khwabon se yun aazad na kar,
Ai ishq hamen barbaad na kar.

Aankhon ko yeh kya aazaar hua, har jazb-e-nihan par ro dena,
Aahang-e-tarab par jhuk jaana, aawaaz-e-fughan par ro dena,
Barbat ki sada par ro dena, mutrib ke bayaan par ro dena,
Ahsaas ko ghum bunyaad na kar,
Ai ishq hamen barbaad na kar.

اختر شیرانی

جی چاہتا ہے اک دوسرے کو یوں آٹھ پہر ہم یاد کریں
آنکھوں میں بسائیں خوابوں کو اور دل میں خیال آباد کریں
خلوت میں بھی ہو جلوت کا سماں وحدت کو دوئی سے شاد کریں
یہ آرزوئیں ایجاد نہ کر
اے عشق ہمیں برباد نہ کر

Akhtar Sheerani

Now we wish to lie reclined lost in amorous thoughts,
With wishful dreams we should people both our eyes and
   hearts,
In seclusion company find, feel together when apart;
Keep thou such thoughts at bay,
Undo us not, O love, I pray.

Ji chaahta hai ik doosre ko yun aath pehar hum yaad karen,
Ankhon mein basaaen khwabon ko aur dil ko khayal aabaad karen,
Khilwat mein bhi ho jalwat ka saman, wahdat ko dooi se shaad
   karen,
Yeh aarzooen eejaad na kar,
Ai ishq hamen barbaad na kar.

اختر شیرانی
جہاں ریحانہ رہتی تھی

یہی وادی ہے وہ ہمدم جہاں ریحانہ رہتی تھی
وہ اس وادی کی شہزادی تھی اور شاہانہ رہتی تھی
کنول کا پھول تھی، سنسار سے بیگانہ رہتی تھی
نظر سے دُور مثلِ نکہتِ مستانہ رہتی تھی
یہی وادی ہے وہ ہمدم جہاں ریحانہ رہتی تھی
انہی صحراؤں میں وہ اپنے گلے کو چراتی تھی
انہی چشموں پہ وہ ہر روز منہ دھونے کو آتی تھی
انہی ٹیلوں کے دامن میں وہ آزادانہ رہتی تھی
یہی وادی ہے وہ ہمدم جہاں ریحانہ رہتی تھی
کھجوروں کے تلے وہ جو کھنڈر سے جھلملاتے ہیں
یہ سب ریحانہ کے معصوم افسانے سناتے ہیں
وہ ان کھنڈروں میں اک دن صورتِ افسانہ رہتی تھی
یہی وادی ہے وہ ہمدم جہاں ریحانہ رہتی تھی
مرے ہمدم، نخلستان اک دن اس کا مسکن تھا
اسی کے خرمئی آغوش میں اس کا نشیمن تھا
اسی شاداب وادی میں وہ بے باکانہ رہتی تھی
یہی وادی ہے وہ ہمدم جہاں ریحانہ رہتی تھی

Akhtar Sheerani
Reehana

This is the vale where, my friend, Reehana used to stay.

She was the princess of the dale, regal was her life,
Lotos-like did she bloom, unconcerned with fret and strife,
Fragrance-like did she reign far from the human eyes;
This is the vale, where, my friend, Reehana used to stay.

Daily did she feed her flock on this grassy wild,
To these springs she would come to wash her face and eyes,
On the slopes of these mounds she led a joyous life.
This is the vale where my friend, Reehana used to stay.

Where you see some scattered ruins aglimmer beneath the palms,
All these ruins tell the tale of her innocent charms,
Here among the ruins she lived like a fairy yarn;
This is the vale where, my friend, Reehana used to stay.

This oasis was, my friend, once her dear abode,
Here she built her simple hut, here she loved to rove,
In this verdant dell she lived, intrepid and unyoked.
This is the vale where, my friend, Reehana used to stay.

Yehi waadi hai woh humdum jahan Reehana rahti thi.

Woh is waadi ki shahzaadi thi aur shahana rahti thi,
Kanwal ka phool thi, sansaar se begana rahti thi,
Nazar se door masl-e-nikhat-e-mastna rahti thi.
Yeh waadi hai woh humdum jahan Reehana rahti thi.

Inhi sahraaon mein woh apne galle ko charaati thi,
Inhi chashmon pe woh har roz munh dhone ko aati thi;
Inhi teelon ke daman mein woh aazaadana rahti thi;
Yehi waadi hai woh humdum jahan Reehana rahti thi.

Khajuron ke tale woh jo khandar se jhilmilate hain,
Yeh sab reehana ke maasoom afsaane sunaate hain,
Woh in khandron mein ik din, soorat-e-afsaana rahti thi;
Yehi waadi hai woh humdum jahan Reehana rahti thi.

Mire humdum, yeh nakhlistaan ik din uska maskin tha,
Isi ke khurmaie aaghosh mein us ka nasheman tha,
Isi shaadaab waadi mein woh be-bakaana rahti thi,
Yehi waadi hai woh humdum jahan Reehana rahti thi.

اخترشیرانی

اسی ویرانے میں اک دن بہشتیں لہلہاتی تھیں
گھٹائیں گھر کے آتی تھیں، ہوائیں مسکراتی تھیں
کہ وہ بن کر بہارِ جنّت ۔ ویرانہ رہتی تھی
یہی وادی ہے وہ ہمدم جہاں ریحانہ رہتی تھی
یہیں آباد تھی اک دن مرے افکار کی ملکہ
مرے جذبات کی دیوی مرے اشعار کی ملکہ
وہ ملکہ، جو برنگِ عظمتِ شاہانہ رہتی تھی
یہی وادی ہے وہ ہمدم جہاں ریحانہ رہتی تھی
صبا شاخوں میں نخلستاں کی جبدم سرساتی ہے
مجھے ہر لہر سے ریحانہ کی آواز آتی ہے
یہیں ریحانہ رہتی تھی، یہیں ریحانہ رہتی تھی
یہی وادی ہے وہ ہمدم جہاں ریحانہ رہتی تھی
فضائیں گونجتی ہیں اب بھی ان وحشی ترانوں سے
سنو، آواز سی آتی ہے ان خاکی چٹانوں سے
کہ جن میں وہ برنگِ نغمۂ بیگانہ رہتی تھی
یہی وادی ہے وہ ہمدم جہاں ریحانہ رہتی تھی

Akhtar Sheerani

Once over this wilderness heaven did preside,
Fleecy clouds came in flocks, winds gently plied,
She brought to the wilderness a touch of paradise.
This is the vale, where my friend, Reehana used to stay.

Here did she live one day, the empress of my thoughts,
Goddess of my feelings, the Muse of poetic art,
The queen blessed with royal might, with regal grace inwrought;
This is the vale where, my friend, Reehana used to stay.

When in this oasis green breezes rustle and blow,
Reehana's voice in whispers soft towards my heart doth flow,
Here, it says, Reehana lived, here she lived and roved.
This is the vale where, my friend, Reehana used to stay.

The vale resounds with her songs right till to-day,
Hark, these brown rocks something seem to say,
The rocks where she lay and loomed like a ditty gay;
This is the vale where, my friend, Reehana used to stay.

Isi weeraane mein ik din bahishten lahlahaati thin,
Ghataaen ghir ke aati thin, hawaaen muskarati thin,
Ke woh ban kar bahar-e-jannat-e-weeraana rahti thi.
Yehi waadi hai woh humdum jahan Reehana rahti thi.

Yehin aabaad thi ik din mire ifkaar ki malika,
Mire jazbaat ki devi, mire ashaar ki malika,
Woh malika jo barang-e-azmat-e-shahaana rahti thi.
Yehi waadi hai woh humdum jahan Reehana rahti thi.

Saba shakhon mein nakhalistan ki jisdum sarsaraati hai,
Mujhe har lahr se Reehana ki aawaaz aati hai,
Yehin Reehana rahti thi, yehin Reehana rahti thi.
Yehi waadi hai woh humdum jahan Reehana rahti thi.

Fazaaen goonjati hain ab bhi un wahshi taranon se,
Suno, aawaaz si aati hai un khaki chatanon se,
Ke jin mein woh barang-e-naghme-e-begaana rahti thi.
Yehi waadi hai woh humdum, jahan Reehana rahti thi.

اخترشیرانی

شمیمِ زلف سے اُس کی مہک جاتی تھی کُل وادی
نگاہِ مست سے اُس کی بہک جاتی تھی کُل وادی
ہوائیں پرفشاں، روحِ مئے و میخانہ رہتی تھی
یہی وادی ہے وہ ہمدم جہاں ریحانہ رہتی تھی
گدازِ عشق سے لبریز تھا قلبِ حزیں اُس کا
مگر آئینہ دارِ شرم تھا روئے حسیں اُس کا
خموشی میں چھپائے نغمۂ مستانہ رہتی تھی
یہی وادی ہے وہ ہمدم جہاں ریحانہ رہتی تھی
اُسے پھولوں نے میری یاد میں بیتاب دیکھا ہے
ستاروں کی نظر نے رات بھر بے خواب دیکھا ہے
وہ شمعِ حُسن تھی پُر صورتِ پروانہ رہتی تھی
پیامِ دردِ دل اخترؔ دیے جاتا ہوں وادی کو
سلامِ رخصتِ غمگیں کیے جاتا ہوں وادی کو
سلام، اے وادیٔ ویراں جہاں ریحانہ رہتی تھی
یہی وادی ہے وہ ہمدم جہاں ریحانہ رہتی تھی

Akhtar Sheerani

Her fragrant locks filled the air with delicious scent,
Her drunken gaze robbed the vale of its wit and sense,
That spirit of wine and tavern did all over extend;
This is the vale where, my friend, Reehana used to stay.

With the heat of love did brim her sad and pensive heart,
But her modest, coy face wouldn't show the inner spark,
The veil of silence served to muffle the music of her heart,
This is the vail where, my friend, Reehana used to stay.

The flowers have seen her, for my sake distraught,
The stars have found her sleepless, distracted in her heart,
Though a taper bright, she burnt like a moth;
This is the vale where, my friend, Reehana used to stay.

Deeply touched and moved, here I quit this vale,
Bidding sad adieu, here I quit the vale,
Farewell, farewell, dale deserted, where Reehana once did stay;
This is the vale where, my friend, Reehana used to stay.

Shameem-e-zulaf se uski mehak jaati thi kul waadi;
Nigaah-e-mast se uski bahak jaati thi kul waadi,
Hawa mein parfishaan, rooh-e-mai-o-maikhana rahti thi,
Yehi waadi hai woh humdum jahan Reehana rahti thi.

Gudaaz-e-ishq se labrez tha qalb-e-hazeen uska,
Magar aaeena dar-e-sharam tha roo-e-haseen uska,
Khamoshi mein chhipaae naghma-e-mastana rahti thi,
Yehi waadi hai woh humdum jahan Reehana rahti thi.

Use phoolon ne meri yaad mein betaab dekha hai,
Sitaaron ki nazar ne raat bhar bekhwab dekha hai,
Woh shama-e-husn thi par soorat-e-parwana rahti thi.
Yehi waadi hai woh humdum jahan Reehana rahti thi.

Payaam-e-dard-e-dil Akhtar diye jata hoon waadi ko,
Salaam-e-rukhsat-e-ghumgeen kiye jaata hoon waadi ko,
Salaam, ai waadi-e-weeran jahan Reehana rahti thi.
Yehi waadi hai woh humdum jahan Reehana rahti thi.

Nazar Mohammed Rashid
(1910-1975)

NAZAR MOHAMMED RASHID
(1910-1975)

Nazar Mohammed Rashid, popularly known as "Noon-Meem Rashid," was born in 1910 at Akalgarh in Gujranwala district (now in Pakistan). He received his early education at his home town, and his college education at Government College, Lahore. Both his father and his grandfather were men of literary taste, well-versed in Persian and Arabic. It was his father, Raja Fazal Ilahi Chishti who introduced him to the poetry of Hafiz, Saadi, Ghalib and Iqbal. While at Government College, Lahore, Rashid was selected to edit the Urdu section of the college magazine, *Ravi*. Later, he edited for sometime Tajwar Najeebabadi's journal, *Shahkaar*. He also served for sometime in the commissioner's office at Multan. At about this time he wrote his first poem in free-verse, "Jurrat-e-Parwaaz,"—which is included in his famous collection: *Maawara*. In 1939 Rashid joined All India Radio as a news-editor, and became, after sometime, the Director of Programmes. He also served in the army on a short service commission. After the partition of India he worked as a regional director in Pakistan Radio. An assignment in the U.N.O. gave him an opportunity to go abroad and stay at New York. He retired in 1973 and settled down in England. Rashid died in a London hospital on October 9, 1975.

Rashid gave evidence of his poetic talent right in his schooldays. Though he began in the conventional way, writing poems in rhymed verse, retaining *radif*, and *qafia*, he soon grew out of the rut to become an accomplished practitioner and a pioneer of free-verse in Urdu poetry. In this transformation, he was influenced by the contemporary poets of England and France. A poem in free-verse which dispenses with the accessories of *radif* and *qafia*, and accommodates long and short lines in the same stanza for giving a naturalistic expression to the undulations of the poet's thought and feeling, was something new for the readers used to the lilting melodies and logical thought-sequences of earlier poetry. Rashid's handling of the new form had a startling effect on the mind of the readers who were thrilled as much by the newness of his technique, as by the daring thought and imagery of his poems. In the manner of Browning's dramatic monologues, Rashid introduced in many of his poems—as for instance, in "Sharabi", and "Be Karan Raat Ke Sannate Mein", the two poems included in this selection—a silent auditor with whom the poet enters into an honest and intimate converse, hitting at the social and moral shibboleths of the day. What stirs his imagination and indignation is the state of man in this age of exploitation—be it the exploitation of the East by the "civilised" West, of the poor by the affluent, of innocent faith by the cunning intellect.

His poems are available under four collections: *Maawara, Iran Mein Ajnabi, Laa—Insaan,* and *Gumaan ka Mumkin.*

ن ۔ م ۔ راشد

شرابی

آج پھر جی بھر کے پی آیا ہوں میں
دیکھتے ہی تیری آنکھیں شعلہ ساماں ہوگئیں
شکر کر اے جاں کہ میں
ہوں درِ افرنگ کا ادنیٰ غلام
صدرِ اعظم یعنی دریوزہ گرِ اعظم نہیں
درنہ اک جامِ شرابِ ارغواں
کیا بجھا سکتا تھا میرے سینہ ٔ سوزاں کی آگ
غم سے مر جاتی نہ تو
آج پی آتا جو میں
جام رنگیں کے بجائے
بے کسوں اور ناتوانوں کا لہو
شکر کر اے جاں کہ میں
ہوں درِ افرنگ کا ادنیٰ غلام
اور بہتر عیش کے قابل نہیں

Nazar Mohammed Rashid
Sharabi (The Drunkard)

Lo, I come once again drunken to my fill!
Why do you glare at me thus with bloodshot eyes?
Thank God, I am, my love,
A humble servant of the Crown,
And not a boss, or overlord, — a mendicant-in-chief.
Or, how could my inner blaze
Be quenched with just a cup of wine?

You wouldn't have been shocked with grief
Had I come to-day,
Drunk not with wine, but blood
Of the poor, helpless folks.

Thank your stars, I am, my love,
The British lords' petty hind,
Unfit for luxury of a superior kind.

Aaj phir ji bhar ke pi aaya hoon main,
Dekhte hi teri aankhen shola saamaan ho gaien;
Shukar kar ai jaan ke main
Hoon dar-e-afrang ka ik adna ghulaam,
Sadar-e-aazam, yaani daryooza gar-e-aazam nahin,
Warna ik jaam-e-sharab-e-arqhawaan
Kya bujha sakta tha mire seena-e-sozaan ki aag?

Ghum se mar jaati na tu
Aaj pi aata jo main,
Jaam-e-rangeen ke bajaae,
Bekason aur naatawaanon ka lahu.

Shukar kar ai jaan ke main
Hoon dar-e-afrang ka ik adna ghula'
Aur behtar aish ke qaabil nahin.

ن۔م۔راشد
بے کراں رات کے سناٹے میں

تیرے بستر پہ مری جان کبھی
بے کراں رات کے سناٹے میں
جذبۂ شوق سے ہو جاتے ہیں اعضا مدہوش
اور لذّت کی گراں باری سے
ذہن بن جاتا ہے دل دل کسی ویرانے کی
اور کہیں اس کے قریب
نیند آغازِ زمستاں کے پرندے کی طرح
خوف دل میں کسی موہوم شکاری کا لئے
اپنے پر تولتی ہے چیختی ہے
بے کراں رات کے سناٹے میں
تیرے بستر پہ مری جان کبھی
آرزوئیں ترے سینے کے کہستانوں میں
ظلم سہتے ہوئے حبشی کی طرح رینگتی ہیں
ایک لمحے کے لئے دل میں خیال آتا ہے
تو مری جان نہیں ۔۔۔۔۔۔۔

Nazar Mohammed Rashid
Be Karaan Raat ke Sannate Mein
(In the Deadly Silent Night)

Stretched on your bed sometime
In the deadly silent night,
Desire-drunk my limbs slip into a delirious state;
And my brain, luxury-weighed,
Becomes a barren marshy ground.

Somewhere near at hand, the sleep,
Like an early winter-bird,
Dreading some hunter's sudden swoop,
Flutters its wings and screams.

In the deadly, silent night,
Stretched on your bed sometime,
Restless longings deep-suppressed in the caverns of your breast,
Like a bonded negro slave, cringe and crawl for life.

A momentary thought disturbs my mind:
You are not my life ....

Tere bistar pe miri jaan kabhi
Be karan raat ke sannate mein
Jazba-e-shauq se ho jaate hain aaza madhosh
Aur lazzat ki Giranbaari se
Zehan ban jaata hai daldal kisi veeraane ki

Aur kahin iske qarib
Neend aagaaz-e-zamistan ke parinde ki tarah
Khauf dil mein kisi mauhoom shikari ka lieye
Apne par tolti hai, cheekhti hai

Be karan raat ke sannaate mein
Tere bistar pe miri jaan kabhi
Aarzooen tire seene ke kuhistaanon mein
Zulm sahte hue habshi ki tarah reengti hain.

Ek lamhe ke lieye dil mein Khayal aata hai
Tu Miri jaan nahin ....

ن ۔ م ۔ راشد

بلکہ ساحل کے کسی شہر کی دو شیزہ ہے
اور ترے ملک کے دشمن کا سپاہی ہوں میں
ایک مدت سے جسے ایسی کوئی شب نہ ملی
کہ ذرا روح کو اپنی وہ سبک بار کرے
بے پناہ عیش کے ہیجان کا ارماں لے کر
اپنے دستے سے کئی روز سے مفرور ہوں میں
ترے بستر پہ مری جان کبھی
بے کراں رات کے سناٹے میں

Nazar Mohammed Rashid

But a damsel of some town on an alien shore,
And I, a soldier of the country now at war with your folks;
Who hasn't for a single night
His weary soul regaled.
Bursting with a spate of longings, thirsting for the feast,
Fleeing from my regiment, I come to seek relief,
Stretched in your bed I muse
In the deadly silent night.

Balke saahil ke kisi shahr ki dosheeza hai
Aur tire mulk ke dushman ka sipaahi hoon main
Ek Muddat se jise aisi koi shab na mili
Ke zara rooh ko apni woh subak baar kare,
Be panah aish ke hejaan ka armaan le kar
Apne daste se kai roz se mafroor hoon main
Tire bistar pe miri jaan kabhi
Be Karaan raat ke sannaate mein.

Sana Allaha Sani Daar Meeraji
(1912-1949)

SANA ALLAHA SANI DAAR MEERAJI
(1912-1949)

Meeraji was born at Lahore on May 25, 1912, and died in Bombay on November 4, 1949. Though he lived for only thirty seven years, his poetic output is astonishing, both in terms of quality and quantity. His complete works *Kulliaat* published in 1988 by Dr Jameel Jaalibi from Urdu Centre, London, contain a rich variety of verse, representing *geet*, *ghazal*, and *nazm*, both of the rhyming and the free-verse type, in addition to translations from foreign languages including English, French, Russian, Japanese, Chinese, Persian, Sanskrit, etc. His favourite topics are love, beauty and death, and his signal contribution lies in giving a new direction to Urdu poetry and poetics. Along with N. M. Rashid, he is a leading poet of the progressive movement in Urdu poetry, which breaks with the convention of *radif* and *qafia*, explores the rich resources of blank verse and free-verse, comes out of the confines of the socially "acceptable" and "respectable" themes, rejects the stranglehold of Persianised "poetical" diction, and explores, with sensitivity and skill, the hitherto forbidden terrritories of sexual and psychological states.

A son of respectable parents (his father, Munshi Mohammed Mahtab-ul-din, was an engineer in Indian railways) and brought up in apparently affluent and affectionate circumstances, Meeraji left his home and family for certain inexplicable reasons, and spent a greater part of his life as a homeless wanderer, staying with his friends, and making his living by writing songs, and by doing editorial work for several urdu magazines: ``Adbi Duniya'' (Lahore), "Saqi" (Delhi) and "Khayaal" (Bombay). As can be made out from the portrait of the poet prefixed to this selection, the poet had adopted a deliberately outlandish style in his looks habiliments. Supporting long, floating hair (which would come and go according to his whims), a dagger-like moustache, oversize earrings, a colourful headgear, an amulet and a string of beads around his neck, Meeraji fits into Coleridge's description of a poet—an inspired being with "flashing eyes and floating hair", who "on honey-dew hath fed/And drunk the milk of Paradise." But beneath this outward appearance of an unworldy ascetic lay a man, sensitive and intelligent, a jilted lover, sad at heart and sick in body, always perplexed, always questing, and turning to poetry for emotional release. As a poet, Meeraji was fully aware of the strength and weakness of Urdu poetry, and fully armed with the requisite energy of thought and style to bring about a transformation in the poetic field.

Both the poems included in this volume—"Mujhe Ghar Yaad Aata Hai" and "Samundar ka Bulawa"—show how this romantic runaway was torn between the two worlds—the cosy world of childhood, when, sitting in the family circle, he would laugh and play with his brothers and sisters, and the outside world of uninhibited freedom, which, however, turned out to be hollow and hypocritical, and in which he floated like a rudderless bark with no shore in sight. And yet this exile from home, who harboured no ill-will against his parents, brothers or sisters, never returned home, not even when he fell seriously ill. Akhtar-ul Iman, the poet's friend, with whom he spent the last days of his life in Poona and Bombay, describes how lonely and miserable was his existence in the end. Excessive drinking, cigarette-smoking, and sexual dissipation had drained away his strength and damaged his liver. Then there came the additional agony of the psychic ailment, for which he had to be admitted to the hospital where he was given electric shocks to cure him of his insanity—a treatment which he dreaded. The end came at 4 p.m. on November 4, in King Edward Memorial Hospital in Bombay. The call had come, the call of the sea, from which, in the poet's own words, "we all spring,/ And to which we all must return."

میرا جی

مجھے گھر یاد آتا ہے

سمٹ کر کس لئے نقطہ نہیں بنتی زمیں؟ کہہ دو؟
یہ پھیلا آسماں اس وقت کیوں دِل کو لبھاتا تھا؟
ہر اک سمت اب انوکھے لوگ ہیں اور ان کی باتیں ہیں
کوئی دل سے پھسل جاتی، کوئی سینے میں چبھ جاتی
انہی باتوں کی لہروں پہ بہا جاتا ہے یہ مجرا
جسے ساحل نہیں ملتا
میں جس کے سامنے آؤں مجھے لازم ہے ہلکی مسکراہٹ میں کہیں یہ ہونٹ
و تم کو جانتا ہوں "، دل کہے،" کب جانتا ہوں میں ؟ "
انہی لہروں پہ بہتا ہوں مجھے ساحل نہیں ملتا۔
سمٹ کر کس لئے نقطہ نہیں بنتی زمیں، کہہ دو،
وہ کیسی مسکراہٹ تھی، بہن کی مسکراہٹ تھی، مرا بھائی بھی، ہنستا تھا
وہ ہنستا تھا بہن ہنستی ہے اپنے دل میں کہتی ہے
یہ کیسی بات بھائی نے کہی، دیکھو وہ اماں اور اَبّا کو ہنسی آئی،
مگر یوں وقت بہتا ہے! تماشا بن گیا ساحل،
مجھے ساحل نہیں ملتا۔

Sana Allaha Sani Daar Meeraji
Mujhe Ghar Yaad Aata Hai
(I Remember My Home)

Why doesn't the earth, tell me, compress into a point?
Why did the open skies then tempt my heart?
I'm now a lonely man amid an alien crowd,
Whose hollow chatter leaves me cold, or stings my heart.
Flowing with the tide of talk drifts along my bark,
Which cannot find the shore.

I'm supposed to smile and say to anyone I meet:
"I know you, sir," though in sooth, I do not know at all;
Carried on these waves I float, but cannot find the shore.

Why doesn't the earth, tell me, compress into a point?
Ah, that sunshine of smiles! my brother laughed, my sister
    smiled,
He laughed that she laughed thinking in her mind,
How her brother's silly talk set their mom and dad agiggle.

But time and tide will not stay, the shore is now a dream
    forgot,
I cannot find the shore.

Simat kar kis lieye nuqta nahin banti zamin? Kah do?
Yeh phaila aasmaan us waqt kyon dil ko lubhata tha?
Har ik samat ab anokhe log hain aur un ki baaten hain,
Koi dil se phisal jaati, koi seene mein chubh jaati,
Inhi baaton ki lahron par baha jaata hai yeh bajra
Jise saahil nahin milta.

Main jis ke saamne aaoon mujhe laazim hai halki muskarahat mein
    kahen yeh hont
"Tumko jaanta hoon," dil kahe, "kab jaanta hoon main?"
Inhi lahron pe bahta hoon mujhe saahil nahin milta.

Simat kar kis lieye nuqta nahin banti zamin, kahdo,
Woh kaisi muskarahat thi, behn ki muskurahat thi, mira bhai bhi
    hansta tha
Woh hansta tha behn hansti hai apne dil mein kahti hai
Yeh kaisi baat bhai ne kahi, dekho woh amman aur abba ko hansi
    aai,
Magar yun waqt bahta hai, tamasha ban gaya saahil,
Muje saahil nahin milta.

میرا جی

سمٹ کر کس لئے نقطہ نہیں بنتی زمیں کہہ دو
یہ کیسا پھیر ہے، تقدیر کا یہ پھیر تو شاید نہیں، لیکن
یہ پھیلا آسماں اس وقت کیوں دل کو لبھاتا تھا؟
حیات مختصر سب کی بہی جاتی ہے اور میں بھی
ہر اک کو دیکھتا ہوں مسکراتا ہے کہ ہنستا ہے
کوئی ہنستا نظر آئے کوئی روتا نظر آئے
میں سب کو دیکھتا ہوں دیکھ کر خاموش رہتا ہوں
مجھے ساحل نہیں ملتا۔

Meeraji

Why doesn't the earth, tell me, compress into a point?
How has it come about? Is it the trick of fate?
But why did the open skies tempt me in the first place?
This our life transient, flows on unchecked, and I too
Gaze on every face, who smiles, who laughs;
This one laughs, that one weeps,
I see them all, I do not speak;
I cannot sight the shore.

Simat kar kis lieye nuqta nahin banti zamin kahdo,
Yeh kaisa pher hai, taqdir ka yeh pher tau shayad nahin, lekin
Yeh phaila aasmaan us waqt kyon dil ko lubhata tha?

Hayat-e-mukhtasir sab ki bahi jaati hai aur main bhi
Har ik ko dekhta hoon muskarata hai ke hansta hai,
Koi hansta nazar aae, koi rota nazar aae,
Main sab ko dekhta hoon dekh kar khamosh rahta hoon,
Mujhe saahil nahin milta.

میرا جی
سمندر کا بُلاوا

یہ سرگوشیاں کہہ رہی ہیں اب آؤ کہ برسوں سے تم کو بلاتے بلاتے
مرے دل پہ گہری تھکن چھا رہی ہے
کبھی ایک پل کو، کبھی ایک عرصہ صدائیں سنی ہیں مگر یہ انوکھی ندا آرہی ہے
بلاتے بلاتے تو کوئی ندا اب تک تھکا ہے نہ آئندہ شاید تھکے گا،
"مرے پیارے بچے" "مجھے تم سے کتنی محبت ہے" "وہ دیکھو، اگر یوں کیا تو بلا مجھ
بڑھ کر نہ کوئی کبھی ہوگا" "وہ خدایا، خدایا!"،
کبھی ایک سسکی، کبھی اک تبسّم، کبھی صرف تیوری
مگر یہ صدائیں تو آتی رہی ہیں
اِنہیں سے حیاتِ دو روزہ ابد سے ملی ہے
مگر یہ انوکھی ندا جس پہ گہری تھکن چھا رہی ہے
یہ ہر اک صدا کو مٹانے کی دھمکی دیئے جا رہی ہے
اب آنکھوں میں جنبش نہ چہرے پہ کوئی تبسم نہ تیوری
فقط کان سنتے چلے جا رہے ہیں

یہ اک گلستاں ہے، ہوا لہلہاتی ہے، کلیاں ٹپکتی ہیں، غنچے مہکتے ہیں اور پھول
کھلتے ہیں، کھل کھل کے مرجھا کے گرتے ہیں، اک فرشِ مخمل بناتے ہیں جس پر
مری آرزوؤں کی پریاں عجب آن سے یوں رواں ہیں کہ جیسے گلستاں ہی اک آئینہ ہے،

Meeraji
Samundar ka Bulawa (The Call of the Sea)

These whisperings urge me: "Come back now, for calling you
    for years
I have tired out my heart.
Now for a while, now for days, I've heard these voices, but 'tis
    a voice strange,
None has ever tired of calling, none perhaps will be.
"Dear, my child, I love you dearly, see, I pray, desist,
God forbid that I should my worst side expose."
Now a sob, now a smile, now a mere frown,
These voices, all the same, have incessantly called;
And linked this life transient with its eternal source.
But this voice unique, worn out, fatigued,
Is threatening into silence the voices from the East.
No frown, no smile now, nor an eye aflicker,
I simply sit and hear this strange compelling call.
This is a garden where breezes blow, buds open, blossoms
    smile,
Flowers fade and fall, and make a velvet floor.
This garden seems a mirror where younglings of desire
    fairy-like strut

Yeh sargoshian kah rahi hain ab aao ke barson se tum ko bulaate
    bulaate
Mire dil pe gahri thakan chha rahi hai.
Kabhi ek pal ko, kabhe ek arsa sadaaein suni hain magar yeh anokhi
    nida aa rahi hai,
Bulaate bulaate tau koi na ab tak thaka hai na aainda shayad
    thakega,
"Mire payare bachche, mujhe tum se kitni mahabbat hai, dekho, agar
    yun kiya tau
Bura mujh se barh kar na koi bhi hoga, Khudaya!"
Kabhi ek siski, kabhi ik tabassum, kabhi sirf teori,
Magar yeh sadaaein tau aati rahi hain,
Inhi se hayat-e-do roza abad se mili hai;
Magar yeh anokhi sada jis pe gahri thakan chha rahi hai,
Yeh har ik sada ko mitaane ki dhamki dieye ja rahi hai.
Ab aankhon mein jumbish, na chehre pe koi tabassum na teori,
Faqt kaan sunte chale jaa rahe hain.
Yeh 'ik gulistaan hai, hawa lahlahati hai, kalian chitakti hain,
    ghunche mahkte hain aur phool
Khilte hain, khil khil ke murjha ke girte hain, ik farsh-e-makhmal
    banaate hain jispar
Miri aarzuon ki parian ajab aan se yun rawan hain ke jaise
    gulistaan hi ik aaeena hai

میرا جی

اسی آئینے میں ہر اک شکل نکھری، سنور کر مٹی اور مٹ ہی گئی، پھر نہ ابھری
یہ پربت ہے خاموش، ساکن،

کبھی کوئی چشمہ ابلتے ہوئے پوچھتا ہے کہ اس کی چٹانوں کے اس پار کیا ہے؟
مگر مجھ کو پربت کا دامن ہی کافی ہے، دامن میں وادی ہے، وادی میں ندی سے ندی میں
بہتی ہوئی ناؤ ہی آئینہ ہے،

اسی آئینے میں ہر اک شکل نکھری، مگر ایک پل میں جو مٹنے لگی ہے تو پھر وہ نہ ابھری'
یہ صحرا ہے پھیلا ہوا، خشک، بے برگ صحرا،
بگولے یہاں تند بھوتوں کا عکسِ مجسم بنے ہیں
مگر میں تو در در ایک پیڑوں کے جھرمٹ پہ اپنی نگاہیں جمائے ہوئے ہوں۔
نہ اب کوئی صحرا، نہ پربت نہ کوئی گلستاں،
اب آنکھوں میں جنبش نہ چہرے پہ کوئی تبسم نہ تیوری
فقط ایک ان لکھی صدا کہہ رہی ہے کہ تم کو بلاتے بلاتے مرے دل پہ گہری تھکن چھا رہی
بلاتے بلاتے تو کوئی نہ اب تک تھکا ہے نہ شاید تھکے گا
تو پھر یہ ندا آئینہ ہے، فقط میں تھکا ہوں،
نہ صحرا نہ پربت، نہ کوئی گلستاں، فقط اب سمندر بلاتا ہے مجھ کو
کہ ہر شکستہ سمندر سے آئی، سمندر میں جا کر ملے گی،

338

Meeraji

Each shape attains to form, dissipates, dissolves, never to come again.
It s a mountain, silent, still,
Where a fount at times upshoots and asks what lies beyond the bourn?
But I'm content to lie on the monutainside, where flows a river with a boat afloat,
This boat is a mirror reflecting many shapes,
Each shape, for a moment, glows, grows, and goes, never to come again.
This is a desert, wide and barren, without a tree or leaf,
Where whirlwinds, like ghosts embodied eddy about and vault,
But I sit unmoved, with my gaze riveted on that distant grove.
The desert, mount, and garden are no longer in sight;
The brow has lost its frown, the eye its flicker, the face its smile,
And I hear one only voice whispering in my ear: calling you for long I've worn out my heart,
Though none has ever tired of calling, none perhaps will be.
This voice then is the mirror, only I am tired.
'Tis the sea that summons me with its final call,
The sea from which we all spring, to which we all return.

Isi aaeene mein har ik shakl nikhri, sanwar kar miti aur mit hi gai, phir na ubhri.
Yeh parbat hai khaamosh, saakin,
Kabhi koi chashma ubalte hue puchhta hai ke us ki chitanon ke us paar kya hai?
Magar mujh ko parbat ka daman hi kafi hoi, daman mein wadi hai, wadi mein nadi hai, nadi mein bahti hui naao hi aaeena hai;
Isi aaene mein har shakl nikhri, magar ek pal mein jo mitne lagi hai, tau phir woh na ubhri.
Yeh sahra hai phaila hua, khushk, be barg sahra,
Bagole yahan tund bhooton ka aks-e-mujassam bane hain,
Magar main tau door ek peron ke jhurmat pe apni nigaahen jamaae hue hoon. -
Na ab koi sahra, na parbat, na koi gulistaan,
Ab aankhon mein jumbish, na chehra pe koi tabassum na teori,
Faqt ik anokhi sada kah rahi hai ke tum ko bulaate bulaate mire dil pe gahri thakan chha rahi hai;
Bulaate bulaate tau koi na ab tak thaka hai na shayad thakega,
Tau phir yeh nida aaeena hai, faqt main thaka hun.
Na sahra na parbat, na koi gulistaan, faqt ab samundar bulaata hai mujhko,
Ke har shai samundar se aai, samundar mein ja kar milegi.

Asrar-ul-Haq Majaz
(1911-1955)

ASRAR-UL-HAQ MAJAZ
(1911-1955)

Majaz was born at Radauli near Lucknow on October 19, 1911. His father, Siraj-ul-Haq was a respectable landlord, and a law graduate from Lucknow university. Majaz's early life was spent in affluent cirumstances. "My life," he says in one of his poems, "was a bed of velvet and brocade." He received his schooling at Lucknow, and his college education at Agra and Aligarh. He had given proof of his poetic talent even during his schooldays at Lucknow, where, under the influence of his friend and counsellor, M. Hassan Jazbi, he had started writing poetry. At Aligarh he was influenced, among others, by Fani Badayuni to whom he took his poems for correction. Majaz also studied at St. Johns College, Agra, where he stayed for sometime in the college hostel. The atmosphere of freedom available in the hostel, combined with the society of his easy-going friends, encouraged his innate tendency to indulge in the sensuous pleasures of love and wine. The habit of drinking later became an addiction, and contributed to the poet's early death. His unsuccessful romance with a "young lady", was the precipitating cause of his first nervous breakdown, which was followed by two more attacks after short intervals of normalcy. Leaving his M.A. (Urdu) studies half-way, Majaz took up employment with All India Radio, where he also edited the radio journal, *Aawaz*. But he had to give up this job after a year due to differences with his boss, Ahmed Shah Bukhari (Pitras). Majaz abjured drinking for a few months, but the habit came back with a vengeance. On the morning of December 5, 1955, he was found lying unconscious on the terrace of a tavern in Lucknow. The end came the same day in a hospital in Lucknow.

Romance and revolt are the two important strands of Majaz's poetry. As Faiz Ahmed Faiz puts it, "saaz-o-jaam, aur shamsheer," i.e., song, sword, and wine are the chief sources of the poet's inspiration. In his real life Majaz had the opportunity to mix with all classes of people, from the lowliest to the richest, and the glaring contrast between the two reminded him of the inequity of the capitalist system. The hero of "Aawara", an unemployed young man, frustrated in love and life, strolls at night the streets of a modern city, apparently glittering and glimmering in the light of the electric bulbs, but dark and deceitful beneath the surface, and inimical to the growth of love and justice. The frustration of the lover finds a powerful expression in the impressionistic imagery of the poem, charged with social and satirical implications. Note in particular the pale moon (in stanza 10) which looks successively like the "mullah's turban", "trader's ledger-book", "a poor man's youth", and the "widow's blighted life". The suppressed anger of the hero finds an outlet in the last two stanzas where he expresses his resolve to burn the thrones and break the swords of the ruling artistocracy, and create a new socialist order out of the prevailing chaos. The poem is a moving cry of an anguished heart, struggling, in vain, to break the bonds of cant and convention.

What is implied in "Aawara" is more explicity stated in "Khwab-e-sehar", which records the poet's feeling of hope and relief at the long-awaited dawn of a new communistic order, which alone, he feels, can deliver man from centuries of slavery to superstition and exploitation. The poem was written to celebrate the anniversary of the Russian revolution.

In his style, Majaz adheres to the conventional kind of rhymed verse, and is not particularly interested in the new forms of blank verse and free verse poems, which were fashionable with his important contemporaries like N. M. Rashid, Miraji, and Ali Sardar Jaafri.

Majaz's collected works are available under the title: *Aahang*.

اسرارالحق مجاز
آوارہ

شہر کی رات اور میں ناشاد و ناکارہ پھروں
جگمگاتی جاگتی سڑکوں پہ آوارہ پھروں
غیر کی بستی ہے کب تک در بدر مارا پھروں
اے غمِ دل کیا کروں اے وحشتِ دل کیا کروں

جھلملاتے قمقموں کی راہ میں زنجیر سی
رات کے ہاتھوں میں دن کی موہنی تصویر سی
میرے سینے پر مگر چلتی ہوئی شمشیر سی
اے غمِ دل کیا کروں اے وحشتِ دل کیا کروں

یہ رُپہلی چھاؤں یہ آکاش پر تاروں کا جال
جیسے صوفی کا تصور جیسے عاشق کا خیال
آہ لیکن کون جانے کون سمجھے دل کا حال
اے غمِ دل کیا کروں اے وحشتِ دل کیا کروں

پھر وہ ٹوٹا اک ستارہ پھر وہ چھوٹی پھلجھڑی
جانے کس کی گود میں آئی یہ موتی کی لڑی
ہوک سی سینے میں اٹھی چوٹ سی دل پر پڑی
اے غمِ دل کیا کروں اے وحشتِ دل کیا کروں

Asrar-ul-Haq Majaz
Aawara (The Vagabond)

Lo, I wander sad and idle in this city at night,
Meander aimless on the roads adazzle with the row of lights;
How long to roam from door to door in this land hostile?
What to do, O aching heart, what to do, O frenzy wild?

A chain of lights on the road before me lies stretched,
The night holds in her arms the day richly dressed,
But I feel a dagger sharp into my breast is thrust;
What to do, O aching heart, what to do, O frenzy wild?

Ah, this silver shade of night, this web of stars on high!
Like the lover's fancy, like the mystic's flight;
Who alas, would know my heart, comprehend my plight?
What to do, O aching heart, what to do, O frenzy wild?

There falls a shooting star, there a sparkler bursts,
This wreath of pearls, I do not know, whose lap has blessed;
But, I feel an ache within, my heart makes a moan suppressed,
What to do, O aching heart, what to do, O frenzy wild?

Shah'r ki raat aur main naashaad-o-na-kaara phiroon,
Jagmagati jaagti sarkon pe aawara phiroon;
Ghair ki bast hai, kab tak dar badar maara phiroon;
Ai ghum-e-dil kya karoon, ai wahshat-e-dil kya karoon?

Jhilmalaate qumqumon ki raah mein zanjeer si,
Raat ke haathon mein din ki mohani tasweer si,
Mere seene par magar chalti hui shamshir si;
Ai ghum-e-dil kya karoon, ai wahshat-e-dil kya karoon?

Yeh roopahli chaaon, yeh aakaash par taaron ka jaal,
Jaise soofi ka tasawwur, jaise aashiq ka khayal,
Aah lekin kaun jane, kaun samjhe dil ka haal;
Ai ghum-e-dil kya karoon, ai wahshat-e-dil kya karoon?

Phir woh toota ik sitara phir woh chhooti phuljhari,
Jaane kis ki god mein aai yeh moti ki lari,
Hook si seene mein uthi, chot si dil par pari,
Ai ghum-e-dil kya karoon, ai wahshat-e-dil kya karoon?

مجاز

رات ہنس ہنس کر یہ کہتی ہے کہ مَیخانے میں چل
پھر کسی شہناز لالہ رخ کے کاشانے میں چل
یہ نہیں ممکن تو پھر اے دوست ویرانے میں چل
اے غمِ دل کیا کروں اے وحشتِ دل کیا کروں

ہر طرف بکھری ہوئی رنگینیاں، رعنائیاں
ہر قدم پر عشرتیں لیتی ہوئی انگڑائیاں
بڑھ رہی ہیں گود پھیلائے ہوئے رسوائیاں
اے غمِ دل کیا کروں، اے وحشتِ دل کیا کروں

راستے میں رک کے دم لے لوں مری عادت نہیں
لوٹ کر واپس چلا جاؤں مری فطرت نہیں
اور کوئی ہمنوا مل جائے یہ قسمت نہیں
اے غمِ دل کیا کروں اے وحشتِ دل کیا کروں

منتظر ہے ایک طوفانِ بلا میرے لیے
اب بھی جانے کتنے دروازے ہیں وا میرے لیے
پر مصیبت ہے مرا عہدِ وفا میرے لیے
اے غمِ دل کیا کروں اے وحشتِ دل کیا کروں

Majaz

The night says with a smile: go, visit the tavern gay,
Or visit the nightly chamber of some beauty flower-faced;
Failing which seek the deserts, scour the barren wastes;
What to do, O aching heart, what to do, O frenzy wild?

Everywhere lie displayed tantalising charms,
Sensuous feasts beckon me, twist, turn and yawn;
Calumnies at every step spread out their arms;
What to do, O aching heart, what to do, O frenzy wild?

To pause and stop on the way goes against my grain,
'Tis not my nature to turn back in vain;
That I may accost a mate, such is not ordained;
What to do, O aching heart, what to do, O frenzy wild?

Many a tempest danger-fraught lies in wait for me,
Many a door lies ajar even now for me,
But this plighted troth of mine will not set me free;
What to do, O aching heart, what to do, O frenzy wild?

Raat hans hans kar yeh kahti hai ke maikhane mein chal,
Phir kisi shahnaaz lala rukh ke kaashaane mein chal,
Yeh nahin mumkin tau phir ai dost weerane mein chal;
Ai ghum-e-dil kya karoon, ai wahshat-e-dil kya karoon?

Har taraf bikhri hui rangeenian, raanaaian,
Har qadam par ishraten leti hui angraaian,
Barh rahi hain god phailae hue ruswaaian;
Ai ghum-e-dil kya karoon, ai wahshat-e-dil kya karoon?

Raaste mein ruk ke dam le loon miri aadat nahin,
Laut kar waapis chala jaaon miri fitrat nahin;
Aur koi humnawa mil jaae yeh qismat nahin;
Ai ghum-e-dil kya karoon, ai wahshat-e-dil kya karoon?

Muntezir hai ek toofaan-e-bala mere lieye,
Ab bhi jaane kitne darwaaze hain waa mere lieye;
Par museebat hai mira ahd-e-wafa mere lieye;
Ai ghum-e-dil kya karoon, ai wahshat-e-dil kya karoon?

مجاز

جی میں آتا ہے کہ اب عہدِ وفا بھی توڑ دوں
ان کو پا سکتا ہوں میں یہ آسرا بھی توڑ دوں
ہاں مناسب ہے یہ زنجیرِ ہوا بھی توڑ دوں
اے غمِ دل کیا کروں اے وحشتِ دل کیا کروں

اک محل کی آڑ سے نکلا وہ پیلا ماہتاب
جیسے ملّا کا عمامہ جیسے بنیے کی کتاب
جیسے مفلس کی جوانی جیسے بیوہ کا شباب
اے غمِ دل کیا کروں اے وحشتِ دل کیا کروں

دل میں اک شعلہ بھڑک اٹھا ہے آخر کیا کروں
میرا پیمانہ چھلک اٹھا ہے آخر کیا کروں
زخم سینے کا مہک اٹھا ہے آخر کیا کروں
اے غمِ دل کیا کروں اے وحشتِ دل کیا کروں

مفلسی اور یہ مظاہر ہیں نظر کے سامنے
سینکڑوں چنگیز و نادر ہیں نظر کے سامنے
سینکڑوں سلطان جابر ہیں نظر کے سامنے
اے غمِ دل کیا کروں اے وحشتِ دل کیا کروں

Majaz

I should break my plighted troth, this is what I feel,
That I can possess my love, I shouldn't believe,
I should snap the thread of hope woven out of flimsy breeze,
What to do, O aching heart, what to do, O frenzy wild?

From behind the palace there, the yellow moon doth rise,
Like the turban of the priest, the ledger of the trader wise,
Like the poverty-stricken youth, like the widow's prime of life;
What to do, O aching heart, what to do, O frenzy wild?

A flame is kindled in my heart, what am I to do?
Brimful is my cup, O Lord, what am I to do?
The wound of heart has come to bloom, what am I to do?
What to do, O aching heart, what to do, O frenzy wild?

In the midst of poverty, such scenes meet my eyes,
Many Changezes, many Naadirs distress my sight;
Many kings and potentates these my eyes descry;
What to do, O aching heart, what to do, O frenzy wild?

Ji mein aata hai ke ab ahd-e-wafa bhi tor doon,
Un ko paa sakta hun main, yeh aasra bhi tor doon,
Haan munasib hai yeh zanjeer-e-hawa bhi tor doon,
Ai ghum-e-dil kya karoon, ai wahshat-e-dil kya karoon?

Ik mahal ki aar se nikla woh peela maahtaab,
Jaise mullah ka amaama, jaise baniey ki ki kitab;
Jaise muflis ki jawani, jaise bewa ka shabab;
Ai ghum-e-dil kya karoon, ai wahshat-e-dil kya karoon?

Dil mein ik shola bharak utha hai aakhir kya karoon,
Mera paimana chhalak utha hai, aakhir kya karoon,
Zakhm seene ka mehak utha hai, aakhir kya karoon;
Ai ghum-e-dil kya karoon, ai wahshat-e-dil kya karoon?

Muflisi aur yeh mazaahir hain nazar ke saamne,
Sainkron Changez-o-Naadir hain nazar ke saamne,
Sainkron sultaan jaabar hain nazar ke saamne,
Ai ghum-e-dil kya karoon, ai wahshat-e-dil kya karoon?

مجاز

لے کے اک چنگیز کے ہاتھوں سے خنجر توڑ دوں
تاج پر اس کے دمکتا ہے جو پتھر توڑ دوں
کوئی توڑے یا نہ توڑے میں ہی بڑھ کر توڑ دوں
اے غمِ دل کیا کروں اے دہشتِ دل کیا کروں

بڑھ کے اس اندر سبھا کا ساز و دسامانپھونک دوں
اس کا گلشن پھونک دوں اس کا شبستاں پھونک دوں
تختِ سلطاں کیا میں سارا قصرِ سلطاں پھونک دوں
اے غمِ دل کیا کروں اے دہشتِ دل کیا کروں

Majaz

I should snatch and break to bits the sword of a Changez,
I should pluck from off the crown the precious stone ablaze,
I at least should break his pride, others may or mayn't break,
What to do, O aching heart, what to do, O frenzy wild?

Let me burn all the trappings of this sensual meet,
Let me burn this nightly chamber, that garden retreat,
Not throne alone, but palace, too, I would burn complete;
What to do, O aching heart, what to do, O frenzy wild?

Le ke ik Changez ke haathon se khanjar tor doon,
Taaj par uske damakta hai jo paththar tor doon,
Koi tore ya na tore main hi barh kar tor doon;
Ai ghum-e-dil kya karoon, ai wahshat-e-dil kya karoon?

Barh ke is indar sabha ka saaz-o-saaman phoonk doon,
Is ka gulshan phoon doon, uska shabastaan phoonk doon,
Takht-e-sultaan kya main saara qasar-e-sultaan phoonk doon,
Ai ghum-e-dil kya karoon, ai wahshat-e-dil kya karoon?

مجاز
خوابِ سحر

مہر صدیوں سے چمکتا ہی رہا افلاک پر
رات ہی طاری رہی انسان کے ادراک پر
عقل کے میدان میں ظلمت کا ڈیرا ہی رہا
دل میں تاریکی، دماغوں میں اندھیرا ہی رہا
اک نہ اک مذہب کی سعئ خام بھی ہوتی رہی
اہلِ دل پر بارشِ الہام بھی ہوتی رہی
آسمانوں سے فرشتے بھی اترتے ہی رہے
نیک بندے بھی خدا کا کام کرتے ہی رہے
ابنِ مریم بھی اٹھے، موسیٰ و عمران بھی اٹھے
رام و گوتم بھی اٹھے، فرعون و ہامان بھی اٹھے
اہلِ سیف اٹھتے رہے، اہلِ کتاب آتے رہے
ایں جناب آتے رہے اور آں جناب آتے رہے
حکمراں دل پر رہے صدیوں تلک اصنام بھی
ابرِ رحمت بن کے چھایا دہر پر اسلام بھی
مسجدوں میں مولوی خطبے سناتے ہی رہے
مندروں میں برہمن اشلوک گاتے ہی رہے

Majaz
Khwab-e-Sehar (Dream of Dawn)

For ages has the radiant sun been shining in the skies,
But human mind has always struggled in the shade of night.

Darkness has held its sway since the world began,
Not a ray was allowed to light the head or heart of man.

Religion too from time to time has made her vain forays,
The rain of revelation too has purified this place.

Angels too from time to time have descended on this earth,
Noble souls have also been displaying their precious worth.

Moses, Umraan, Mary's Jesus—all showed their spiritual might,
Ram, Gautam, Faroun, Haaman, all have their hands tried.

Wielders of the pen and sword have also walked this globe,
The world has been graced by unnumbered reverend folks.

For centuries has the human heart to idols been a prey,
Islam too, like vernal cloud, has fertilized this clay.

Mullahs have been sermonizing in the holy mosques,
Brahamins have been chanting hymns in their synogogues.

Mehar sadion se chamakta hi raha iflaak par,
Raat hi taari rahi insaan ke idraak par.

Aql ke maidaan mein zulmat ka dera hi raha,
Dil mein taariki, dimaaghon mein andhera hi raha.

Ik na ik mazhab ki sai-e-khaam bhi hoti rahi,
Ahl-e-dil par baarish-e-ilhaam bhi hoti rahi.

Aasmaanon se farishte bhi utarte hi rahe,
Nek bande bhi khuda ka kaam karte hi rahe.

Ibn-e-Mariam bhi uthe, moosa-o-umraan bhi uthe,
Ram-o-Gautam bhi uthe, Faroun-o-Haaman bhi uthe;

Ahle-e-saif uthte rahe, ahl-e-kitab aate rahe,
Een janab aate rahe, aur aanjanab aate rahe.

Hukamraan dil par rahe sadion talak isnaam bhi,
Abr-e-rahmat ban ke chhaya dahr par islaam bhi.

Masjidon mein maulvi khutbe sunate hi rahe,
Mandiron mein brahamin ashlok gaate hi rahe.

مجاز

آدمی منت کشِ اربابِ عرفاں ہی رہا
دردِ انسانی مگر محرومِ درماں ہی رہا
اک نداک درپرجبیں شوقِ گھستی ہی رہی
آدمیت ظلم کی چکی میں پِستی ہی رہی
رہبری جاری رہی پیغمبری جاری رہی
دین کے پردے میں جنگِ زرگری جاری رہی
اہلِ باطن علم کے سینوں کو گرماتے رہے
جہل کے تاریک سائے ہاتھ پھیلاتے رہے
یہ مسلسل آفتیں، یہ یورشیں، یہ قتلِ عام
آدمی کب تک رہے اوہام و باطل کا غلام
ذہنِ انسانی نے اب اوہام کے ظلمات میں
زندگی کی سخت طوفانی اندھیری رات میں
کچھ نہیں تو کم سے کم خوابِ سحر دیکھا تو ہے
جس طرف دیکھا نہ تھا اب تک ادھر دیکھا تو ہے

Majaz

Man has been supplicating saints and sages wise,
Human misery, all the same, has all recipes defied.

Human brow has always bent at this or that threshold,
Humanity has always suffered inequities untold.

There has been no dearth of leaders, or of prophets wise,
Greed for gold has plied its trade wearing religious guise.

Feeling hearts have tried to leaven knowledge with the light of love,
The clouds of darkness, nevertheless, have always hung over this earth,

Such struggle, such suffering, such heinous carnage!
How long has man been to superstition a slave!

Human mind has at last awakened from its heavy sleep,
In the stormy night of life, in the superstitious deep,

Has at least dreamt a dream of the golden dawn,
Looked at least towards the East, where none before had glanced.

Aadmi mannat kash-e-arbaab-e-irfaan hi raha,
Dard-e-insaani magar mehroom-e-darmaan hi raha.

Ik na ik dar par jabeen-e-shauq ghisti hi rahi,
Aadmeeat zulam ki chakki mein pisti hi rahi.

Rahbari jaari rahi, paighambari jaari rahi,
Deen ke parde mein jang-e-zargari jaari rahi.

Ahl-e-baatin ilm ke seenon ko garmaate rahe,
Juhal ke taarik saae haath phailaate rahe.

Yeh musalsal aafaten, yeh yorishen, yeh qatal-e-aam,
Aadmi kab tak rahe ohaam-e-baatil ka ghulaam!

Zehn-e-insaani ne ab ohaam ke zulmaat mein,
Zindagi ki sakht toofaani andheri raat mein,

Kuchh nahin tau kam se kam khwab-e-sehar dekha tau hai,
Jis taraf dekha na tha ab tak udhar dekha tau hai.

Faiz Ahmed Faiz
(1911-1984)

FAIZ AHMED FAIZ
(1911-1984)

Faiz Ahmed Faiz was born at Sialkot, also the birthplace of Iqbal, and was educated, like Iqbal, at Lahore, where he studied English literature and philosophy. He began his career as a lecturer in English at Amritsar. During World War II, he joined the Welfare Department of the Army and became a Lt. Colonel. However, with his strong sense of independence, and a commitment to the socialist ideology, he could not for long brook the shackles of military discipline. He turned to journalism and distinguished himself as the editor of *The Pakistan Times*. He was charged with complicity in the Rawalpindi conspiracy case and was condemned to 4 years' imprisonment in 1951. The jail-term gave him a first-hand experience of the harsh realities of life, and provided him with the much-needed leisure and solitude to think his thoughts and transmute them into poetry. Two of his books, *Dast-e-Saba*, and *Zindan Nama*, are the products of this period of imprisonment.

As a poet Faiz began with the conventional themes of love and beauty, but soon these conventional themes get submerged in the larger social and political issues of the day. The traditional griefs of love get fused with the travails of the afflicted humanity, and Faiz uses his poetry to champion the cause of socialistic humanism. Consequently, the familiar imagery of a love-poet acquires new meanings in the hands of Faiz. The conventional figures of the beloved or mistress come to represent the poet's cause, or country or people. Separation from the beloved implies separation from the poet's cherished ideals. The garden and the rose-bud symbolise the poet's homeland and people; wine becomes the wine of political truth or insight, or it may signify the self-sacrificing madness induced by progressive political ideas. This turning away from romance to realism, from EROS to AGAPE, is beautifully suggested in his poem, "Mujh se Pehi si Mahabbat Miri Mehboob Na Maang", here translated as: "Ask me not, my Love, for the love of former days." This poem is meant to give a jolt to the traditional view which regards love as the source and centre of life, to the exclusion of all other interests. But life is not love alone. There are other pressing problems of life—hunger, want and social inequity—which have even stronger claims on our minds and hearts. The idea harks back to Ghalib who, in one of his verses, makes a similar point:

تیری وفا سے کیا ہو تلافی کہ دہر میں
تیرے سوا بھی ہم پر بہت سے ستم ہوئے

How can your love alone offer recompense?
I've suffered many blows besides those of love.

In the matter of diction and style, Faiz may be called the inheritor of the tradition of Ghalib. His admiration of Ghalib is also reflected in the title of his first published work, *Naqsh-e-Faryadi*, which comes straight from the opening line of the first *ghazal* of "Dewan-e-Ghalib." Although he has written poems in a simple, conversational style, he has a marked preference for polished, Persianised diction, the diction of the elite rather than of the commoners. But because of the universality of his thought and a sympathetic vision, and because of his consummate art, his poetry is read and admired in both parts of the Indian subcontinent.

Faiz is a "committed" poet who regards poetry as a vehicle of serious thought, and not a mere pleasurable pastime. He does not accept the maxim of "art for art sake." An admirer of Karl Marx and a poet of the people, Faiz was honoured by Soviet Russia with the prestigious Lenin Award for Peace, and his poems have been translated into Russian language. His poetical collections include *Naqsh-e-Faryadi*, (1943), *Dast-e-Saba*, (1952), *Zindan-Nama*, (1956), *Dast-e-Tah-e-Sang*, (1965), *Sar-e-Wadi-e-Seena*, (1965), *Sham-e-Shahr Yaraan*, *Mire Dil Mire Musafir*, and *Ghubar-e-Ayaam*. The first two poems of this selection, *Mujh se Pehli si Mahabbat* and *Mere Humdum, Mire Dost*, occur in *Naqsh-e-Faryadi* while *Lahu Ka Suragh* comes from *Sar-e-Wadi-e-Seena*.

فیض احمد فیضؔ

مجھ سے پہلی سی محبت مری محبوب نہ مانگ

مجھ سے پہلی سی محبت مری محبوب نہ مانگ
میں نے سمجھا تھا کہ تو ہے تو درخشاں ہے حیات
تیرا غم ہے تو غمِ دہر کا جھگڑا کیا ہے
تیری صورت سے ہے عالم میں بہاروں کو ثبات
تیری آنکھوں کے سوا دنیا میں رکھا کیا ہے؟
تو جو مل جائے تو تقدیر نگوں ہو جائے
یوں نہ تھا، میں نے فقط چاہا تھا یوں ہو جائے
اور بھی دکھ ہیں زمانے میں محبّت کے سوا
راحتیں اور بھی ہیں وصل کی راحت کے سوا
اَن گنت صدیوں کے تاریک بہیمانہ طلسم
ریشم و اطلس و کمخواب میں بنوائے ہوئے
جا بجا بکتے ہوئے کوچہ و بازار میں جسم
خاک میں لتھڑے ہوئے خون میں نہلائے ہوئے
لوٹ جاتی ہے ادھر کو بھی نظر کیا کیجے
اب بھی دلکش ہے ترا حُسن، مگر کیا کیجے
اور بھی دکھ ہیں زمانے میں محبّت کے سوا
راحتیں اور بھی ہیں وصل کی راحت کے سوا

360

Faiz Ahmed Faiz
Mujh se Pehli si Mahabbat (Ask me not, my love...)

Ask me not, my love, for the love of former days,
I had thought, with you around life 'uld be dazzling bright,
With your griefs to fill my heart, other griefs would vaporize,
Your beauty keeps the spring alive,
The world contains naught else but your starry eyes,
To own you is to own the fortune's richest prize.
It wasn't so; I simply wished it could be so!
Besides the griefs of love, there're other griefs in life,
Besides the joy of union there're other delights.
The dark, devilish spells, o'er several centuries cast,
Woven in silks and satins, in brocade finely wrought;
Human bodies for sale in every street and shop,
Bodies bathed in blood, splashed with gory spots,
I cannot help but see them all.
Your beauty still attracts the heart; but what to do?
There are other griefs in life,
Besides the joy of union, there're other delights.

Mujh se pehli si mahabbat miri mehboob na maang!
Main ne samjha tha ke tu hai tau darakhshan hai hayaat,
Tera ghum hai tau ghum-e-dahar ka jhagra kya hai,
Teri soorat se hai aalam mein bahaaron ko sabaat,
Teri aankhon ke siwa duniya mein rakha kya hai?
Tu jo mil jaae tau taqdir nigoon ho jaae,
Yun na tha, main ne faqt chaha tha yun ho jaae.
Aur bhi dukh hain zamane mein mahabbat ke siwa,
Raahaten aur bhi hain wasal ki raahat ke siwa;
An ganit sadion ke taarik, bahimaana talism,
Resham-o-atlas-o-kamkhwaab mein bunwae hue,
Ja baja bikte hue koocha-o-bazaar mein jism,
Khak mein lithre hue, khoon mein nahlaae hue,
Laut jaati hai idhar ko bhi nazar, kya kijeye,
Ab bhi dilkash hai tira husn, magar kya kijeye?
Aur bhi dukh hain zamane mein mahabbat ke siwa,
Raahten aur bhi hain, wasal ki raahat ke siwa.

فیض احمد فیض

مرے ہمدم، مرے دوست

گر مجھے اس کا یقیں ہو مرے ہمدم، مرے دوست
گر مجھے اس کا یقیں ہو کہ ترے دل کی تھکن
تیری آنکھوں کی اداسی، ترے سینے کی جلن
میری دلجوئی، مرے پیار سے مٹ جائے گی
گر مرا حرفِ تسلّی وہ دوا ہو جس سے
جی اُٹھے پھر ترا اُجڑا ہوا بے نور دماغ
تیری پیشانی سے دُھل جائیں یہ تذلیل کے داغ
تیری بیمار جوانی کو شفا ہو جائے
گر مجھے اس کا یقیں ہو مرے ہمدم، مرے دوست
روز و شب، شام و سحر میں تجھے بہلاتا رہوں
میں تجھے گیت سناتا رہوں ہلکے، شیریں
آبشاروں کے، بہاروں کے، چمن زاروں کے گیت
آمدِ صبح کے، مہتاب کے، سیّاروں کے گیت
تجھ سے میں حسن و محبّت کی حکایات کہوں
کیسے مغرور حسیناؤں کے برفاب سے جسم
گرم ہاتھوں کی حرارت میں پگھل جاتے ہیں

Faiz
Mere Humdum, Mere Dost (My Love, My Life!)

If I were sure of this, O my love, my life!
If your weary heart and breast, your despondent eyes,
Soothed by my love and care would indeed revive;
If my word of solace could act as anodyne,
To relume your darkened brain, uplift your mind,
Wash away the blot of shame from your brow depressed,
And restore to its health, this your faded prime;
If I were sure of this, O my love, my life!
I would entertain you day and night, morn and eve,
For ever sing for your delight songs light and sweet,
Of spring and gardens, and of waterfalls,
Of rising sun, the sailing moon, and the shining stars.
And I would relate to you tales of love and youth,
How the frigid beauties proud,
Melt in the heat of warm embrace,

Gar mujhe iska yaqin ho, mire humdum, mire dost,
Gar mujhe iska yaqin ho ke tire dil ki thakan
Teri aankhon ki udaasi, tire seene ki jalan,
Meri diljooi, mire payaar se mit jaaegi,
Gar mira harf-e-tasalli woh dawa ho jis se,
Ji uthe phir tira ujra hua be noor dimagh,
Teri paishaani se dhul jaaen yeh tazlil ke dagh,
Teri beemaar jawani ko shifa ho jaae,

Gar mujhe iska yaqeen ho, mire humdum, mire dost!
Roz-o-shab, sham-o-sahr main tujhe bahlaata rahun,
Main tujhe geet sunaata rahun, halke, sheerin,
Aabshaaron, baharon ke, chaman zaaron ke geet,
Aamad-e-subah ke, mahtaab ke, sayyaaron ke geet,
Tujh se main husn-o-mahabbat ki hikayaat kahun,
Kaise maghroor haseenaaon ke barfaab se jism,
Garm haathon ki hararat mein pighal jaate hain,

فیض احمد فیض

کیسے اِک چہرے کے ٹھہرے ہوئے مانوس نُقوش
دیکھتے دیکھتے یک لخت بدل جاتے ہیں
کس طرح عارضِ محبوب کا شفّاف بلور
یک بیک بادۂ احمر سے دہک جاتا ہے
کیسے گلچیں کے لئے جھکتی ہے خود شاخِ گلاب
کس طرح رات کا ایوان مہک جاتا ہے
یونہی گاتا رہوں، گاتا رہوں تیری خاطر
گیت بنتا رہوں، بیٹھا رہوں تیری خاطر
پر مرے گیت ترے دُکھ کا مداوا ہی نہیں
نغمہ جرّاح نہیں، مونس و غم خوار سہی
گیت نشتر تو نہیں، مرہم آزار سہی
تیرے آزار کا چارہ نہیں نشتر کے سوا
اور یہ سفّاک مسیحا مرے قبضے میں نہیں
اس جہاں کے کسی ذی روح کے قبضے میں نہیں
ہاں مگر تیرے سوا، تیرے سوا، تیرے سوا

Faiz

How the settled looks and face,
Suddenly change their hue and shape;
How the mirror of beauty's face,
The purple goblet sets ablaze;
How the rose-sprig, itself, for the flower-plucker falls,
And the nightly meet at once acquires a fragrant grace.

I'll sing for your sake songs without respite,
Weave and weave the verbal web for your sole delight.
But my songs can't provide a cure for your grief,
Song is no surgeon, yet can cause relief;
Not a lancet sharp, it yet can help and heal.
Nothing short of lancet, though, your malady needs.
And this relentless saviour is beyond my reach;
Beyond, as a matter of fact, any human's reach;
You, albeit, and none but you, can this grief defeat.

Kaise ik chehre ke thahre hue maanoos naqoosh,
Dekhte dekhte yak lakht badal jaate hain;
Kis tarah aaraz-e-mehboob ka shaffaf bilour,
Yak ba-yak baada-e-ahmar se dahak jaata hai,
Kaise gulcheen ke lieye jhukti hai khud shaakh-e-gulab,
Kis tarah raat ka aiwaan mahak jaata hai.

Yunhi gata rahun, gata rahun teri khatir,
Geet bun-ta rahun, baitha rahun teri khatir.
Par mire geet tire dukh ka madawa hi nahin,
Naghma jirrah nahin, moonis-e-ghumkhwaar sahi,
Geet nishtar tau nahin, marham-e-aazaar sahi,
Tere aazaar ka chara nahin nishtar ke siwa,
Aur yeh saffak maseeha mere qabze mein nahin,
Is jahan ke kisi zi rooh ke qabze mein nahin,
Haan magar tere siwa, tere siwa, tere siwa!

فیض احمد فیض
لہو کا سراغ

کہیں نہیں ہے کہیں بھی نہیں لہو کا سراغ
نہ دستِ و ناخنِ قاتل نہ آستیں پہ نشاں
نہ سرخیِ لبِ خنجر نہ رنگِ نوکِ سناں
نہ خاک پر کوئی دھبّا نہ بام پر کوئی داغ
کہیں نہیں ہے کہیں بھی نہیں لہو کا سراغ
نہ صرفِ خدمتِ شاہاں کہ خوں بہا دیتے
نہ دیں کی نذر کہ بیعانۂ جزا دیتے
نہ رزم گاہ میں برسا کہ معتبر ہوتا
کسی علم پہ رقم ہو کے مشتہر ہوتا
پکارتا رہا، بے آسرا، یتیم لہو
کسی کو بہرِ سماعت نہ وقت تھا نہ دماغ
نہ مدّعی، نہ شہادت، حساب پاک ہوا
یہ خونِ خاکِ نشیناں تھا، رزقِ خاک ہوا

Faiz
Lahu ka Suragh (Trail of Blood)

Not a trace of blood is left, no trail at all,
The assassin's hands or nails or sleeves do not carry a single stain,
The point of spear, the edge of sword are free of blood or blame;
No patch of blood on the ground, nor on roof a blot,
Nowhere the blood is left, nowhere at all!

It wasn't shed for the king's sake, where it could earn reward,
It wasn't spent for religious faith where it could win applause,
It did not flow in the battlefield to win public acclaim,
Nor did it wet the battle flag to broadcast its fame;
It was the poor, orphaned blood, it cried out in vain,
None had time or inclination to hear this voice in pain;
No witness, no complainant,—so the case was closed;
It was the blood of lowly folks, down the drain it flowed.

Kahin nahin hai, kahin bhi nahin lahu ka suragh,
Na dast-o-nakhun-e-qatil, na aasteen pe nishan,
Na surkhy-e-lab-e-khanjar, na rang-e-nok-e-sanan,
Na khak par koi dhabba, na baam par koi dagh,
Kahin nahin hai, kahin bhi nahin hai lahu ka suragh.

Na sarf-e-khidmat-e-shahaan, ke khoon-baha dete,
Na deen ki nazr, ke bai-aana jaza dete,
Na razm gah mein barsa ke moatbir hota,
Kisi alam pe raqm ho ke mushtehar hota,
Pukarta raha be aasra yatim lahu,
Kisi ko bahr-e-samaat na waqt tha na dimagh,
Na muddai, na shahadat, hisab paak hua,
Yeh khoon-e-khak-e-nasheenan tha, rizq-e-khak hua.

Abdul Haie Sahir Ludhianvi
(1922-1980)

ABDUL HAIE SAHIR LUDHIANVI
(1922-1980)

Sahir was the son of a rich landlord, known for his love of pleasure and luxury. He had married several times, but had only one male issue—Sahir—to perpetuate his race. After he fell out with Sahir's mother, the landlord father went to the court to claim guardianship of his son. But Sahir preferred to stay with his mother, foregoing a life of luxury in favour of a more contented and honourable existence. Sahir had his education at Government College, Ludhiana, from where, however, he was externed perhaps for his non-conformist behaviour. But his native city is proud of his prodigal son as is proved by the re-naming of a street in Ludhiana as "Sahir Ludhianvi Road."

Though Sahir gave ample evidence of his poetic abilities right in his college days, he really shot into fame with the publication, in 1943, of his poetical collection: *Talkhian*. Two poems of this volume, "Taj Mahal" and "Chakley" (both of which are included in this anthology), became immediately popular. In the former, the poet elicits our sympathies for the artisans and labourers without whose skill and industry such a dream in marble could not have been concretised. In "Chakley", the poet peeps behind the veil of boasted Eastern piety, and shows us the stinking brothels and their unfortunate inmates, for whose tragic fate only the society is to blame.

Apart from the enlightened vision which informs his poetry, Sahir wins our admiration through his simple, unaffected style, which, without breaking with the tradition of rhyme, *radif*, and metre, seems fresh and forceful, unencumbered with far-fetched conceits, pseudo-mystical thought, or over-embellished diction.

Whether he writes *nazms, ghazals,* or songs, he articulates his thoughts with sincerity, spontaneity, and directness.

Goaded by economic necessity, Sahir went to Bombay and started writing film songs. He made a signal contribution towards improving the quality of these songs, by enricing their content, and toning up their language. Cinema brought him fame and money, but it obstructed, one feels, the full growth of his poetic genius, so that the public had to wait in vain for another collection as authentic and artistic as *Talkhian*. His film songs were published under the title: "Gata Jaae Banjara." But film songs, written to suit a particular mood and measure are different from lyrical poetry, which springs as naturally as a water spring. His long poem, "Parchhaiaan", is an impressive anti-war document. The insistent note of pain and pathos heard in his *nazms* and *ghazals* is the result of both environmental and personal frustration, for, despite his romantic temperament, and despite the opportunities that came his way, Sahir was a lonely man, who remained unmarried all his life. He died in 1980 at the age of 58.

عبدالحیٔ ساحر لدھیانوی

تاج محل

تاج تیرے لئے ایک مظہرِ الفت ہی سہی
تجھ کو اس وادیِ رنگین سے عقیدت ہی سہی
میری محبوب کہیں اور ملا کر مجھ سے
بزمِ شاہی میں غریبوں کا گزر کیا معنی
ثبت جس راہ میں ہوں سطوتِ شاہی کے نشاں
اس پہ الفت بھری روحوں کا سفر کیا معنی
میری محبوب پسِ پردہٴ تشہیرِ وفا
تونے سطوت کے نشانوں کو تو دیکھا ہوتا
مردہ شاہوں کے مقابر سے بہلنے والی
اپنے تاریک مکانوں کو تو دیکھا ہوتا
ان گنت لوگوں نے دنیا میں محبت کی ہے
کون کہتا ہے کہ صادق نہ تھے جذبے ان کے
لیکن ان کے لئے تشہیر کا ساماں ہی نہیں
کیونکہ وہ لوگ بھی اپنی ہی طرح مفلس تھے

Abdul Haie Sahir Ludhianvi
Taj Mahal

The Taj, mayhap, to you may seem, a mark of love supreme,
You may hold this beauteous vale in great esteem;
Yet, my love, meet me hence at some other place!

How odd for the poor folk to frequent royal resorts;
'Tis strange that the amorous souls should tread the regal
    paths
Trodden once by mighty kings and their proud consorts.
Behind the facade of love my dear, you had better seen,
The marks of imperial might that herein lie screen'd
You who take delight in tombs of kings deceased,
Should have seen the hutments dark where you and I did
    wean.

Countless men in this world must have loved and gone,
Who would say their loves weren't truthful or strong?
But in the name of their loves no memorial is raised,
For they, too, like you and me belonged to the common throng.

Taj tere lieye ik mazhar-e-ulfat hi sahi,
Tujh ko is waadi-e-rangeen se aqeedat hi sahi,
Miri mahboob kahin aur mila kar mujh se.

Bazm-e-shahi mein gharibon ka guzar kya maani,
Sabt jis raah pe hon satwat-e-shahi ke nishan
Us pe ulfat bhari roohon ka safar kya maani?
Meri mahboob pas-e-parda-e-tashhir-e-wafa,
Tu ne satwat ke nishanon ko tau dekha hota.
Murda shahon ke muqabir se bahlne wali,
Apne taarik makanon ko tau dekha hota.

An ganit logon ne duniya mein mahabbat ki hai,
Kaun kahta hai ke saadiq na the jazbe unke?
Lekin un ke lieye tashhir ka samaan hi nahin
Kyonke woh log bhi apni hi tarah muflis the.

ساحر لدھیانوی

یہ عمارات و مقابر یہ فصیلیں یہ حصار
مطلق الحکم شہنشاہوں کی عظمت کے ستون
سینۂ دہر کے ناسور ہیں کہنہ ناسور
جذب ہے ان میں ترے مرے اجداد کا خوں
میری محبوب! انھیں بھی تو محبت ہوگی
جن کی صناعی نے بخشی ہے اسے شکلِ جمیل
ان کے پیاروں کے مقابر رہے نام و نمود
آج تک ان پہ جلائی نہ کسی نے قندیل

یہ چمن زار یہ جمنا کا کنارہ، یہ محل
یہ منقش در و دیوار یہ محراب یہ طاق
اک شہنشاہ نے دولت کا سہارا لے کر
ہم غریبوں کی محبت کا اڑایا ہے مذاق
میری محبوب کہیں اور ملا کر مجھ سے

374

Sahir Ludhianvi

These structures and sepulchres, these ramparts and forts,
These relics of the mighty dead are, in fact, no more
Than the cancerous tumours on the face of earth,
Fattened on our ancestors' very blood and bones.

They too must have loved, my love, whose hands had made,
This marble monument, nicely chiselled and shaped,
But their dear ones lived and died, unhonoured, unknown,
None burnt even a taper on their lowly graves.

This bank of Jamuna, this edifice, these groves and lawns,
These carved walls and doors, arches and alcoves,
An emperor on the strength of wealth,
Has played with us a cruel joke.
Meet me hence, my love, at some other place.

Yeh imaraat-e-muqabir, yeh fasilen, yeh hissar,
Mutliq-ul-hukm shahnshahon ki azmat ke satoon,
Seena-e-dahr ke naasoor hain kuhna naasoor
Jazb hai in mein tire mire ajdad ka khoon.

Meri mahboob! unhen bhi tau mahabbat hogi,
Jin ki sannai ne bakhshi hai ise shakl-e-jameel,
Un ke payaaron ke muqabir rahe be naam-o-namood,
Aaj tak un pe jalaai na kisi ne qandil.

Yeh chaman zaar, yeh jamuna ka kinara, yeh mahal,
Yeh munaqqish dar-o-deewar, yeh mahraab, yeh taaq,
Ik shahnshah ne daulat ka sahara le kar,
Hum gharibon ki mahabbat ka uraya hai mazaaq.
Meri mahboodb kahin aur mila kar mujh se!

چکلے

ساحر لدھیانوی

یہ کوچے یہ نیلام گھر دلکشی کے
یہ لٹتے ہوئے کارواں زندگی کے
کہاں ہیں کہاں ہیں محافظ خودی کے
ثناخوانِ تقدیسِ مشرق کہاں ہیں

یہ پُر پیچ گلیاں یہ بے خواب بازار
یہ گمنام راہی یہ سکّوں کی جھنکار
یہ عصمت کے سودے یہ سودوں پہ تکرار
ثناخوانِ تقدیسِ مشرق کہاں ہیں

تعفّن سے پُر نیم روشن یہ گلیاں
یہ مسلی ہوئی ادھ کھلی زرد کلیاں
یہ بکتی ہوئی کھوکھلی رنگ رلیاں
ثناخوانِ تقدیسِ مشرق کہاں ہیں

وہ اُجلے دریچوں میں پائل کی چھن چھن
تنفّس کی الجھن پہ طبلے کی دھن دھن
یہ بے روح کمروں میں کھانسی کی ٹھن ٹھن
ثناخوانِ تقدیسِ مشرق کہاں ہیں

Sahir Ludhianvi
Chakley (Brothels)

These lanes, these marts of rich delights,
Precious lives, undone, defiled;
Where are the defenders of virtuous pride?
Where are they who praise, the pious eastern ways?

These sinuous streets, these doors ajar,
The clinking coins, the moving masks,
Deals of honour, hagglings fast,
Where are they who praise, the pious eastern ways?

These dimly-lighted, stinking streets,
These yellowing buds, crushed and creased,
These hollow charms, for sale and lease;
Where are they who praise the pious eastern ways?

The jingling trinklets at casement bright,
Tambourins athrob 'mid gasping life;
Cheerless rooms with cough alive;
Where are they who praise the pious eastern ways?

Yeh kooche, yeh neelam ghar dilkashi ke,
Yeh lut-te hue kaarwaan zindagi ke,
Kahan hain kahan hain muhaafiz khudi ke;
Sanakhwaan-e-taqdees-e-mashriq kahan hain?

Yeh purpech galian, yeh be-khwaab bazaar,
Yeh gumnaam rahi, yeh sikkon ki jhankar,
Yeh ismat ke saudey, yeh saudon pe takrar;
Sanakhwaan-e-taqdees-e-mashriq kahan hain?

Ta-affun se pur, neem roshan yeh galian,
Yeh masli hui adh-khili zard kalian,
Yeh bikti hui khokhli rang-ralian;
Sanakhwaan-e-taqdees-e-mashriq kahan hain?

Woh ujle dareechon pe payal ki chhan chhan,
Tanaffus ki uljhan pe table ki dhan dhan,
Yeh be-rooh kamron mein khansi ki than than;
Snakhwaan-e-taqdees-e-mashriq kahan hain?

ساحر لدھیانوی

یہ گونجے ہوئے قہقہے راستوں پر
یہ چاروں طرف بھیڑ سی کھڑکیوں پر
یہ آوازے کھنچتے ہوئے آنچلوں پر
ثنا خوانِ تقدیسِ مشرق کہاں ہیں
یہ پھولوں کے گجرے یہ پیکوں کے چھینٹے
یہ بیباک نظریں یہ گستاخ فقرے
یہ ڈھلکے بدن اور یہ مدقوق چہرے
ثنا خوانِ تقدیسِ مشرق کہاں ہیں
یہ بھدی نگاہیں حسینوں کی جانب
یہ بڑھتے ہوئے ہاتھ سینوں کی جانب
لپکتے ہوئے پاؤں زینوں کی جانب
ثنا خوانِ تقدیسِ مشرق کہاں ہیں
یہاں پیر بھی آ چکے ہیں جواں بھی
تنو مند بیٹے بھی آبا میاں بھی
یہ بیوی بھی ہے اور بہن بھی ماں بھی
ثنا خوانِ تقدیسِ مشرق کہاں ہیں

Sahir Ludhianvi

Boisterous laughs on public paths,
Crowds at windows, thick and fast,
Vulgar words, obscene remarks;
Where are they who praise, the pious eastern ways?

The betel spittal, the floral wreaths,
Audacious looks and filthy speech,
Flaccid figures, looks diseased;
Where are they who praise, the pious eastern ways?

Lecherous eyes in beauty's quest,
Extended hands chasing breasts,
Springing feet on stairs pressed;
Where are they who praise, the pious eastern ways?

This is the haven of young and old.
Aging sires, and youngsters bold,
Wife, mother and sister—she plays a triple role.
Where are they who praise, the pious eastern ways?

Yeh goonje hue qahqahe raaston par,
Yeh chaaron taraf bhir si khirkion par,
Yeh aawaze khinchte hue aanchlon par,
Sanakhwaan-e-taqdees-e-mashriq kahan hain?

Yeh phoolon ke gajre, Yeh peekon ke chheente,
Yeh be-baak nazren, yeh gustaakh fiqre,
Yeh dhalke badan aur yeh madquq chehre;
Sanakhwaan-e-taqdees-e-mashriq kahan hain?

Yeh bhooky nigahen haseenon ki jaanib,
Yeh barthe hue haath, seenon ki jaanib,
Lapakte hue paaon zeenon ki jaanib;
Sanakhwaan-e-taqdees-e-mashriq kahan hain?

Yahan pir bhi aa chuke hain, jawan bhi,
Tanomand bete bhi, abba mian bhi.
Yeh biwi bhi hai aur behn bi hai, maan bhi;
Sanakhwaan-e-taqdees-e-mashriq kahan hain?

ساحر لدھیانوی

مدد چاہتی ہے یہ حوّا کی بیٹی!
یشودھا کی ہم جنس رادھا کی بیٹی
پیمبر کی اُمت، زلیخا کی بیٹی
ثناخوانِ تقدیسِ مشرق کہاں ہیں
ذرا ملک کے رہبروں کو بلاؤ
یہ گلیاں، یہ کوچے، یہ منظر دکھاؤ
ثناخوانِ تقدیسِ مشرق کو لاؤ
ثناخوانِ تقدیسِ مشرق کہاں ہیں

Sahir Ludhianvi

Help, O help, this daughter of Eve!
Radha's child, Yashoda's breed;
The prophet's race, Zuleikha's seed;
Where are they who praise, the pious eastern ways?

Call, O call the leaders wise,
Let them see these streets, these sights,
Where are the champs of eastern pride?
Where are they who praise, the pious eastern ways?

Madad chahti hai yeh houaa ki beti,
Yashodha ki hum jins, Radha ki beti,
Paimber ki ummat, Zuleikha ki beti;
Sanakhwaan-e-taqdees-e-mashriq kahan hain?

Zara mulk ke rahbaron ko bulaao,
Yeh kooche, Yeh galian, yeh manzir dikhaao,
Sanakhwaan-e-taqdees-e-mashriq ko laao,
Sanakhwaan-e-taqdees-e-mashriq kahan hain?

Index of First Lines

(The name of the poet is mentioned at the end of the line)

A strange tale, lo I inscribe, SHAUQ LUCKNAVI	101
Ask me not, my love, for the love of former days, FAIZ	361
Be not proud, O love, of your beauteous brow, QULI QUTAB SHAH	17
Brimful with the wine of Truth is the cup of Indian thought, IQBAL	219
Exhilarating is the air! HAFEEZ JULLUNDHARY	291
For ages has the radiant sun been shining in the skies, MAJAZ	353
Friends, 'tis a terrible thing to fall a prey to age, NAZIR AKBARABADI	71
He alone is happy whom we do not know, MIR TAQI MIR	27
He who is a king crowned, is but a man, NAZIR AKBARABADI	63
Here where even the day reflects the shades of night, MEHROOM	239
How to describe the heat intense of the battle day, ANEES	145
If I were sure of this, O my love, my life! FAIZ	363
In London I had married a silver-bodied dame, AKBAR ALLAHABADI	171
In the evening, twilight-tinged, the river gently flows, JOSH MALIHABADI	263

It looks so charming, my Gori's beaming face, QULI QUTAB SHAH	15
Leave your lust and greed, O man, wander not in distant lands, NAZIR AKBARABADI	55
Let us celebrate Basant, the fest of love and life, QULI QUTAB SHAH	19
Lo, I come once again drunken to my fill! NAZAR MOHAMMED RASHID	323
Lo, I wander sad and idle in this city of night, MAJAZ	345
Mind ye not, O Brahman if I tell the truth, IQBAL	217
Not a trace of blood is left, no trail at all, FAIZ	367
Nothing like our Hindustan in the world entire, IQBAL	215
O mothers, daughters and sisters, you're our wealth and pride, HALI	155
Stretched on your bed sometime NAZAR MOHAMMED RASHID	325
The cavalcade of spring arrives, IQBAL	205
The Prophet's grandson, moved along, debating in his mind, DABIR	137
The Taj, mayhap, to you may seem, a mark of love supreme, SAHIR LUDHIANVI	373
The word springing from the heart surely carries weight, IQBAL	193
There she sweats on the road, a beauteous, restless lass, JOSH MALIHABADI	271
These lanes, these marts of rich delights, SAHIR LUDHIANVI	377
These whisperings urge me: "Come back now, for calling you for years" MEERAJI	337
This is the vale where, my friend, Reehana used to stay. AKHTAR SHEERANI	313

383

Thus he parted from his sire, calling upon his God,
    CHAKBAST   225

Thus spoke Laila's mother to Majnun one day:
    AKBAR ALLAHABADI   175

Western clouds are gathering fast,
    HAFEEZ JULLUNDHARY   281

When chapaties fill a man's stomach right to the brim,
    NAZIR AKBARABADI   89

Why comest thou to tease us love, why arouse
    the slumbering folks? AKHTAR SHEERANI   305

Why doesn't the earth, tell me, compress into a point?
    MEERAJI   333

Why should I abet the loss, why forget the gain,
    IQBAL   181

With the birth of rainy season begins the reign of buds,
    QULI QUTAB SHAH   21

Woman lends a glow to life, love,
    honour and faith, AKHTAR SHEERANI   301

Yeah, Rebellion! fire, tempest, thunder,
    ruin are my names? JOSH MALIHABADI   251

VBD
11913
14/11/24